# "Beyond Borders:
# A Guide to Financial
# Success for Expats"

Dan Dobry

Beyond Borders © Copyright 2023 Dan Dobry

For more information, email Dan@globalnetuk.co.uk

ISBN: 979-8-89109-216-7 - paperback

ISBN: 979-8-89109-217-4 - ebook

# Dedication

This book "Beyond Borders" was written as a heartfelt response to an inner calling. It compelled me to share the wealth of knowledge and experience I've garnered while serving families over 45 years. Through these pages, my intention is to empower them with the tools needed to embrace a life characterized by dignity and security, even amidst the ever-evolving landscape of our world.

Thanks, my cherished wife, Jenny, hailing from the vibrant heart of our beloved city of London. This endeavour reflects the unity and diversity that has shaped us.

This book is in profound dedication to the enduring spirit of my family, across generations and continents, I present this book on cross-border financial advice.

A tribute to my beloved father and mother, Alex and Kitty, whose roots stretch across Poland, Russia, Spain, Croatia, Bulgaria, Iraq, England, Australia, India, and Israel.

To my remarkable children, Leeron, Amit, and Oren, born amidst the warmth of Israel, your presence has illuminated our lives with joy and purpose. As we bridge nations through our histories and experiences, this book stands as a legacy of our shared journey, underscoring the importance of navigating financial landscapes with wisdom and insight.

May the wisdom within these pages be a testament to our family's values, our diverse origins, and the shared pursuit of knowledge and progress. With love and gratitude, this book is dedicated to you all, a symbol of unity across the world.

# Acknowledgements

During my life's journey, I have come to recognize the delicate balance that separates right from wrong, the often-unconventional interpretations of values, and the curious conduct of business. Through these experiences, I have encountered individuals who, while influencing my path, might not have consistently exemplified fairness or integrity in their interactions, even with me. It has become evident that power has the potential to lead to corruption, and achievement can foster a sense of superiority. Nonetheless, I've come to appreciate that personal values are subject to diverse interpretations.

I would like to extend my heartfelt acknowledgements to a group of exceptional professionals who have significantly shaped my journey. Among them, my initial partners, Sephy Peled and Yossi Cohen, stand out as both remarkable colleagues and steadfast friends. Their prowess in their respective fields was matched only by their remarkable qualities as individuals. From them, I garnered invaluable lessons and insights that left an indelible mark on my life's trajectory. Their influence has been immeasurable, and I am deeply grateful for the impact they have had on my personal and professional growth.

During my collaboration with Sephy Peled and Yossi Cohen, I encountered an individual of extraordinary significance, Ram Amit. Ram held the esteemed position of Head of Long-Term Savings and Assistant General Manager at Zion Insurance Company. In an era where the industry seemed fixated on achieving sales at any cost, Ram's unique character and approach were truly remarkable. Amidst a sea of sales-oriented individuals, he stood out as a genuine professional.

Ram Amit's impact on me was profound and enduring. He introduced me to a set of values that resonated deeply with me and that I carried throughout my entire career. In an environment that often-prioritized short-term gains, Ram's commitment to professionalism and ethical conduct left an indelible impression on me. His guidance and mentorship enriched my perspective and contributed immeasurably to my personal and professional development. I am forever grateful for the privilege of learning from such a distinguished figure in the industry.

Subsequently, I had the distinct privilege of collaborating with several luminaries within the industry. Benny Gaon, the former CEO of Koor Industries, and Itzhak Chalamish, the former Chairman of the Israeli Stock Exchange, joined forces with me as I transitioned from a sales-centric approach to a methodology centered around familial objectives.

The partnership with Benny and Itzhak marked a significant juncture in my journey. Working alongside them, I embraced a perspective that prioritized family goals above all else. Their leadership and insights were invaluable, propelling me toward a more holistic and purpose-driven approach.

Following Benny's untimely passing due to cancer, I embarked on an eight-year consulting career alongside my devoted partner, Moshe Laron. Together, we extended our guidance to global banks, regulators, and played a pivotal role in establishing the Union of Financial Planners and the College of Financial Planning. Our collaboration with esteemed professionals in fields such as banking, asset management, risk management, and education was instrumental in our own growth and development.

During this transformative period, I was fortunate to receive tutelage from one of the industry's luminaries, Dr. Boaz Barack. His expertise and guidance deeply enriched my understanding and paved the way for a lasting partnership between us. The knowledge and insights gained during these experiences further solidified my commitment to the principles of ethical conduct, professionalism, a more proficient understanding of behavioral finance and holistic financial planning.

In my most recent endeavor, I have been incredibly fortunate to collaborate with my esteemed partner, Ohad Weigman. Ohad is not only a beacon of trustworthiness but also stands at the pinnacle of our profession. Our partnership is built on a foundation of shared values, propelling us forward with a united purpose. Ohad's contributions to my journey have been invaluable, as he has introduced a wealth of skills and knowledge that have enriched my professional world.

I am confident that Ohad Wigman's trajectory will lead him to become one of the industry's great luminaries. His dedication to our shared values and his steadfast commitment to excellence make him a standout figure in our field. Together with Boaz and our amazing CEOs Guy Iluz and Teddy Lin, we continue to strive toward upholding the highest standards of professionalism and ethical conduct, confident in the positive impact we can collectively make on the industry and the individuals we serve.

Finally, but undoubtedly of paramount importance, I am deeply grateful for the unwavering support and love of my incredible family.

My wife, Jenny, has been a cornerstone in my journey, granting me the freedom to pursue my aspirations. Our partnership has been characterized by mutual growth, as we have embarked on shared endeavors while allowing each other to flourish individually. Jenny's remarkable achievements, including attaining two master's degrees in social work and Disaster Management (Master of Public Health) from the faculty of medicine, are a testament to her dedication and intellect.

In her specialization in gerontology, she has proven herself to be an expert in enhancing the lives of the elderly, offering them guidance and tools to lead lives of dignity. Through every step of my journey, she has stood steadfastly by my side, offering invaluable advice and insightful suggestions. Her unwavering support and contributions have played an indispensable role in my accomplishments, and I am profoundly thankful for her presence in my life. Together, as a family, we have navigated the challenges and triumphs of our respective paths, forging a bond that remains an enduring source of strength and inspiration.

I am truly blessed to have been surrounded by a family that consistently inspires me. My children, Leeron, Amit, and Oren have been a wellspring of motivation as I've observed them mature and witnessed their values come to life in the world.

Amit's dedication to his role as a computer programmer and his commitment as a loving father to my two wonderful grandchildren have filled me with immense pride. His endeavors serve as a testament to his character and the values he embodies.

Leeron and Oren, who have chosen to work alongside me, have been indispensable assets to our business and the future trajectory of our company. Their contributions have proven invaluable, and their dedication, talent and expertise have played a pivotal role in propelling our company forward.

As I reflect on the path we've walked together as a family, I am filled with gratitude for the opportunity to witness their growth and to be part of their journey. Their presence and the values they uphold have added immeasurable richness to my life and have spurred me onward in my own pursuits.

# About the Author

I have an extensive background in the financial industry, spanning forty-three years. Throughout my career, I have focused on finding innovative and effective solutions to help clients navigate the challenges of an evolving world.

In Israel, I founded the Union of Financial Planners in Israel (UFPI) and served as its inaugural Chairman and President. I also represented Israel as the Global Council Representative for the Global Community (FPSB) from 2012 to 2018. Additionally, from 2019 to 2021, I was a member of the Committee for Standards and Qualifications for the European Union (SQC).

I am the primary shareholder in Global Net Investment Group, which specializes in providing investment strategies and structures for professionals and families worldwide. I have offered guidance to affluent individuals on various financial matters, including cross-border issues, international planning, trusts, real estate, and multinational family structures.

As an educator, I taught for the Graduate Degree in Financial Gerontology at Haifa University. This field of study combines research on aging and human development with finance and business concerns. I also serve on the boards of financial companies internationally, including some in Switzerland, Isle of Man, Luxembourg, and Israel.

I hold the Certification Certified Financial Planner TM (CFP®), which I take pride in. In addition, I studied economics at Tel Aviv

University and obtained the CLU degree from the College of Insurance. Additionally, I have pursued the Associate Professional Risk Manager designation (APRM) to enhance my expertise in risk management.

I have published over 700 articles in national professional journals and have been a frequent speaker at both national and international events. I also published many articles on a blog on the Times of Israel website, where I shared my insights and perspectives. You can find this blog at https://blogs.timesofisrael.com/author/dan-dobry/.

# My Cross Border life

My life has never been defined by borders and as President Obama once said, "We are not defined by our borders but by our bonds".

I was born in Hong Kong into an extreme international community. I grew up with children that came from multiple cultures.

My family was also part of the small but diversified local Jewish community in Hong Kong. Kith and kin came from Russia, Japan, Australia, Iraq, India, Britain, and Israel.

I went on to reside in Israel and then in the United Kingdom where I now live.

Growing up in a multicultural society provided me with valuable insights and perspectives that can be applied to various aspects of my life, including work. Here are some potential lessons you may experience from your cross-border life:

**Appreciation for diversity**: Experiencing different cultures and interacting with people from various backgrounds can foster an appreciation for diversity. You will have learned to value and respect different perspectives, traditions, and ways of life, which can be an asset in today's globalized world.

**Adaptability and flexibility**: Moving between different countries and cultures requires adaptability and flexibility. Living in different environments and experiencing different social norms can enhance your ability to adapt to new situations and find common ground with people from diverse backgrounds.

**Cross-cultural communication skills**: Growing up in a multicultural community hones your cross-cultural communication skills. You will have learned how to navigate language barriers, understand non-verbal cues, and communicate effectively with people from different cultural backgrounds. These skills can be valuable in professional settings, especially in international collaborations or working with diverse teams.

**Global perspective**: Having exposure to multiple cultures can broaden your worldview and provide a global perspective. You may have developed a deeper understanding of global issues, intercultural dynamics, and international relations. This perspective can be advantageous in various professional fields, such as diplomacy, international business, or nonprofit work.

**Tolerance and empathy**: Living among diverse communities often fosters tolerance and empathy. You may have developed the ability to empathize with people from different backgrounds and appreciate their unique challenges and perspectives. These qualities can be valuable in fostering inclusive environments and promoting collaboration in the workplace.

**Multilingualism or language skills**: Growing up in a multicultural environment may have exposed you to multiple languages, enabling you to become proficient in more than one. Being multilingual or having strong language skills can be a significant asset in today's interconnected world, opening opportunities for international careers and cross-cultural communication.

The experiences and skills we gain can contribute to building a diverse and inclusive work environment, fostering effective communication, and navigating global challenges.

## Understanding differences in cultures and accepting them

I do not think that other people's values aren't as important or valid because they're not my own. I have my multicultural environment I grew up in, to thank for that.

Western cultures are mostly based on individualism rather than collectivism. In many societies, there is an emphasis on individual rights rather than placing the whole society above oneself. Western families are usually comprised of a nuclear family that strives to be independent. Children in the western world tend to live separately from their parents after graduating and marriage often in separate cities or even countries. They often disagree with their elders.

In Asian and many other cultures, the family is an extended unit where the oldest members are the most respected ones, and it is unlikely for young family members to argue with or disobey their parents even if they live separately.

In the Western world we are taught to ask questions and to propose alternative methodologies.

A good example is while I was a member of the Global Council for Financial Planning (we met once every six months), the global board voted on changes to the certification process of Financial Professionals that included a "Pathway Program". A resolution was made, and we were all instructed to implement the decision in our countries.

Six months later we met again. In the Western Countries the decision had not been implemented as the members objected offering alternative strategies. In the Asian communities (China, Japan, Korea) as obedience is part of their culture the decision had been implemented, and they already had thousands of professionals certified into this "Pathway Program".

Understanding and accepting cultural differences is an important aspect of fostering harmony and inclusivity in today's diverse world. Here are a few key points to consider when it comes to understanding and accepting cultural differences:

**Recognize the value of cultural diversity**: Every culture has its unique perspectives, values, and practices that have evolved over centuries. Embracing diversity allows for a richer exchange of ideas, promotes understanding, and encourages collaboration between different communities.

**Avoid judgment and ethnocentrism**: Ethnocentrism is the tendency to view one's own culture as superior to others. It is essential to overcome this mindset and approach other cultures with an open mind, acknowledging that different ways of life can be equally valid and meaningful.

**Educate yourself**: Take the initiative to learn about different cultures, their histories, traditions, and values. Engage in respectful conversations with people from different backgrounds to gain insights into their experiences. This knowledge will help you develop a broader perspective and foster empathy towards others.

**Be mindful of cultural relativism**: Cultural relativism is the understanding that different cultures operate based on their unique contexts and values. It means that certain practices may be acceptable or important in one culture but may not be so in another. Respecting cultural relativism involves refraining from imposing one's own values or judgments onto others.

**Practice empathy and active listening**: When interacting with individuals from different cultures, listen actively to their experiences, perspectives, and concerns. Show empathy by trying to understand their point of view, even if it differs from your own. This will promote effective communication and mutual respect.

**Avoid stereotypes and generalizations**: Recognize that cultural diversity encompasses a wide range of beliefs, practices, and attitudes within each culture. Avoid making assumptions or relying on stereotypes, as they often oversimplify and fail to capture the complexity of any culture or individual.

**Engage in cultural exchange**: Actively seek opportunities to engage with people from different cultures. Participate in cultural festivals, events, or community activities that promote cross-cultural understanding. Building relationships with individuals from diverse backgrounds fosters mutual learning and appreciation.

By adopting an open-minded and respectful approach, you can contribute to a more inclusive and harmonious society, where cultural differences are celebrated rather than feared or judged.

# Contents

# Introduction to Beyond Borders by Dr. Boaz Barack

Financial service providers play a vital role as the economic lubricant, facilitating connections between savers seeking profitable investments and companies in need of optimal borrowing terms for expansion. This perspective was highlighted by John Bruton, a former Prime Minister of Ireland. Dan Dobry possesses a deep understanding of this connection and has amassed extensive expertise across all facets of the financial services sector, positioning himself to contribute his knowledge for the benefit of all.

The realm of financial services continues to expand within the fabric of everyday life. Encompassing banking, credit, insurance, investment, mortgages, and advisory services, financial interactions are pervasive, engaging millions globally in the industry. The evolution of fintech and Big Data, however, is reshaping consumption patterns. Nevertheless, our engagement as consumers merely scratches the surface of a sprawling network comprising markets, institutions, and regulatory bodies.

This book undertakes a multidisciplinary exploration, delving into the cross-border complexities faced by investors and the enabling environment that propels them into the realm of influential financial entities. By participating in contemporary capitalism, these investors garner attention from multiple angles, shedding light on their origins, roles, motivations, power dynamics, and future trajectories within present-day financial markets.

Dan draws upon insights gained through a diverse life journey spanning various countries and perspectives. These insights help elucidate the context and significance of investors in modern financial markets, thereby unearthing the potential for a transformed financial landscape characterized by broader participation on a smaller scale.

While numerous books about financial services target corporate finance education, "Beyond Borders: A Practical Guide" distinguishes itself by shifting focus toward the end-users – the customers – who are often overlooked despite being the linchpin of retail financial services markets. The author's intent is to provide a roadmap for consumers to adeptly navigate the inherent risks and uncertainties associated with global financial products and services.

This book holds appeal for a multidisciplinary and interdisciplinary readership comprising financial market investors, financial regulators, political economists, public administrators, macroeconomists, corporate governance experts, and scholars in finance philosophy and sociology.

Cross-border financing harbors inherent political and currency risks. Over nearly three decades of collaboration, Dan Dobry has imparted his wisdom to empower consumers in obtaining diverse products and services, elevating their quality of life. I express my gratitude to him for broadening horizons and offering fresh perspectives to all individuals.

*Dr. Boaz Barack has over 35 years of experience in global banking and investment firms. His international career has focused on asset management and transforming innovative financial products into bankable solutions. Barack was on the senior management team of the two leading Swiss banks, Credit Suisse and UBS. Barack is the Founder and CEO of Bonart Financial Performance Ltd., an independent Swiss strategic advisory and execution firm.*

# Chapter One

## Living an International Life.

---

L iving an international life is a dynamic and ever-evolving experience, as people continue to cross borders in search of new opportunities and experiences. In this rapidly changing world, where individuals redefine their sense of belonging, there arises a tremendous need for reliable financial and investment advice backed by academic research.

The United Nations statistics reveal that nearly three hundred million people are now classified as expatriates, individuals who reside outside their native country. Typically, expatriates are educated professionals, skilled workers, or artists who either independently choose to relocate or are sent abroad by their employers.

Moving to a foreign country and embracing the expatriate lifestyle is a transformative event that necessitates access to knowledge and experience. While being an expat can be an exhilarating adventure filled with learning and personal growth, it also presents unique challenges associated with acclimating to a new culture, language, and legal system. This book aims to prepare you for the difficulties you may encounter as an expat and guide you in overcoming the challenges of living in a multi-jurisdictional world.

In addition to the three hundred million expatriates, there are countless others who engage in business or investment activities outside their home jurisdictions without fully comprehending the legal and tax implications. The lack of awareness surrounding international financial matters can lead to unfavorable outcomes and financial pitfalls. Recognizing this, the importance of providing individuals with reliable information and advice becomes evident.

Reflecting on my own journey, I realize that when I began my career in 1980, I had no inkling of the profound impact my work would have on people's lives. Opening my first business at the age of 29, my former boss, who became my partner, asked a crucial question: "How will we make a living?" My naive response was rooted in a belief that if we wholeheartedly cared for our clients, they would reciprocate by supporting us. Fortunately, luck was on our side, and our approach proved successful.

Throughout my career, I have consistently worked to effect positive change. I have advocated for education, encouraging families to understand the value of reliable financial advice and solutions. At one point, I had the opportunity to lecture at Haifa University, teaching financial Gerontology for graduate students.

It was during this time that the head of the faculty, my professor, referred to us as the "social workers of the financial profession." This notion resonated with me, as I understood that true success entailed not only comprehending the lives and aspirations of families but also experiencing them firsthand.

To guide families, we must all empathize with their challenges, opportunities, fears, and sources of their pride. Only then can we embark on a journey to help them develop a comprehensive strategy that leads them toward their desired lives and the fulfillment of their dreams.

Over the course of my career, I have been involved in various aspects of the financial industry, ranging from academia, where I crafted syllabuses and taught, to managing organizations and collaborating with numerous professionals. I have assisted global banks, investment houses, regulators, family offices, and software companies. However, my true dedication has always been towards serving families. I believe that to bring about real change, I must have direct access to families and actively participate in their journeys to understand their unique challenges.

Many people perceive financial planning as a task involving Excel spreadsheets, asset allocations, and investment tracking. However, it encompasses much more than that. When I engage with families and discuss their goals, it becomes an emotional experience. Never have I encountered a situation where a family responded to the question of their life's aspirations by stating a desire for a 10% return on capital. Instead, they share stories about their children, grandchildren, and the inherent challenges they face.

Financial planning is indeed about much more than just numbers and spreadsheets. It's about understanding the dreams, hopes, and fears of individuals and families and helping them achieve their goals.

By taking the time to truly listen to families and understand their unique circumstances, I was able to provide them with tailored financial solutions that align with their values and aspirations. This personal touch goes beyond the technical aspects of financial planning and creates a strong bond between myself and the families I had the honor of serving.

Emotional experiences are common when discussing goals and aspirations because money is often intertwined with our deepest desires and concerns. By creating a safe and empathetic space for families to express their emotions, I was not only helping them with their financial well-being but also supporting their overall happiness and fulfillment.

Being there for my clients and demonstrating that I genuinely care about their well-being is invaluable. While investment outcomes are important, the trust and confidence my clients had in my support and guidance can make a significant difference in their lives. My commitment to being present and dependable allowed my clients to feel reassured that they had a partner who is invested in their success.

The quote from the Dalai Lama perfectly encapsulates the power of compassion. *"By practicing empathy and understanding in your work, you not only contribute to the happiness of others but also cultivate your own happiness"*. It's a beautiful reminder that our actions and intentions can have a profound impact on the well-being of those around us.

# Chapter Two

## The History of Money

Money has allowed people to trade goods and services indirectly. It helps communicate the value of goods, and it provides individuals with a way to store their wealth.

It seems that in 770 BC the first coins were introduced in China, in 700 BC the first paper currency was implemented there. By 600 BC in Lydia Greece the first official currency was minted.

One of the greatest achievements of the introduction of money was the increased speed at which business, whether it involved hunting or fishing or monument-building, could be done.

The world has evolved since then and the 21st century has given rise to two novel forms of currency: mobile payments and virtual currency. Mobile payments are money rendered for a product or service through a portable electronic device, such as a cellphone, smartphone, or tablet device.

To begin this book, it is important to understand the scale of the change.

Money, whether it's represented by a seashell, a tulip bulb, a silver or gold coin, a piece of paper, or an electronically mined computer code, has a value. The total global worth today is estimated to be around $418 trillion.

It is important to understand that money is a faith. For money to have value we need to believe in it. What is behind the numbers we read on the computer that define our wealth and the value of our assets? Just faith, we believe that our currency is of value and therefore it is.

The world, as we discussed before, is changing rapidly.

In 1977 a string of 12 characters ushered in a new age of global finance.

Until then a bank that was wiring money abroad needed to relay up to ten instructions on public phone lines, which were then typed into forms, taking time, and causing errors. Then payments began to be facilitated by a code and secure network created by the Society for Worldwide Interbank Financial Telecommunications (SWIFT), a club originally of some 500 banks.

Today more than $140trn is transmitted across borders every year, equivalent to more than 152% of global GDP. Analysts reckon about 90% of that was transferred by SWIFT. Its 11,000 members in 200 countries ping each other 42 million times a day.

### The history of the financial world and planning.

The first organized financial markets emerged in Europe starting with Antwerp in the 1400s which found itself between the Germans, who traded furs and rye, and the Italians who brought gems from the Far East.

Innkeepers in the city would provide shelter, while also helping travelers exchange goods with one another. Over time, they began to create exchange rates and by the 16th century, they were trading more promissory notes than exchanging goods.

Then, in Amsterdam in 1602, The Dutch East Trading Company became the first publicly traded company by offering an IPO to "all residents of these lands" inviting all Dutchmen the ability to invest in them.

Fast forward to 1792, stockbrokers met on Wall Street and devised the "Buttonwood Agreement" for selling stocks and bonds. This would eventually become the New York Stock Exchange.

Charles Dow created the Dow Jones Industrial Average in 1896. Then in 1923, Henry Barnum Poor released the pre-version of the S&P, followed by MFS Massachusetts Investors Trust introducing the beginning of modern mutual funds in 1924.

While these United States markets were maturing, they remained almost completely unregulated until the stock market crash of 1929.

In the 1920s, if an individual wanted to buy stock in a company they had to go in person to a stockbroker for the purchase.

It was simple, if a person wanted to buy stock in a company, they went to a broker who would make it happen.

The key was information flow. In those days it was very slow and those who had access to, for instance, newspaper printing presses were able to act faster on the news.

Over time a problem developed, people close to the information were giving tips to friends who were also passing on the message. This created the first bubbles as hordes of people were acting on information. This phenomenon would drastically change the landscape of investing in the coming decade.

Then came the crash of 1929. The 'Roaring Twenties' came to a sudden end.

The unstable economy during the 1920s and then the Wall Street Crash in 1929 led to an unprecedented depression in the USA and globally.

Big businesses and banking collapsed. The crash brought financial ruin for many businessmen and financiers. America's GNP dropped by almost 50 per cent. Car production fell by 80 per cent and building construction by 92 per cent.

Firms went bankrupt. Between 1929 and 1932 109,371 businesses failed. Some businessmen committed suicide.

Banks collapsed. Statistics show 659 banks closed in 1929. This increased to 2,294 in 1931. They collapsed because people withdrew their savings for fear of losing money. Their closures, in turn, led to the remainder of savers losing their cash as well.

Those banks which remained refused loans to struggling firms, leading to bankruptcies.

People who bought "on the margin" were also in debt. There was loss of confidence in businesses.

The public lost confidence in the economy and hope in the future. They blamed big businesses and banks for the problems. Suicides went up 50 per cent.

In an effort to prevent another crash, Congress passed the Securities Act, which President Franklin D. Roosevelt signed in 1933. It was the first time the federal government passed legislation to regulate the nation's stock markets. The federal government intended the law to protect investors, create transparency of corporations and their finances, and prevent misrepresentations and fraud.

Following the Securities Act Directive, the Government established the SEC (Securities and Exchange Commission), then the NASD (National Association of Securities Dealers), and still more legislation over the coming decades. Financial regulation was born.

It was the development that motivated the Nobel Winning economist Harry Markowitz to come up with "Modern Portfolio Theory" in 1952.

In less than 50 years after that legislation the world would see the creation of commissions, corporations, societies, colleges, new investment strategies and tax incentives as a direct outcome of those federal laws.

The creation of new laws, theories and strategies laid the framework for the public's need for a financial advisor.

On June 19, 1969, a man named Loren Dunton started the Society for Financial Ethics. This society recognized individuals who were legally and ethically helping the public with financial counselling.

Six months later, Dunton met with 12 other men in Chicago on December 12, 1969. The group of attendees mainly had a background in mutual funds and insurance and met during a bad economic cycle.

They were seeking to find positive solutions to navigate the new economic situation. Out of this gathering came the International Association of Financial Planning and the College of Financial Planning.

Within four years, the college released a five-course curriculum and graduated their first class with the CFP designation. This certification continues today through the Certified Financial Planner Board of Standards. The meeting of the "Chicago 13" now receives a public consensus as to the start of financial planning.

In the beginning, the role looked very different from todays. Investors focused less on stocks and more on real estate, limited partnerships (private equity) and annuities.

Tax planning was at the heart of the plan. Inflation, taxes, and interest rates were high, and these investments served to defer taxes and assist families maximize their asset returns.

In those days the stock market performed poorly as investors wanted little to do with it, still remembering the "crash" of 1929.

As the world emerged into the 1980s, households started to realize they may need assistance because of new tax laws, pension laws and a stock market that finally began to take off again.

# Chapter Three

## Creating an International Future and becoming an Expat (Expatriate)

The situation in many countries regarding the tax burden on the middle class is sometimes so significant that families accumulating wealth to live or retire with dignity need to transfer their abode to a cheaper more tax efficient jurisdiction.

For example, in the UK the first 142 days of working income of the average citizen will be paid to the state if income is over 125,000 GBP. This calculation includes income tax, National Insurance, Council Taxes, VAT, and duties on consumer goods.

In Germany, more than 50% of income will go to taxes so one pays 192 days out of 365 of income.

In Austria, it is even a few days longer than that. This means that you work for the state for more than half of the year.

And how do governments thank you for it? They make sure that you work for them for even longer and look for creative ways to make you pay them more without complaining.

But as you groan under the tax burden, you are far from sharing your fate with all your fellow inhabitants in this world.

Remember the saying: Only two things in life are certain: "taxes and death".

This saying is, in fact, very wrong. Many, many people in the world are living in a more lucrative tax environment.

To achieve this, you do not have to live on a yacht in the middle of the ocean, all you should do is settle down in a suitable country and enjoy a relaxed life there.

You have a very large selection of countries to choose from that have significant benefits for expats.

You may look at the alternative to working and living abroad as the solution.

The world population is on the move, and we can make the best of it for our families.

There are over 300 million people living outside of their nation of origin today and if they organized themselves as an imaginary nation, 'Expatria' – they would have a population of over 300 million, rising from 154 million in 1990 and 175 million in 2000, according to UN statistics.

This would rank our imaginary country "Expatria" around the third most populous nation on the planet, over four times the number of people in the United Kingdom and very similar to the population of Indonesia or Brazil – and more than half the population size of the European Union.

The average age of the citizens of Expatria would be 38. UN statistics estimate that 48% of the population would be women and 26 million of the residents aged 65+ years of age – that's proportionally greater than in the world population.

We read in the newspaper about celebrities who reside in tax shelters (Björn Borg, Novak Djokovic, Bono, - all in Monaco) but you really don't have to be a celebrity to be a part of this community.

Since 2013, New World Wealth, a research outfit based in South Africa, has been tracking High Net Worth families migrations by culling property records, visa programs, news media reports and information from travel agents and others who cater to the wealthy.

Out of 15 million people they tracked, each worth more than $1 million in net assets, nearly 100,000 changed their country of residence in 2021 searching for tax relief and a better life.

Some twenty-three countries have no income tax, and another thirty-nine have tax-exemption on foreign income. Tax-free foreign income means that you can still live tax-free in the destination country if you earn your money outside of that country. And best of all: many of them offer an extremely high quality of life and very easy-to-obtain residence permits.

Amongst these countries are the United Kingdom, Japan, and Portugal. These attract wealthy entrepreneurs and businesspeople as well as high tech professionals.

Israel too, has a program to encourage immigration of wealthy families. It provides exemption on all income not created in Israel and no need to report on worldwide assets for up to 10 years.

Our lives are very difficult and challenging, and we alone are responsible for our futures and destinies, so young professionals and the wealthy are asking the question "How can I build for my family a future with dignity and security when I could have to pass over more than half the money I earn to the government?"

These people are looking at working and living in another country as the solution, despite facing challenges different from those faced in the country of origin.

## Key Advantages of becoming an Expat.

### The Tax Opportunity

On of the perks of being an expat is the opportunity to plan your taxes which may result in a significantly improved situation for your family.

For example, the largest, and potentially most important tax opportunity available to American expats is the Foreign Earned Income Exclusion (FEIE). The FEIE potentially enables American expats to avoid paying tax on the first $120,000 of foreign earnings in 2023 providing the following criteria are met.

Physical Presence Test: To pass this test, all the following must be true:

You have foreign-earned income- This would include a salary, wages, bonus, or self-employment income. Note that this does not include dividends, interest, pension distributions, or capital gain.

You are taxed as a resident in a foreign country. A resident is where an individual is permanently or indefinitely engaged in work—regardless of where their original residence was. To establish a tax residency, you must have a work engagement expected to last at least one year.

You have been physically present in a foreign country for at least 330 days out of any 12-month period. This does not have to be on a calendar-year basis and can be adjusted over a two-year span as needed to qualify. An important thing to note is that you must spend 330 full days in the foreign country, as partial days and time spent traveling does not count. It's critical that you track travel days carefully if planning to use the Physical Presence Test, as you'll need to be able to show details to the IRS if requested.

Using the Bona Fide Resident Test: To pass this test, all the following must be true:

You have foreign-earned income– This is the same requirement as for the Physical Presence Test. You must have income earned in a foreign country to pass the test and use the FEIE to save on your US taxes while abroad.

You pay tax in a foreign country– Again, this is the same requirement for using the Physical Presence Test to qualify. You must establish a tax residency and live full-time with no intention of returning to the US.

You have been a bona fide resident for a full tax year. The definition of a "bona fide resident" can be murky. The biggest factor here for passing the test is that you must demonstrate that you are permanently living abroad with no immediate plans to return to the US. This would include having a long-term lease or owning a home, having local bank accounts and utility bills, etc

## Key Concerns for Expats and International Families.

There are many challenges for a family who relocate and live overseas.

Some of the challenges are functional and these I will discuss in detail.

For example:

Tax challenges

New Reporting obligations

Strategies made available by multiple jurisdictions.

Retirement

Accrued obligations.

Distribution strategies

Understanding tax treaties

Understanding tax residency

Understanding offshore opportunities.

FATCA PFIC and the challenges of US citizens living abroad.

FATCA and PFIC for US Taxpayers

Many citizens of foreign countries also happen to hold a U.S. citizenship without ever residing in the U.S. They may have it because they were born in the U.S. or received it from their parents.

Regardless of how the US citizenship was obtained, they are still required to file an annual tax return with the IRS on their worldwide income. This is the same as U.S. citizens who live in America.

In addition, under FATCA legislation US citizens living abroad are required to report annually their assets held in foreign banks and Financial Accounts. (FBAR).

The penalties are severe and include a penalty of 10,000 USD for failure to file each year and an additional 10,000 USD each month after the taxpayer is aware of the delinquency and 10% of the value of the asset/s. If the reporting error is deemed willful (that the taxpayer was aware that he had to report and chose not to or reported falsely on purpose) the penalty could be up to 100,000 USD a year and 100% of all the assets.

This can be corrected by a voluntary disclosure program.

US Citizens residing overseas and saving and investing.

US citizens residing overseas have special investment challenges and tax issues that expose US citizens to significant tax exposures.

## The challenge of a PFIC (Passive Foreign Investment Company)

A passive foreign investment company (PFIC) is a foreign-based corporation that exhibits either one of two conditions. The first condition, based on income, is that at least 75% of the corporation's gross income is "passive," income that is derived from investments rather than from the company's regular business operations. The second condition that determines a company as a PFIC, based on assets, is that at least 50% of the company's assets are investments that produce income in the form of earned interest, dividends or capital gains.

All foreign investment managers and companies are PFICs, and all investment vehicles managed by Foreign Companies are PFIC.

In this capacity all managed accounts, mutual funds, provident funds and pension funds are PFIC and subject to severe tax penalties including:

Tax must be paid on all income derived each year regardless of if the asset has been sold or is still being held, at the highest level in the US (40%) and regardless of the tax rate or exemptions in the country of the origin of the residing US citizen.

The taxpayer cannot deduct bad years losses from good year gains.

The IRS came to a treaty with the UK Government and Malta regarding the accumulation of retirement assets in a pension account that would exempt the pension fund from FATCA and PFIC requirements, based on this precedence accountants worldwide especially in countries with mandatory contribution laws consider a pension fund or retirement vehicle that is mandatory (not voluntary) to be FATCA and PFIC exempt. This however does mean that contributions by an employer will not be taxed in the US as notional income therefore all withdrawals of notional monies or monies that have received local tax exemptions will be taxed in the US as income in the US when they are withdrawn.

## Banking and investment challenges

- Foreign exchange / International Money transfers

- Opening accounts, managing accounts in home jurisdictions, understanding bank costs and how banks think and work.

- Global Anti Money Laundering

- Assets Held for Investment

- Identifying a brokerage firm that works internationally.

## Real estate challenges

- Purchase of and management of real estate and other alternative assets

- How to buy real estate / obtain mortgage in foreign country.

## Estate planning challenges

1. Creating compliant wills and trusts and plans to administer assets post-death.

2. Asset protection strategies

3. Insurance

4. Relative strengths of different countries policies

5. Client Knowledge, Behavior and Other

- Healthcare planning

- Client Service and Administrative Support

**The Emotional Challenge of being an Expat.**

Additional Benefits for Becoming an Expat

Put simply, you live only once. If you can get out there, into the wider world, and discover new places and cultures, new people, and experiences, you'll find that this enriches you and brings lots of new experiences and satisfaction.

Broadening your horizons means taking yourself outside your comfort zone, meeting people who you'd never have met in normal circumstances, making connections that could completely change your life, and experiencing moments and lifestyles that were previously limited to Facebook or Television.

You'll witness new cultures, new ways of life, new styles of cuisine.

Expatriates the world over are often seen as existing in cosseted bubbles, living, and interacting only with those who share their nationality or language. But the reality, like the nature of the expat world itself, is complicated and changing. Nowadays expats are just as likely to be Asian as they are Western and an increasing number of professionals are moving abroad independently, instead of on a company-sponsored posting.

You can, if you choose, live in a complete bubble with communities from your place of origin, but you would be losing as much as you gain. If you want to get something out of being an expat; the food, the culture, you must get to know local people.

## Life in a bubble

Of course, in some places, where the expat population far exceeds the local one, sticking within the bubble isn't so difficult. In Dubai, the overall foreign population makes up about 88% of those living there, according to the International Organization for Migration. In nearby Qatar, it's 76%, the IOM data shows. Unsurprisingly, in these places' expats are more likely to socialize with each other (65% in Qatar and similar levels in the UAE and other Gulf states), according to InterNations, the global expat networking group.

In a country like Saudi Arabia, the demographics aren't so stark, but strict rules govern society, making it hard for expats to make friends among the local community. Some 61% of the expats InterNations surveyed there said they found it difficult to make local friends. In Kuwait, 31% went as far as to describe the process of making local friends as "very difficult."

The nature of the host country — be it a developed nation or an emerging economy, an open culture or a more guarded one — can also affect the kind of social circle an expat develops.

It's easy to meet other expats — through the office, kids' schools and even around the playgrounds and pools of their apartment complexes. But the internet has hugely expanded the opportunities for those who want to meet people outside their own community, including like-minded locals.

For example, at InterNations, which operates in 390 cities around the world, about 30% of its membership are local. At a recent event in London, British citizens were among the 100 different nationalities who signed up.

"People like meeting other expats who might have had the same problems and dealt with them," "But they also want to meet locals who know the location even better and want to share their culture."

Singapore, New Zealand, and Canada topped the HSBC Expat Explorer Survey in 2022, partly because expats saw the three countries as welcoming places where it was easy to integrate into the local community. For the second year in a row, Canada was named the most welcoming. More than three quarters of all expats there said they were integrating well into the local culture, compared with a global average of 61%.

## Getting comfortable being out of your comfort zone

While a contradiction in terms, many expats find they become used to getting out of their comfort zone and begin to see it as a thrill rather than a threat. The experience of setting up a bank account without speaking the local language or finding your way around a bustling city, when you are used to the quiet life in the suburbs, helps new expats realize their true potential, away from the routine of everyday life.

## Becoming an expat: cheaper than you'd think.

Of course, the cost of living depends on where you live. If you're living in London or Paris right now, prepare to be amazed by costs in Hong Kong and Singapore! But you may be surprised at just how cheaper you could live your life abroad.

Expats often reference the reduced cost of living as a primary factor in moving abroad. Typically, money earned at home goes further abroad, and additional disposable income makes many experiences and adventures more accessible to expats.

## New kinds of food

If your new home is in a major city like London, you'll never be far from a fantastic range of restaurants. Often, this is part and parcel of International city living.

The sheer adventure of local novel cuisine really does make for an amazing experience. Food, cooking, and eating are so wrapped up in the fiber of our cultures and societies, and they'll be your gateway into new experiences and understanding your new home.

While you may be moving abroad alone, eating out becomes the de facto shared experience of expats, and a great way to meet new people.

## Being more culturally aware

If you are moving from a multicultural city like Toronto, London or Paris, you are likely to have a lot in common with others in your city. You are familiar with societal norms and 'how things are done' in your home country.

When you move overseas, your eyes will be opened to how different countries operate. You will need to be aware of and possibly adapt to these cultural differences to get things done, professionally and personally. This will improve how you work with colleagues when you repatriate.

## Better education prospects

Many expats move to other countries with their families to give their children better prospects for learning and development. Countries in North America and Western Europe are rightly famed for their world-leading education systems, and we are accustomed to seeing high proportions of foreign students enrolling in highly valued private educational institutions.

Knowing that your children are experiencing a high-quality education is great for your peace of mind. Plus, living abroad introduces the possibility for them of learning a new language, a skill which cannot but help your children lead a better life.

## Better Employment Opportunities

One of the main reasons that people move abroad is employment. Perhaps you are stagnating in your company, or perhaps you're a remote worker who is no longer tied down to any time zone. Or perhaps you've just decided to take a chance abroad.

Wrapped up in our home countries, it's easy to forget that life exists and flourishes elsewhere, foreign economies could be booming, and opportunity abounds everywhere. If you're setting up a business or looking for a new position of employment, it's certainly worth considering where the best country is and even continent for your prospects. In addition there are a lot of opportunities to live overseas and still work digitally (by zoom for instance) in the company that you worked from originally.

## Learning to be more patient

We are all used to an element of routine in our day-to-day lives. When we make a move to another country we must start again from scratch. This could involve organizing utilities for your new accommodation, enrolling your children in school, or working out your new commute. Things are bound to be complicated, there may be miscommunication, misunderstandings or time spent lost in an unfamiliar city. Although this may prove frustrating initially, you will learn to be more patient and allow more time for many things you would consider routine in your home country.

## Love for city or remote living

Depending on your assignment, you might be moving from the suburbs to live in a busy city or from a busy city to a very remote location. No matter what the change is for you, it may feel intimidating initially but once you settle in, you may develop a love for a fast city life or the relaxed pace of rural living.

## Better at nurturing and maintaining relationships.

There is no doubt, living away from the support of friends and family is challenging. But during your time overseas you may develop ways of maintaining those relationships that make your relationships stronger. It could be a weekly Skype (skype is being phased out) call where you spend quality time really talking and listening to each other. While maintaining these connections you can also create new, expat relationships with others who are in a similar situation to yourself in your new location.

It is also very common for new very intimate relationships to develop while living as an expat. Away from families and friends we tend to develop new alternative families with relationships that are more intimate and mutually dependent.

## An Opportunity to relax.

When you move abroad, you'll find yourself sucked into an administrative machine. You'll certainly have your work cut out, what with sorting out visas, banking, and paperwork.

But this is a perfect opportunity to let go of the stress and let your new environment take over. Becoming an expat can relax you, as you realize that you can't control everything.

Just let your new way of living take over and focus only on what you can control. It can be rather liberating!

## Build your confidence.

Strangely, you may find yourself becoming more confident as an expat. When you move abroad, you're making a huge change and this is a great achievement: you've moved away from friends and family, you've temporarily (possibly) cut ties with your home country, you're moving into new accommodation and taking a new occupation.

Taken together and combined under the context of moving abroad, these changes can take on massive proportions! The achievement of moving abroad will make you feel like you can take on anything. It's an exciting time, and you'll feel stronger and more independent about it.

## Lose your attachment to material Assets.

Wherever you are relocating to, you will be forced to cull some of your belongings when you move, or at least leave them behind. This is liberating and is one of the key reasons why so many people change for the better when they move.

You will lose your attachment to material things and become more aware of people and nature and what they can offer you.

The stress of moving and adjusting to the new country can lead to anxiety and depression and other psychological problems. Often the hardest thing for new residents in a new country is coping with the loss of family and friends.

It certainly is a huge decision to live abroad, whether you are following your dreams or moving for other reasons.

It also could be one hell of a new start, bringing all the excitement that goes along with going on a big adventure, meeting many new people, becoming more tolerant as you experience other people from other cultures, a whole new country to explore with new travel opportunities, you will grow as a person from the experience as living abroad introduces you to alternative ways of thinking and behaving, You will learn about a new culture, its history, and maybe even a new language, it certainly will be a new challenge.

But on the other hand,

It will be difficult as you leave your old life behind, you will leave family and friends behind. If you have offspring, you will be asking them to leave their friends and schools behind too with very little say in the matter.

Experts think that the most stressful things in life are divorce, death and moving home, but one life-changing event they missed off the list is migrating from the country of your origin. These countries are often on the other side of the world from most migrants and in a totally different time zone. The psychological impact of moving to such a faraway place and different culture is often very significant.

Moving abroad is not an easy decision. Lots of individuals and families prepare well for the task of emigrating overseas though there are some psychological aspects of immigration that it's difficult to prepare for.

One of the hardest parts of relocating is undoubtedly living simultaneously in two different countries. And as much as most families and individuals would like to keep ties with their home country, there are emotional drawbacks to living your life in different countries at the same time.

Once you have made the move, you may find it even harder to reconcile the rules, environments, and behaviors of your two different countries, and this can place stress on your mind and body.

Individuals often find themselves torn between two homes– and the price is often a breakdown of emotional stability.

In addition to this it can also cost a lot of money to move depending on how much of your life you are taking with you.

There can be language barriers, at least until you get a grasp of the new tongue. Add in the time it will take to devote to learning the language too.

You may find it a shock to settle into a new country, with a different way of living and facing new problems.

Simple daily tasks (such as shopping or making appointments) can become very difficult and challenging to achieve, especially at the outset. Everything will take more time and effort to do.

You are stepping right out of your comfort zone – there are positives to doing that as well though.

You may go through a period of feeling misunderstood, especially if there is a language barrier or a different culture, and that could be quite frustrating.

## There is also a Reverse culture shock when going back home.

Many people expect the culture shock that comes with moving abroad. It can take months to overcome language barriers and social differences while dealing with leaving behind your family and friends. However, the reverse culture shock, which can follow, may come as a surprise.

Things that were once familiar might seem unusual. You may have to re-acclimatize to a warmer or colder climate. Your friends and family members could be in different stages of their lives.

The important thing to remember is that it's also normal to feel disconnected when you return to the country of your origin; keep in mind that this feeling will pass. Staying in touch with the latest news from your home country in the weeks leading up to moving home can help.

## Personal Safety and Crime

Many expats cite personal safety and crime as a concern for them before moving to a new host country. This is an even bigger consideration for those moving to African countries, where closer to two thirds consider this a major factor. There is always a fear for one's own safety when traveling to an unknown place, but there are a few measures that can be taken to mitigate this worry.

Most places in the world publish detailed crime statistics that are freely available to the public. When choosing a place of residence, make sure to study the surrounding locality and historical trends relating to criminal activity there. Most cities have areas that are widely regarded as unsafe by locals, and so accordingly should be avoided.

Local expat forums and social media platforms are good ways to connect and figure out where the safest areas to stay are. Some cities might be dangerous for women and children to be out alone at night, so getting a good idea of the native culture is important to staying protected. Also make it a point to get details and contact information for the local law enforcement infrastructure.

## Language Barriers

Learning the local language is an important part of feeling at home in many host countries. Not knowing the local language can certainly have a negative impact on one's ability to integrate with the local community, and most expats in fact learn it. In an international survey, not many expats were concerned that learning a new language would be a burden on them.

Fortunately, with learning tools now freely available across a variety of media, it's easier and less expensive than ever. It's advisable to get a head start before you make the move, and many mobile apps, websites and books can help you get accustomed to the new language. You can go further by getting a language tutor, or finding someone who speaks the native language in your current home and practicing with them.

## Healthcare and Potential Health Risks

Many expats are concerned about the potential quality of, and access to, healthcare in the country they were moving to. This is of greater significance to retirees who were more likely to need medical attention, and to parents who were concerned for their children's wellbeing.

The cost of private healthcare continues to rise globally, while the quality of public healthcare can often leave much to be desired.

Not having adequate healthcare provisions in place for your family can be a very costly mistake in the event of an unforeseen emergency. It's also possible that hospitals will refuse treatment if you do not have an accepted form of health insurance, so it's essential to know what the policies are.

Potential health hazards in a new country are also a legitimate cause for concern. It's best to check with a qualified health agency about whether you are required to take any specific precautions or inoculations before travelling.

Research the various healthcare and insurance policies available to you and choose the one which best suits your family's needs. It's advisable to spend a little time and money upfront to get fully covered, so that you are prepared if medical treatment becomes necessary.

## Purchasing Health Insurance for Expats

Health insurance for expats is a crucial aspect of ensuring their well-being and peace of mind while living in a foreign country. As they venture far from their home country, the uncertainties and risks associated with unfamiliar healthcare systems can be daunting. Purchasing adequate health insurance becomes paramount to safeguarding against unforeseen medical expenses and accessing quality healthcare services. These are some key considerations when making this essential purchase.

Health insurance for expats provides coverage for medical expenses, including hospitalization, doctor's visits, medications, and emergency treatments. Without proper insurance, expats might find themselves facing exorbitant bills, limited access to healthcare facilities, or even denial of treatment in some cases. By having a comprehensive health insurance plan, expats can minimize financial burden and focus on their personal and professional endeavours in the new country.

The first step in purchasing health insurance for expats is to research and compare various insurance plans. Factors to consider include the coverage scope, the network of healthcare providers, the premium cost, and the deductible. Expats should also examine whether the insurance covers pre-existing conditions, maternity care, and emergency medical evacuations, which can be vital in critical situations.

An essential consideration is whether to opt for international health insurance or a local plan from the host country. International plans generally offer more extensive coverage, flexibility to seek treatment worldwide, and smoother claims processes. On the other hand, local plans might be more affordable, especially in countries with lower healthcare costs, but they could limit coverage outside that country.

Understanding the healthcare system of the host country is crucial for selecting the right insurance policy. In some nations, public healthcare might be of high quality and affordable, while in others, private healthcare facilities could be the preferred choice. Expats should also check if their insurance policy requires direct billing arrangements with healthcare providers or if they need to pay upfront and claim reimbursement later.

Additionally, expats should consider their personal health needs and lifestyle. If they engage in high-risk activities or have existing health conditions, a more comprehensive and specialized insurance plan may be necessary. Moreover, if they plan to travel frequently or relocate to different countries, a policy with international coverage and portability will be advantageous.

Before finalizing the purchase, it's crucial to read and understand the policy documents thoroughly. Pay attention to exclusions, waiting periods, and any additional services, such as wellness programs or mental health support. Seeking advice from insurance experts or consulting with other expats who have firsthand experience can provide valuable insights and recommendations.

In conclusion, purchasing health insurance for expats is an essential investment in their well-being and security while living abroad. It protects against unexpected medical expenses and ensures access to quality healthcare services. By carefully evaluating different plans, understanding the host country's healthcare system, and considering individual health needs, expats can make informed decisions to find the most suitable health insurance policy. Having this coverage in place allows expats to focus on embracing new experiences and opportunities in their chosen foreign destination with confidence and peace of mind.

## Examples of Providers and their Business Models

Global healthcare providers operate with various models to deliver medical services worldwide. These models can differ based on the scope of services, ownership structure, funding mechanisms, and target clientele. Here are some examples of global healthcare providers with different models:

**International Private Healthcare Groups**: Companies like Bupa, Cigna, and Aetna are well-known examples of international private healthcare providers. They offer comprehensive health insurance plans and medical services to individuals, families, and corporate clients in multiple countries. These providers maintain a global network of healthcare facilities and partner with local clinics and hospitals to ensure access to medical care wherever their clients are located.

**Medical Tourism Companies**: Medical tourism companies, such as Apollo Hospitals in India and Gleneagles Hospital in Singapore, cater to international patients seeking medical treatment in specific countries. They offer packages that include medical procedures, travel arrangements, and accommodations. These providers often focus on specialized treatments, elective surgeries, and medical procedures that are cost-effective or not readily available in the patient's home country.

**Non-Governmental Organizations (NGOs)**: Some NGOs operate global healthcare programs to deliver medical services to underserved populations in developing countries. For instance, Doctors Without Borders (Médecins Sans Frontières) deploys medical teams to provide emergency medical care and humanitarian aid in regions affected by conflict, epidemics, or natural disasters.

**International Health Organizations**: Global health organizations like the World Health Organization (WHO) and the World Bank play a critical role in shaping and coordinating healthcare policies and initiatives worldwide. They provide technical assistance, research, and funding to support healthcare infrastructure development and disease prevention programs in various countries.

**Telemedicine Providers**: Telemedicine companies, such as Teladoc Health and Doctor on Demand, offer virtual medical consultations and remote healthcare services to patients across the globe. Through online platforms and mobile applications, patients can access qualified healthcare professionals for non-emergency medical advice, diagnosis, and treatment.

**International Hospital Chains**: Hospital chains like Mediclinic International and Ramsay Health Care operate multiple healthcare facilities across different countries. They standardize medical practices, maintain high-quality care, and attract medical tourists seeking reliable medical services with international accreditation.

**Public-Private Partnerships (PPPs)**: In some cases, governments collaborate with private healthcare providers to improve healthcare access and infrastructure. These partnerships can take various forms, such as the construction and management of public hospitals by private companies or the provision of specific medical services through contracted private providers.

Each of these global healthcare providers operates with distinct models, but they all contribute to the delivery of healthcare services on an international scale. Their presence and diversity play a vital role in addressing the diverse healthcare needs of people around the world, promoting medical advancements, and ensuring health equity on a global level.

Examples of Global Healthcare Providers who provide direct access to healthcare and providers that require the Expat to pay and then be reimbursed.

Global healthcare providers offering direct arrangements with healthcare providers (no need to pay and ask for reimbursement):

**Bupa Global**: Bupa is an international private healthcare group that provides health insurance and medical services across the globe. Bupa has a network of healthcare providers in various countries with whom they have direct billing arrangements. This allows their members to access medical services without paying upfront; instead, the bill is settled directly between Bupa and the healthcare provider.

**Aetna International**: Aetna International is another major global health insurance provider that offers direct billing arrangements with a network of healthcare providers worldwide. Their members can avail medical services without having to pay upfront, as Aetna handles the billing process directly.

**Cigna Global Health**: Cigna Global Health provides health insurance solutions for expats and globally mobile individuals. They have an extensive network of healthcare providers and offer direct billing services, making it convenient for their members to access medical care without worrying about upfront payments.

Global healthcare providers who require upfront payment and require you to claim reimbursement later:

**GeoBlue**: GeoBlue is a provider of international health insurance plans primarily catering to expats. In some cases, GeoBlue members may need to pay for medical services upfront, especially if they seek treatment outside their network of preferred providers. After receiving the medical care, they can file a claim for reimbursement, and GeoBlue will cover eligible expenses as per the policy terms.

**Allianz Care**: Allianz Care offers health insurance plans for expats and global citizens. Depending on the specific plan and location, some medical services may require upfront payment, especially if the healthcare provider is not part of their direct billing network. Allianz Care members can submit reimbursement claims to receive coverage for eligible expenses.

**AXA Global Healthcare**: AXA Global Healthcare provides health insurance solutions for individuals and families living or working abroad. Like some other providers, the reimbursement model applies when policyholders receive treatment from non-network providers or in countries where direct billing arrangements are not established.

It's essential for individuals seeking global health insurance to carefully review the terms and conditions of their chosen policy to understand the billing process and reimbursement procedures. While direct billing arrangements offer the convenience of not paying upfront, the reimbursement model may require policy-holders to have sufficient funds to cover initial medical expenses until they can claim reimbursement from their insurance provider.

## Your Relationship with your Partner

It's common for expats to make a move to be concerned about the impact it will have on their existing relationships.

If you're a spouse accompanying a working individual, if can be difficult to adapt to a new environment. A radical shift can expose cracks in a relationship, and there are instances where a spouse wants to return to the comforts of their home country. Communication is vital to ensuring that both partners are on the same page and pulling in the same direction.

Fortunately for couples, most expats who moved abroad because their partner accepted a job believed that the move strengthened their relationship. Overall, expats usually say that the journey overseas has brought them closer together.

Relationships back home can be a little trickier to maintain. But with the various video messaging and chat applications like Skype, WhatsApp and Facetime available nowadays, it's probably easier than ever before to stay in touch. It's imperative to take the lead in connecting regularly, whether it's by calling in or catching up on a social network. Hearing from friends and loved ones also helps to alleviate any loneliness or homesickness you may be experiencing in a new country.

## Guidance on Networking for an expat

Networking and making friends can be a valuable tool for expats to build connections, establish professional relationships, and access opportunities in their new country. Remember many expats find comfort in their new friendships. Here are some guidance points for networking as an expat:

- Join Local Professional Networks: Research and join professional associations, industry-specific groups, and networking events in your new country. These organizations often offer opportunities to connect with professionals in your field and gain insights into the local job market.

- Attend Social and Cultural Events: Engage in social and cultural activities to meet people from various backgrounds and build a diverse network. Attend local festivals, community gatherings, and expat meetups to connect with like-minded individuals and establish friendships.\

- Leverage Online Networking Platforms: Utilize online platforms such as LinkedIn, professional forums, and expat communities to expand your network. Join relevant groups and actively participate in discussions to showcase your expertise and connect with professionals in your industry.

- Reach Out to Alumni Networks: If you attended a university or educational institution, explore the possibility of connecting with alumni in your new country. Alumni networks often organize events and provide platforms for networking and mentorship.

- Seek Out Expat Support Groups: Join expat support groups or forums where you can connect with fellow expats who have experienced similar challenges. These groups can offer valuable advice, support, and potential networking opportunities.

- Attend Workshops and Seminars: Participate in workshops, seminars, and conferences related to your field of interest. These events provide opportunities to learn, gain industry knowledge, and meet professionals who share your interests.

- Volunteer and Engage in Community Service: Volunteering can help you connect with locals, contribute to the community, and expand your network. Look for volunteer opportunities aligned with your interests or professional skills.

- Be Open and Approachable: Approach networking with an open and positive mindset. Be proactive in initiating conversations, listening actively, and showing genuine interest in others. Be approachable, friendly, and respectful of cultural differences.

- Offer Help and Support: Networking is a two-way street. Be willing to help, advise, or support to others when appropriate. Building a reputation as a helpful and reliable professional can open doors for future collaborations and opportunities.

- Maintain Relationships: Networking is not just about making initial connections; it's about nurturing and maintaining relationships over time. Stay in touch with your contacts, send follow-up messages after meetings or events, and offer support whenever possible.

- Remember, networking takes time and effort, so be patient and persistent. Building a strong network as an expat can provide valuable support, professional opportunities, and a sense of belonging in your new environment.

# Chapter Four

## "Laying the Foundation: Key Preparations for Your Expat Journey"

### Creating a budget

Adapting to a new reality and the cost of living brings one of the most common considerations of expats, with many admitting to not having given enough thought before moving abroad. This is reasonable, as the usual promise of a larger salary or less tax doesn't necessarily translate to a larger disposable income if you move to a country with a higher cost of living. Matters are further complicated by differences in currency values, and it can all be quite difficult to comprehend initially.

There are many costs to consider when planning a budget, such as housing, utilities, travel, food, and taxes. It's often wise to get advice on managing financial matters and keeping a generous buffer to meet unexpected costs that are sure to arise in a new location. Some careful research can help in estimating costs to a certain degree, and expat forums can often provide helpful cost-cutting advice too. The sooner you can familiarize yourself with your new surroundings, the easier it will be to find cheaper local alternatives and so alleviate some of the pressure on your finances.

Surveys reveal that three out of every four expats worldwide were challenged by an aspect of money management abroad. They reported that dealing with multiple currencies, complicated tax systems and moving money between countries were some of the most common financial problems they faced.

## How to prepare a budget

To begin with, you'll need to look at what you have in terms of money coming in and going out, (Income and Expenses).

Look at all sources of income, including salary, dividends, advisory fees, and others that come in every month. Divide this into two categories, income created in the country of your new residence and passive income (dividends, royalties, rental income and investment income)

Then look at your expenditure:

How much do you spend each month in total?

How much do you put on a credit card?

How much do you spend on utilities?

How much on food, entertainment, discretionary spending, etc?

Build a picture of your income versus expenditure and make a record of it.

How you choose to record the information doesn't really matter provided you do it.

You could use a spreadsheet, or an app or even specific financial software. Or pencil and paper.

The purpose of this step is to give you the chance to understand where you are now and identify potential problem areas before moving on to the next step.

## Defining Goals

Now we want to build some clarity and focus on where you are going.

It's about identifying your financial goals, otherwise known, and your 'wants' and 'needs'.

Do you need to build an emergency fund? (If you don't have one, then the answer to this question is categorically 'yes'. Having accessible cash available for emergency situations is an important part of solid financial planning foundations.)

Are you thinking about your retirement needs?

This is where you set the framework for your budget or financial plan.

Allocate your income to the things you need, i.e., rent/mortgage payments, food, bills, debt payments, clothing, etc.

List them in order of importance including investing free from restraints income.

How much you allocate to savings varies from person to person, but 10-20% of your disposable monthly income is a perfectly achievable goal for most people.

The key point here is to set yourself up with a structure. You can adjust later as you go along.

Once you have done this, you have basically created your budget.

When I leave my country of origin should I sell or rent out my home

Deciding whether to sell or rent your house in your country of origin when moving overseas is a significant decision that depends on several factors. Here are a few considerations to help you make an informed choice:

Financial Considerations: Evaluate the potential financial gains and risks of each option. Selling the house can provide you with a lump sum of money that you can use for your new life abroad. On the other hand, renting it out can provide a steady income stream, especially if the rental market is strong and the property is in a desirable location.

Long-Term Plans: Consider your long-term plans for the property. If you intend to return to your country of origin in the future, you might prefer to keep the house and rent it out. Renting allows you to retain ownership and potentially benefit from future property value appreciation.

Rental Market: Research the rental market in your area to gauge demand, rental rates, and vacancy rates. If the rental market is favorable and you can find reliable tenants, renting might be a viable option. However, if the market is weak or saturated, it could be challenging to secure tenants or achieve the desired rental income.

Property Management: Reflect on your willingness and ability to manage the property from a distance. Renting out a property comes with responsibilities, including finding tenants, managing mainte- nance and repairs, dealing with potential issues, and ensuring legal compliance. If you don't want the hassle or if you'll be unable to manage the property effectively, selling might be a more suitable choice.

Emotional Attachment: Consider your emotional attachment to the property. If the house holds sentimental value or has been in your family for generations, you might prefer to retain ownership and pass it on to future generations.

Tax Implications: Consult with a tax professional to understand the tax implications of selling or renting your property in your country of origin. Different countries have varying tax laws and regulations regarding property sales, rental income, and capital gains.

Ultimately, the decision to sell or rent your house when moving overseas depends on your unique circumstances, financial goals, long-term plans, and personal preferences. It's advisable to seek professional advice from a real estate agent, financial advisor, or tax consultant to make an informed decision based on your specific situation. Don't forget, if you sell, you may not be able to afford to repurchase the property.

## "Navigating the Advisor Landscape": Choosing the Perfect Partner for Your Expat

### Finances

When working with advisers, you should ask first, are you the client or is your money the client? This is the most critical question you need to ask. So, what really sets good people apart from "distributors and product salespeople."

For most, the money is the client, and so their systems, methodologies and procedures are all about classifying the money (low, medium, and high risk, for example,) and advice on the product. The value for the client- that's you - is limited.

The Goal of a good adviser is not to help a client commit to purchasing a product, but to help families achieve their defined life goals. A good adviser will not be limited to providing thoughts within the limits of regulated thinking, she or he will take on all the challenges of the family globally.

Every day, the family's location in the world becomes less and less important. In the past, people lived in a region, and it made up their entire world. Today a person's location no longer restricts them from experiencing the rest of the world. Our environment is constantly changing, due to the development of vehicles, ships, and airplanes.

These inventions significantly affected human relations, travel, and the economy. Land phones, hand-held devices, computers, technologies and most importantly, the internet, have made it possible for people to communicate with other people, whom they wouldn't have been able to communicate with otherwise. With the help of computers, people can now acquire information from all around the world and smart phones have made the internet easily accessible.

## The Information-Sharing Age

While the development of transportation, technology, the internet, and smart phones have made accessing information very easy, there still are challenges especially for expats. In addition to having access to our monies, investments and savings plans we need to have access to information and understand cross-border issues and understand platforms and assets in a global environment. We need to choose a professional who is trained to help us with this.

## International Finance

These days, coordination among financial products such as retirement and inheritance products are prevalent. Professionals limited to local knowledge and experience (however broad) are not likely to supply significant value to us expats. We need to look for advisers who can provide significant value, who have a wider range of expertise and work experience. They need to understand international trends relating to and being able to identify domestic equivalents of financial products, for people who are arriving in or departing from a country.

## Can access to International Knowledge benefit Your Business and Life?

Things you should think about:

**Are your assets in the right jurisdiction?** Where is your money sitting? In today's world governments must address and are addressing the issue of taxation on assets and freedom of movement of assets for assets that are placed in a jurisdiction that is not the domiciled home of the owner.

**Legislation in the European Union** (EURBS) Britain (QROPS and QNUPS) and the US allow some freedom of movement of assets – these opportunities for clients can have significant economic outcomes for clients with assets in pension funds in the US, Europe and Britain, for example exemption from inheritance tax and more efficient tax planning on income from assets that can result in hundreds of thousands of Euro or Dollars in savings towards a better lifestyle or transferring assets to the next generation.

**Do you have a Diversified Asset Allocation?** The purpose of asset allocation is to achieve maximum returns with the lowest exposure to risk. This is not an easy task. In the past we based the building of our portfolios on a risk-free core asset base, but does that exist anymore? If US Government bonds are no longer risk free then what is risk free? The last risk-free meal in the investment world is diversification. Diversifying assets over geographic regions, economic sectors and non-correlated assets is essential for less overall exposure to risk.

## Have you considered Life Planning?

If you don't know where you are going – what is the chance that you will get there? Life planning means understanding assets and what the family wants to achieve with the assets. Money is never a goal; what money can buy is the goal. Mapping out life goals and matching assets to goals (understanding what returns are essential to life the life we dream of and then looking for investments that match best our needs) is starting a process of becoming the person you most want to be.

## Do you have access to Global Tax Planning?

Once it was said that global tax planning was the province of ultra-high net worth individuals only. This is jargon for the super-rich.

This is not true anymore. While ultra-high net worth individuals understand and highly value global tax planning, it is now essential for all of us especially for expats. In a world where we alone are responsible for our futures, we can accumulate significant assets and must have a global view on our assets and our tax obligations. We must look at this as fast as possible as good tax planning can increase our tax-free assets, making more available to life the life we dream of.

Before you even consider choosing a financial planner or adviser to help you on your journey, you need to determine what you want to accomplish in terms of long and short-term goals.

Though most may not seem financially oriented at first, many goals are probably related to money: retiring, purchasing a home, helping your children attend college or just giving them a hand. A good financial planner can help you to reach those desirable areas.

Defining life goals can be emotional, possibly mundane, but it can be life changing. We all deal with personal challenges that are part of everyone's journey but once we start documenting specific goals, we start a process where we become the person we want to be.

So, take an evening or weekend to write down your specific money-related goals, whether it be buying a bigger house, paying off debt, or setting up a college savings plan for your child. It also may be helpful to list where you want to be in 5 years, 10 years, even 50 years.

Once you have done this, this will help your adviser with a more well-rounded view of where you'd like to be financially. Then they can help you get there.

## Find a Financial Planner that understands the challenges of an expat.

When you move abroad or invest internationally, one of the questions that you will often ask yourself is "how do I ensure I'm managing my global finances in the most tax efficient manner possible".

Just like in your home country, seeking professional advice from experts that understand your challenges is vital when it comes to managing your finances to ensure that you're on the right side of the law while remaining as tax efficient as possible. When it comes to finding the best financial planner for your purposes, there are steps you can take to ensure that they have your best interests at heart, and it's not all about finding ways to separate you from your money.

## Ask about education, licenses and who regulates them.

The financial advisory ecosystem can be surprisingly complex. Nearly anyone can call themselves a financial advisor, financial planner, or financial coach, with minimum or no qualifications required. Consequently, it's important to be careful and thoughtful when selecting a professional to help you save, grow, and protect your savings.

Here are some things to consider when shopping for a financial advisor.

## Education and Experience

Review your prospective advisor's educational background and experience to learn why that person may be uniquely positioned to help you. Seek advisors who have demonstrated they have acquired the knowledge and can apply this knowledge to develop a strategy for you.

The website and articles published could be a good starting point to learn about his/her qualifications, experience, and how she/he thinks but a referral from someone you trust who has worked with him/her may be even better.

Check on the internet, this may sound mundane, but you can learn a lot about a person easily just by searching for the name, if you find nothing that too can be a warning sign, if he/she was involved in litigation on issues involving advice that too can be a warning sign for you to avoid.

Don't just put your money with the first financial planner you meet with. Do your research and ask around. Often, word of mouth is the best way to find a great financial planner.

Ideally, you should ask friends or relatives who have similar goals and strategies regarding finances. This will help you find a financial planner who is a better fit.

## Certifications

Try to see what steps your proposed advisor has taken to increase their knowledge base and how often they achieve this. One way is through the various certifications he/she may hold. Specifically, take the time to learn about both the upfront requirements needed to attain a certification and the ongoing requirements for maintaining it.

For example, the Certified Financial Planner designation (CFP®) is considered an excellent standard in financial planning circles.

To get the CFP® designation, planners must take extensive, specialized coursework, pass an exam, and accrue three years of relevant experience. Every two years, those with certificates must complete many hours of continuing education (usually 30 hours per annum).

Other worldwide common designations that could be relevant include Certified Public Accountant (CPA), Chartered Financial Analyst (CFA), for advisors that specialize in portfolio management and investing, and the Accredited Financial Counselor (AFC®), for advisors who may focus on financial coaching and counseling.

### Trust and relationships.

When working with anyone, chemistry is important, and each planner is unique. In many cases, simply providing good advice may not be enough. It is also important that you can build a personal relationship with your adviser. A good planner is not just someone who understands you and your goals, he will be your confidant and he should care about your journey as if it is his own.

It's hard to quantify exactly how important trust is when working with an advisor. In business, a lack of trust can be the biggest liability. Without trust, transactions cannot occur, influence is destroyed. Trust and relationships, much more than money, are the currency of financial planning.

Trust is the natural result of thousands of actions, words, thoughts, and intentions. Trust usually does not happen at once as gaining trust takes work. It might take years for you to really trust a professional.

So, it is important to make sure that whoever you choose will act in your best interests.

If you consider that some investments will be extremely long term what you don't want to be doing is transferring your assets from one solution to another because you've had to change your adviser.

It is likely however that with every transfer, the adviser will take some form of commission as payment. This creates a conflict of interest. You may want to work with a professional who is compensated by you directly via a fee structure and not from the product. At the very least, advisers must be completely transparent and tell you what they are earning and how.

While you build a relationship with your adviser, your adviser must try to understand your personality, values, what kind of a person you are and what kind of a person you want to be, understand in detail your risk profile so he/she can make decisions on your behalf, if you so wish.

Once that level of trust is established, much of the pressure of keeping an eye on your assets will be removed and you can live in comfort knowing that your best interests are being withheld.

## Sorting them out

There are thousands of professional advisers around the world. Some are exceptional, some are little more than agents who sell financial products.

## So how can you spot the good from the bad?

The first thing you can do is some due diligence with their existing clients. So, before you make any formal arrangement, ask to speak to several existing clients to find out how they feel. Make sure the client's profiles are like yours (being an expat). Beware of those who either cannot or do not wish to provide you with references. The professional may claim that he must be discreet and that clients will not agree to disclose their relationships, and this may be true but usually if the planner has happy clients, they are willing to share their experiences.

It is also worthwhile to run a google search on the professional and the firm he works for/owns. Sometimes a simple search can give you confidence or warn you.

It's also important that you don't simply go with what is on the websites and you speak to the people directly. While time consuming, it might just enable you that additional peace of mind before deciding.

Most importantly, don't go with the first adviser you come across, even if they seem perfect. Quite often, good salespeople can fool anyone, so the safest option is to get a second - or even third - opinion on any planner. Most advisers will offer a free consultation up front to enable them to understand more about you. Take advantage of this.

Thirdly, if they claim to be regulated, make sure you double check the register. And even then, if you or they are not in the jurisdiction of the regulatory body, it may not mean anything anyway. But at least you know that they are regulated somewhere.

Finally, don't just go with the cheapest or most expensive. When you evaluate the agreements and costs, ensure you know everything and get it in writing. It's far more important to be cost effective in the long run than keep costs low - or go with an expensive option because you think the price is a guide of quality.

## Don't let a professional drive you to action by using fear.

Whether you currently have a financial planner or not, making snap decisions normally ends in disaster. If an adviser is using fear to get you to react, take a step back and consider again. You should never be rushed into a decision which could have a major effect on your long-term financial health.

In addition, you must be aware that no financial planner is a prophet, and occasionally investments will not perform exactly as they wish, so rather than making an impulsive decision, sit with your adviser, discuss the situation and try and adjust your plan accordingly with him/her. This is where trust comes into play.

Remember, all investments come with some degree of risk - and there is no such opportunity which is a sure thing. Even the best professionals can get it wrong. The key to working together Is to mitigate these risks as much as possible.

## Too good to be true?

Last and by no means least, if something appears too good to be true, it usually is.

## Our Professionals are changing and our expectations from them should alter as well.

Over the last 20 years, financial planning has evolved, from trading in manual calculations and paper trails to software and interactive digital tools.

But evolution does not begin nor end with technology. Disruption and change within the financial industry will continue at the same pace over the next few decades, and those changes won't be restricted to technological capabilities.

Instead, clients' expectations are forcing professionals to expand the boundaries of the financial professional's role, forcing them into new territories, and encouraging deeper levels of connection with clients.

We define creating a financial plan as a communication that demonstrates a holistic understanding of our finances, desired objectives, and assumptions. It conveys an analysis of future outcomes on one or more financial topics that include recommendations and action items.

As our preferences and expectations evolve, we seek relationships with those who can help us connect, from achieving our financial goals to achieving targets in other aspects of our lives as well.

When financial planning was in its infancy, financial professionals worked primarily with wealthy clients. Much of their day was spent manually crunching numbers and executing repetitive tasks.

Today, the client experience has moved front and centre. The question of paying commissions or fees or agreeing to profit sharing on the profitability of the investment may be marginal to the managing of tax efficiency, exposure to new asset classes and to understanding the developments of the sectors of tomorrow.

In the future, new methods of advice delivery will once again change the planning profession for your benefit.

## What should we expect from a financial Plan?

A financial plan is the lens through which all our financial activities are examined and executed.

As we plan for our estate to change hands generationally, our chosen advisors need to understand and deliver value for us.

## The transition to a fee-based model

Regulators worldwide are working to align clients' interests with the interests of those who advise them. Regulators want to avoid conflicts of interests, linking the compensation of professionals to your best interest, encouraging them to develop new skills and pursue knowledge that will benefit those who are receiving the advice.

## The rise of the fee based and hybrid models.

Cerulli Associates (who for over 30 years, have been at the forefront of the financial services industry, delivering market intelligence and strategic business recommendations.) in their recent research report state that today 56 percent of investors are working with a fee-based model —a 5 percent increase.

## The rise of Cross Border Service for Expats

As the growing international economy and prevalence of virtual communication continue to flatten the world, we realize that you we part of a community of hundreds of millions of individuals who have crossed borders from native countries for opportunities to work and live abroad.

Crossing international borders introduces several unique issues and challenges, from opening bank accounts, transferring money from country to country, working with and buying and selling multiple currencies, financial reporting obligations, tax complexities, to moving retirement benefits between countries.

One of the major questions you will pose is what can you trust in this process?

## "Embracing the Academic Approach: Building Trust in the Expat Decision-Making Process"

To address all these very important and complex issues we must not only put trust in a professional of choice but in an academic process backed by research and implemented by qualified professionals.

The process has six standard components. They are: Financial Management, Asset Management, Risk Management, Tax Planning, Retirement Planning, and Estate Planning.

The professional you choose should be proficient and educated to address these issues.

## Financial Management

The purpose of Financial Management is to understand and define your life goals, income and expenses, assets, and liabilities. They should help identify strategies and techniques to optimize short- and midterm cash flows, assets, as well as liabilities.

## Asset Management

Creating an investment management strategy provides you with the framework for making investment decisions. It ensures that your decision-making process with respect to portfolio management is consistent, even when unexpected market fluctuations tempt distraction. The development of an effective investment management strategy is the basis for building a family's future.

## Risk Management (Profiling) and Stress Testing

Creating a "Risk Profile "tests your willingness, capacity, and ability to take on risks. A risk profile is important for determining a proper investment asset allocation for a portfolio.

Controversially, it is accepted that if an individual expresses a desire for the highest possible return—and is willing to endure large swings in the value of the account to achieve it—there is a high willingness to take on risk. However, it really means that the risk could expose you to the possibility of total loss.

"Scenario techniques" enable stress scenarios to be addressed. (What if for example the dollar loses 20% of its value, what if there is a crisis in the stock market etc.) —in addition to realistic economic performance scenarios. This can therefore be an effective tool for constructing stress-resilient portfolios.

While risk profiling and scenario management are very important, the priority is to work on individuality and specific life goals, dreams, values, and aspirations. Hence you align asset allocation accordingly.

## Tax Planning

The principles of tax planning form an integral part of any wealth-building strategy. The overall objective is to structure affairs to legally minimize the amount of tax to pay. You can accomplish this by adhering to what are known as the 4D's of taxation: deduct, defer, diminish, and divide.

Deduct – maximize all tax deductions and credits.

Defer – Defer paying tax if possible. A tax dollar deferred is often a dollar saved.

Diminish – Position investments in investment vehicles, which attract the least amount of tax, having full regard for your risk tolerance and asset allocation strategy.

Divide – Split income among family members to the maximum degree possible while considering other personal objectives.

## Retirement Planning

Retirement Planning is planning for the day we stop accumulating assets and start living off the assets we have accumulated.

By identifying all sources of income and all expenses and recognizing the timing of each, you can identify in any year when you will have a shortfall (more expenses than income). In those shortfall years, the monies invested can be used to cover these shortfalls. These controllable variables include:

- Controlling expenses as much as possible.

- Reducing taxes

- Improving the rate of return on the investment portfolio by changing investment strategy

- Reducing or eliminating one or more of your goals in the future if need be.

By making one or more of these changes, you can go from a shortfall to a surplus. When you have a surplus, it means that you would achieve all your goals and objectives, with something left over at the end of your planning horizons.

# Chapter Five

## "Welcome to Expatria: Embracing Our New Home"

There are over 300 million people living outside of their nation of origin today and if they organized themselves as an imaginary nation, 'Expatria' – they would have a population of over 300 million.

### The Challenge of Global Banking for expats

The world has been facing unprecedented challenges in the banking sector over the past decade and analysts find themselves in uncharted waters,

The global banking crises of 2008-09 and again in 2020-21 due to the COVID-19 pandemic and after that the impacts (positive and negative) of rising interest rates are challenging the sector again and again.

As we move forward, the banking industry is still facing many challenges that need to be addressed to ensure the stability and resilience of the global financial system.

This has been creating a challenge for expats who have left their country of origin and want to manage cross border banking.

Finding and opening an account with the best bank can be a challenge for expats.

Increasingly, banks are implementing stricter account opening requirements and more complex due diligence procedures, making it more difficult for expats to open accounts or transfer monies from jurisdiction to jurisdiction.

Mostly this is because of the headache of submitting the proper required documentation to meet the banks' requirements and in addition many expats simply apply to the wrong banks.

The most common challenges for expats who want to open accounts are:

As an expat you could be restricted because of your country of residence.

The bank does not work with expats (in some banks only specific branches are qualified to work with expats).

You are faced with exorbitant fees as an expat.

Unable to meet the strict account opening requirements.

Excluded from remote opening of an account as you are an expat.

Unable to support the monthly account balance.

Charged unexpectedly with crazy foreign transfer fees.

As you see there are many challenges, and the solution may lie in first choosing the right jurisdiction for your account. It may in addition to a local account opening a global account in places that are expat friendly for example Switzerland, Isle of Man, Singapore, or the US.

## Transferring Money for expats

Expat bank accounts are special accounts designed for people living an international lifestyle away from their home country. Many high street banks will offer specific international expat bank accounts but will often have strict requirements for opening an account as a new customer and may also be restricted depending on the country of residence.

## Offshore Banking

Expat offshore banking is a solution offered by international banks to expats in foreign jurisdictions and helps them retain one central account for the duration of time they work abroad. It's important to remember though, if you have left the UK to work abroad, you are provisionally considered a non-resident from the day you leave.

Some offshore regions are known for minimal taxation rates, making them attractive options for global expats. International bank account owners can transfer funds between countries and currencies smoother. Another benefit to banking offshore as an expat is there is a higher chance of being able to find financial services which are attuned to the internationally-minded, including a range of currency facilities – allowing you to save, and borrow, in other currencies.

## Transferring Money

Families and businesses have come up against the challenge of cross-border payments for years, but in the past few years' compliance with money laundering directives and the pandemic have truly changed the game.

## Money Laundering Directives

Money laundering is the process of concealing the origin of money obtained from illicit activities such as drug trafficking, gambling and prostitution by converting it into a legitimate source. It is a crime in most jurisdictions – although with varying definitions.

In the past, the term "money laundering" was applied only to financial transactions related to organized crime. Today its definition is often expanded by government and international regulators to mean "any financial transaction which generates an asset or a value as the result of an illegal act", which may involve actions such as tax evasion or false accounting. In the UK, it does not even need to involve money, but anything such as property or jewelry. Courts involve money laundering committed by private individuals, drug dealers, businesses, corrupt officials, members of criminal organizations such as the Mafia and even states.

The directive while having noble roots, is the source of many challenges and frustration for families who find themselves dealing with compliance experts in banks globally who interpret the directives as they see fit and, in many circumstances, take a very extreme opinion blocking money transfers for the elderly who cannot afford or warrant protection or advice and are left helpless dealing with bureaucrats who simply do not care.

While banks operating in the same country generally must follow the same anti-money laundering laws and regulations, financial institutions all structure their anti-money laundering efforts differently.

Today, most financial institutions globally, and many non-financial institutions, are required to identify and report dodgy dealings to the financial intelligence unit in the respective country. For example, a bank must verify a customer's identity and, if necessary, monitor transactions for suspicious activity. This process comes under know your customer measures, which means knowing the identity of the customer and understanding the kinds of transactions in which the customer is likely to engage. By knowing one's customers, financial institutions can often identify unusual or suspicious behavior, or "anomalies", which may be an indication of money laundering. This practice is the source of much frustration for expat families worldwide who just want to transfer money to their home base or to their accounts overseas.

In addition to this, the directives have become a challenge for families investing overseas. A simple investment can become complicated when redeeming funds. There are many financial institutions involved in a simple transaction for example.

A client makes a redemption of a fund in Country X and instructs them to transfer the money into their account in their country of Jurisdiction.

In this very simple scenario, the process today is as follows:

The Custodian of the fund ("payer") will transfer the money into the Payers bank who will transfer the money into a Correspondent Bank who will transfer the monies to a fund clearance organization (such as Euroclear owned by S&P). This in turn will transfer the monies to the Payee's bank (usually in bulk) who will usually deposit the money into a clearance account until internal accounting allocates the monies back to the client.

If a problem arises and any of these financial institutions delay the process, usually blaming compliance, it can be very challenging to work out what happened, why, and how the problem should be solved.

Bank employees, such as tellers and customer account representatives, are trained in anti-money laundering and are instructed to report activities that they deem suspicious, and this suspicion is sometimes allocated not to those involved in criminal activity but also to the weak and defenseless, maybe on minor transactions.

Additionally, anti-money laundering software filters customer data, classifies it according to level of suspicion, and inspects it for anomalies. Such anomalies include any sudden and substantial increase in funds, a large withdrawal, or moving money from a bank in a tax-free jurisdiction. (This is relevant to all funds as they must establish themselves in tax free jurisdictions to avoid inflicting double taxes on investors)

Smaller transactions that meet certain criteria may also be flagged as suspicious. The software also flags names on government "blacklists" and transactions that involve countries under sanction (Such as Russia today and many Russians). Once the software has mined data and flagged suspect transactions, it alerts the bank management, who must then determine what their course of action should be.

It is highly recommended to try and keep records on the source of monies received to avoid this and make the process easy and efficient.

## The effect of the Pandemic on money transfers

By pushing consumers to purchase online instead of in-store, the pandemic removed the geographical boundaries that usually confine commerce. As a result, cross-border E-commerce trans-actions grew by 17% during the pandemic in 2020. Consumers now easily buy from overseas companies that provide a positive purchasing experience.

It's not just consumers who are involved in this trend. Companies understand that the shift to remote work is not a temporary reality with many employees wanting either a fully remote or hybrid job. This could mean working for an employer in another country where the salary must be sent across a border.

The Top Challenges for Cross-Border Payments

Here are some of the top cross-border payments challenges:

## High Costs

Every transaction incurs a fee, but cross-border payments frequently incur several. This is because more players are involved in an international transaction than a domestic one, and they all want to be paid for their services.

Depending on the geographic region, a single transaction may have to travel to three or four countries. With each region governed by its own laws and restrictions, there is also a myriad of currency conversion fees and regulatory fees. Navigating these different protocols adds up and someone must bear the cost, either the provider or the customer.

## Slow Transactions

A multi-stage transaction necessarily takes longer than a simple direct transfer. As cross-border payments involve multiple entities, each of which must process the payment — these transactions can take several days to complete, leaving the recipient waiting on the payment to go through. This prolonged process is inconvenient at best and unsustainable at worst, especially for small businesses or when transferring large sums of money.

## A Lack of Transparency

Unfortunately, cross-border payments lack both speed and transparency. Multiple intermediaries, geographical distance, and differing regulations can create a complicated transaction path. Then there are the extra fees, some of which are necessary but cannot be traced, leaving customers to wonder what they're paying for.

## Solving Cross-Border Payment Problems

The whole outdated system must and will be overhauled. Inefficient technology built around a crumbling framework is creating a frustrating process for all parties involved.

With the right technological support, such as a third-party provider, merchants and customers can benefit from expert guidance. These providers can handle regulation compliance, currency conversion, and other cross-border complications. They're also more likely to have direct relationships with providers in other regions, minimizing the necessary stages in the transaction journey. The shorter the journey, the quicker and less expensive it is.

Lastly, a collaboration between international entities is critical to the success of cross-border payments.

## The Road Map for Money Transfers going Forward.

The journey to painless cross-border payments will not be easy. There are so many factors and players involved that a change would take time, but the good news is that a transformation is in the cards. It is important to understand the process, procedures, and challenges in moving monies and for the time being patience and keeping orderly records are of great importance.

With the right infrastructure, regulatory landscape, and standards in place, cross border payments will evolve.

Cross-border payments are expected to undergo significant evolution in the future, driven by advances in technology, changing regulatory landscapes, and increasing global connectivity. Here are a few potential ways in which cross-border payments may evolve:

Faster and Real-Time Transactions: Traditional cross-border payments can be slow and subject to multiple intermediaries. With the emergence of technologies like blockchain and distributed ledger technology (DLT), there is potential for faster and near-instantaneous cross-border transactions. This could reduce settlement times and improve overall efficiency.

Reduced Costs and Fees: Traditional cross-border payments often incur high fees, foreign exchange costs, and intermediary charges.

As digital payment solutions and FinTech innovations continue to grow, there is a possibility of reducing these costs. This could be achieved using cryptocurrencies, stablecoins, or digital assets, which can provide more cost-effective and transparent payment options.

Increased Security and Transparency: Blockchain and DLT offer enhanced security and transparency through features like immutable transaction records and smart contracts. These technologies have the potential to reduce fraud, improve data integrity, and provide better audit trails for cross-border payments.

Regulatory Changes and Standardization: Governments and regulatory bodies worldwide are recognizing the need for modernizing cross-border payment systems. Initiatives such as the European Union's Payment Services Directive 2 (PSD2) and the Society for Worldwide Interbank Financial Telecommunication (SWIFT) global payment innovation (GPI) are driving standardization, interoperability, and compliance across borders. Future regulations may further streamline cross-border payment processes.

Enhanced Customer Experience: The future of cross-border payments may prioritize improved customer experiences. Innovative solutions, such as mobile wallets, biometric authentication, and simplified user interfaces, could enhance convenience and accessibility for individuals and businesses making cross-border payments.

It's important to note that the evolution of cross-border payments will depend on various factors, including technological advancements, regulatory developments, industry collaborations, and the adoption of new payment infrastructures. While the future landscape is uncertain, these trends provide insights into potential directions for cross-border payments.

## Can the banking crisis affect me?

The crisis has been triggered by a range of factors, including rising debt levels, historically low but now fast rising interest rates, and the ongoing impacts of the COVID-19 pandemic. These factors have combined to create a volatile and unstable financial system, with many banks struggling to meet their obligations and remain afloat.

One of the main causes of the crisis has been the increasing levels of debt held by both individuals and corporations. Low-interest rates made it easier for people and businesses to borrow money, leading to a surge in debt levels. This, in turn, has created a situation where many borrowers are struggling to repay debts, putting pressure on the banking system.

The COVID-19 pandemic has also played a significant role in the crisis. Lockdowns and restrictions on travel and commerce led to a sharp decline in economic activity, with many businesses struggling to stay afloat. This led to a wave of defaults and bankruptcies, putting further pressure on the banking system.

The effects of the banking crisis are likely to be severe and far-reaching. One of the main effects is likely to be a sharp decline in economic growth, as businesses struggle to access credit and consumers cut back on spending. This, in turn, could lead to rising unemployment and social unrest.

Another effect of the crisis is likely to be a wave of bank failures and government bailouts, as banks struggle to meet their obligations and stay afloat. This could lead to a loss of confidence in the banking system, making it harder for banks to raise capital and access funding.

Remedies to control bank risk for the public:

It is virtually impossible to forecast the demise of a bank but there are things that we can do to mitigate the risk.

1. Work in jurisdictions that are heavily regulated and will back their banks (the US has declared that it will not let their banks fall, Switzerland, Ireland and the UK have demonstrated their commitment to the stability of their financial institutions, so these places are safer than others.

2. Diversification. Try and diversify between jurisdictions and banks.

3. For governments to control the banking crisis, a range of remedies will need to be implemented. One main remedy is to increase the level of capital that banks are required to hold. This will help to make banks more resilient to financial shocks, reducing the risk of bank failures and government bailouts. Before opening an account, check to see the level of capital the bank has and what kind of investments the bank has made. (In this scenario boring and no exposure to clever financial structures are better for us).

4. Look for an emphasis on transparency and accountability within the banking system.

5. Look for a focus on risk management within the banking industry. This means better risk models and tools and ensuring that banks have robust systems in place to manage and mitigate potential losses.

The banking crisis both now and coming is likely to have far-reaching effects on the global financial system. To control the crisis, a range of remedies will need to be implemented, including an increase in capital requirements, greater transparency and accountability, and a greater focus on risk management but for expats this means especially care when working with banks or financial institutions.

## The rise of Globalization

Globalization is increasing and the world is becoming ever more connected, driven by companies expanding globally, technology companies importing specialized talent and a growing open border policy by nations around the world.

Despite the challenges of global banking, financial globalization continues. The global stock of foreign investment relative to GDP has changed little since 2007, standing at roughly 180 percent of world GDP. In absolute terms, total foreign investments have grown to $132 trillion in 2016, up from $103 trillion in 2007. More than one-quarter of equities around the world are owned by foreign investors, up from 17 percent in 2000. In global bond markets, 31 percent of bonds were owned by a foreign investor in 2016, up from 18 percent in 2000. Foreign lending and other investment is the only component of foreign investment assets and liabilities that has declined since the crisis.

While foreign investment stocks remain highly concentrated among a handful of advanced economies, more countries are participating. My Financial Connectedness Ranking shows the total stock of foreign investment and liabilities for 100 countries, as well as their composition and growth. Advanced economies and international financial centres are the most highly integrated into the global system. The United States, Luxembourg, the United Kingdom, the Netherlands, and Germany top the ranking.

Cross border clients require specialized financial planning delivered through a personal relationship with a knowledgeable financial planner. Key areas of focus are:

- Understanding investment platforms that are aligned with different jurisdictional requirements.

- Understanding personal risk need, capacity, and tolerance

- Understanding the impact of an asset allocation aligned with our life goals.

- Understanding of Global Stock option and equity compensation

- Global Tax strategies and optimization of investment portfolios to maximize tax efficiency.

- Retirement readiness and financial projections

- Review of real estate and other alternative assets

- Advanced retirement planning related to estate planning, asset protection and insurance etc.

- Client Service and Administrative Support

Because of the complexities involved, cross border investors also require advanced knowledge or access to knowledge in:

- Purchasing property abroad: Understanding the challenge of owning property in multiple jurisdictions. repetition

- Understanding Inflation: Understanding the impact of multi-jurisdictional inflation.

- Understanding the impact of volatile global interest rates.

- Understanding the challenges of International Banking. Opening accounts, managing accounts in home jurisdictions, understanding bank costs and how banks think and work.

- Foreign Currency exchange.

- International Money transfers.

- Comparing international costs of Living.

- Global Anti Money Laundering

- Global Trusts and foundations.

## Cross Border Investing

This unique situation of families with cross border challenges has led to an occurrence where cross border professionals have very limited options to find sensible sustainable investment solutions. Many investment firms and large banks (all over the world) choose to avoid this market completely because they are ill-equipped and not staffed appropriately to service these clients.

New laws, focused not on protecting these clients but on taxing them, makes this challenge more complex. These laws are not completely understood by the lawmakers and are very open to opinion.

Banks and investment firms think that relative to their core client base, the number of these client opportunities is small and come with a higher level of risk and reporting complexity, therefore mostly they are not yet looking at this market segment seriously.

Compounding this lack of solutions is the movement by custodians and banks to exit this part of the industry due to the complexities involved, regulatory concerns and other issues. New policies and procedures put in place because of new regulations are not allowing them to service these accounts, and many are ultimately restricting all accounts that have a foreign address or a foreign citizen owner.

## Cross Border Estate Planning

Given the increased mobility of clients and globalization of assets, property at death may occur in several jurisdictions. This means that a great number of clients will require coordinated estate planning using multi-jurisdictional wills and separate situs wills (that is, wills concerning assets located in one legal jurisdiction (situs) and typically executed in that jurisdiction in accordance with its law).

## Cross Border Tax Planning

There is also the trend of growing government transparency and information sharing, leading to new regulations and rules globally that impacts tax planning; foreign financial institutions are now required to identify all clients with a "connection" to the U.S. (soon in additional jurisdictions) and to report details of their financial holdings. As a result, investors are rapidly changing their undisclosed accounts to fully disclosed accounts. This contributes to the rapid growth of investible assets in the cross-border niche.

## Trust the Process and the Results will Come

Trust the process, no matter how difficult it is. Easier said than done, right?

We all have financial goals that we want to achieve but setting them isn't enough. If you really want to make a change in your life, you need to commit to a process guided by a professional financial professional who works aligned with an academic proven methodology.

Do you know someone who is trying to get in better physical shape? Maybe they've spent months researching various workout regimens and diets but haven't taken any meaningful action. Perhaps they've even created a comprehensive plan to lose those extra pounds and improve their overall health. Until they act though, the plan is just a plan, many of which fade into oblivion despite well-meaning intentions.

Financial wellness works similarly. Sometimes a plan is a binder filled with pages of charts, goals, analysis, assumptions. I've seen plans that are hundreds of pages long, I've even created a few. I imagine most of these stacks of paper sit on a shelf or in a drawer until tossed into recycling or shredded years later. Plans of that size can be overwhelming and intimidating.

The more I've talked with clients, experienced financial events myself, and worked with other advisors, the more I've realized that most of the value isn't in the plan itself; it's in the planning process.

## Aligning Values with Finances

It's easier not to think about finances (in the short term anyway). Money talk can be stress-inducing. Since we have minimal information about the future, we're throwing darts at a board of possible outcomes. It doesn't have to be this way, though. We don't have to try to predict every life event. We can acknowledge that there will be surprises, big and small, good, and bad. That's what makes life so interesting.

Another way to approach planning is to consider your values and goals. It's not just about finding your retirement "number" and backing into a plan. Life by spreadsheet isn't a way to exist.

Instead, think about what you are living for. What excites you? What do you genuinely enjoy? What keeps you up at night? These discussions help ensure that your financial plan makes your life fulfilling. The goal isn't to die the richest; it's to live the life you dream off.

## Adjust your plans as needed.

In my career during which I have organized many courses and seminars, and a great deal of the success is preparation. The organizing team charts the seminar program from their starting location to their destination and every minute in between. They even check the weather forecast and ensure they're aware of all possibilities of changes.

Despite considering all the variables, sometimes things just do not work out (Who could forecast the COVID crisis or the Ukraine war?)

You may think your life is standard, with minimal variability. And maybe it has been, but experience shows surprises are lurking around the corner. Don't worry; these can be unexpected positive events. Life sometimes presents pleasant financial surprises despite our tendency to only consider the bad and the ugly, focusing on events that could derail our plan. It might be hard to believe now, especially if you're experiencing hardship, but something unexpected could improve your financial situation down the road.

So, we must have something that is clear and that is the methodology.

## Establish and define a relationship

The adviser informs the client about the financial planning process, and services on offer. The financial planning professional and the client determine whether the services offered by the financial planning professional and his or her competencies meet the needs of the client.

The financial planning professional considers his or her skills, knowledge and experience in providing the services requested or likely to be required by the client.

The financial planning professional determines if he or she has, and discloses, any conflict(s) of interest. The financial planning professional and the client agree on the services to be provided. The financial planning professional describes, in writing, the scope of the engagement before any financial planning is provided, including details about: the responsibilities of each party (including third parties); the terms of the engagement; and compensation and conflict(s) of interest of the financial planning professional. The scope of the engagement is set out in writing in a formal document signed by both parties or formally accepted by the client and includes a process for terminating the engagement. This has nothing to do with investing.

## Collect information.

The financial planning professional and the client identify the client's personal and financial objectives, needs and priorities that are relevant to the scope of the engagement before making and/ or implementing any recommendations. The financial planning professional collects sufficient quantitative and qualitative information and documents about the client relevant to the scope of the engagement before making and/or implementing any recommendations.

## Analyze and assess your financial status.

The financial planning professional analyses the client's information, subject to the scope of the engagement, to gain an understanding of the client's financial situation. The financial planning professional assesses the strengths and weaknesses of the client's current financial situation and compares them to the client's objectives, needs and priorities. Develop the financial planning recommendations and present them to you.

The financial planning professional considers one or more strategies relevant to the client's current situation that could reasonably meet the client's objectives, needs and priorities; develops the financial planning recommendations based on the selected strategies to reasonably meet the client's confirmed objectives, needs and priorities; and presents the financial planning recommendations and the supporting rationale in a way that allows the client to make an informed decision.

## Implement the financial planning recommendations.

The financial planning professional and you agree on implementation responsibilities that are consistent with the scope of the engagement, the client's acceptance of the financial planning recommendations, and the financial planning professional's ability to implement the financial planning recommendations. Based on the scope of the engagement, the financial planning professional identifies and presents appropriate product(s) and service(s) that are consistent with the financial planning recommendations accepted by the client.

## Review our situation.

The financial planning professional and client mutually define and agree on terms for reviewing and reevaluating the client's situation, including goals, risk profile, lifestyle and other relevant changes. If conducting a review, the financial planning professional and the client review the client's situation to assess progress toward achievement of the objectives of the financial planning recommendations, determine if the recommendations are still appropriate, and confirm any revisions mutually considered necessary.

So, my advice to just embrace the process and not only the plan, be optimistic and steady, and finances can be empowering and not anxiety inducing.

# Chapter Six

## "Embracing the Expat Family Journey: Overcoming Challenges Together"

With the high incidence of divorce and remarriage, or even without the reality of multiple spouses in a lifetime, modern families are a complex structure. It is common now for a family to live in multiple jurisdictions, and for both spouses to be significant earners.

Unlike the traditional family, there are many aspects of the modern family that require careful and honest evaluation, including how to blend finances, especially when one (or both) spouses bring significant assets to a new relationship. The main challenges for expat families are as follows:

1. Managing Joint Expenses: It is common for the new modern family to approach the merger of interests, income, and assets in different ways for example:

- "One single joint account"—In this scenario both spouses deposit all their income into, and all expenses are paid from this joint accounts. Typically, the account is funded with an equal contribution from each spouse from other assets, including but not limited to, distributions from retirement accounts.

- "Household account"—Both spouses fund a joint account with a like amount each month, quarter or annually to share equally in the common household expenses. In addition, each spouse maintains their remaining accounts and assets separately.

- "Drawing straws"—Both spouses determine, by drawing, luck or voluntarily, which expenses will be paid directly by each spouse and all accounts are maintained separately.

2. Estate Planning challenges

- **Balance**—Balancing the desire to provide for a surviving spouse during his/her lifetime with the desire to provide for the children during their lifetimes can be a significant challenge. This challenge is further heightened when there is a minimal difference between the age of subsequent spouse and the ages of the children.

- **Avoiding the Will/Trust Contest**—Avoiding a costly, emotionally draining will or trust contest is one of the greatest challenges in estate planning for modern families. Without an effective plan in place, the estate may be the subject of a long battle that significantly reduces its value and places those we love the most at odds. This is a common occurrence that all too often pits a new spouse against the children.

- **Unintended Disposition**—If you pass away without a will your assets will pass under the laws of intestacy. These laws will result in a disposition of your estate that may surprise your new spouse and leave him/her without sufficient assets to care for themselves during their lifetime. Moreover, it will most likely not result in a disposition of your estate per your wishes.

- **Children of Multiple Marriages**—Providing for children of multiple marriages can be a significant challenge. Will your new spouse's children from a previous marriage be treated the same as your own, or will you provide that your assets pass only to your children? These questions require honest, candid conversations with your spouse and seeking counsel if needed from an estate planning attorney.

- **Beneficiary Designations**—Ensuring your beneficiary designations align with your overall wishes and provide the appropriate balance between your new spouse and children is a significant challenge that requires effective coordination and careful planning.

# Chapter Seven

## "Protecting the Vulnerable: Financial Planning for Those in Need"

If in our family, there are people who could be defined as having vulnerable circumstances. They are at risk of not receiving competent treatment from their financial services providers and advisors.

The solution is to make sure that the professional is taking all this into account and is working with a methodology that will give us the confidence that no one will be taken advantage of. The biggest challenge is to define "a vulnerable individual".

### Who are vulnerable individuals?

A vulnerable individual is someone who, due to their personal circumstances, is especially susceptible to detriment.

Vulnerability can come in a range of varieties, and can be temporary, sporadic, or permanent in nature. Many people in vulnerable situations would not diagnose themselves as 'vulnerable'. The clear message is that we could all become vulnerable.

To identify potential vulnerability and prioritize their efforts, one option is to think of scenarios of bereavement, diagnosis of illnesses, that could be considered risk factors, or sudden changes in circumstances could be indicators.

Individuals who cope with difficult situations with limited resources could be defined as vulnerable. Stress can affect the state of mind and the ability to manage finances or make decisions effectively. In such conditions, being confronted by a complex issue delivered in complex text or trying to receive service with complex processes and procedures can affect the chances of our family achieving the goals we strive for and losing control over our assets and our destiny.

## A suitability standard or a fiduciary standard

As it is virtually impossible to pinpoint a "vulnerable" individual the key to working and understanding the scenario is in the process. One solution is not to focus on creating a standard to match suitable solutions to "vulnerable" clients' reality but to focus on the methodology of the advice.

The most realistic solution for us is finding a professional who adopts a fiduciary standard and is required by law to act our best interest and to implement a methodology of processes and proce-dures that consider special circumstances and plan accordingly. (All this is part of stress testing the plan).

**Understanding the proposed process and procedures.** The first and most important exercise is understanding goals, values, fears, and challenges.

What are our realities, what stage are we in our life journey? What do we want to achieve? What assets/liabilities do we have and how can anyone match these goals to a resource?

The next stage will be understanding our capacity to lose money: In this exercise we will want to understand what can happen to our family in the scenario of a market downfall or any other scenario we want to explore.

This process is called a sensitivity study where it can be explained what the probability for a market correction could be to someone's life (not their portfolio) and whether the capacity is there for being exposed to market risk.

The next step will be understanding the family's attitude to exposure to risk: Only after it is understood what the family's need for risk and capacity is for taking risk, can anyone do anything about it.

This is best explained not by defining categories such as risk averse or aggressive but by understanding probabilities. (For example, one could say: In this diversified asset allocation with non-correlated asset classes the probability of achieving your life goals is ....... and the probability of your family losing money in a crisis is ...).

# Chapter Eight

## "Mind over Money: Understanding the Behavioral Dynamics of Planning Our Expatriate Future"

People often view financial planning and investing as over-whelming, intimidating, and scary, especially if they must tackle these tasks on their own. They are fearful of making costly mistakes that could influence both their well-being. Their fear often stems from a lack of background, education, or experience to help them cope with the financial side of living.

The world of financial planning and investing can be highly complex and difficult. What should investors do?

Investors sometimes find themselves in a similar position to Alice in Lewis Carroll's *Alice's Adventures in Wonderland* who, when coming to a fork in the road, asks the Cheshire Cat:

**Alice:** "Would you tell me, please, which way I ought to go from here?"

**Cat:** "That depends a good deal on where you want to get to."

**Alice:** "I don't much care where."

**Cat:** "Then it doesn't matter which way you go."

Unlike Alice, investors should make decisions based on their goals and then determine the appropriate path to get there. We should develop a financial strategy that incorporates values and needs.

Assuming we have well-defined goals, they we can take one of two major paths to achieve them. One is to acquire the knowledge needed to do one's own financial planning and investing. According to Benjamin Franklin, "An investment in knowledge pays the best interest." Nothing is likely to pay off more than gaining a financial education and engaging in the necessary research, study, and analysis before making any financial decisions. Otherwise, the result could be regrettable.

Another is to use the services of an investment professional or advisor who already has the requisite knowledge, skills, and abilities to conduct these important tasks for us. Both options involve trade-offs, but each offers the potential for long-term success.

Successful planning is much more than crunching numbers, listening to popular opinion, and understanding the latest market trends. As much as people need to know about financial markets and investments, they also need to know about themselves. A large part of planning our future involves investor behaviour. Emotional processes, mental mistakes, and individual personality complicate financial decisions.

As we all know as markets go up, people enter the market. When markets go down people redeem their investments occasionally at a great loss. As markets go up you are being exposed to the greatest market risk, after markets go down you are exposed to the greatest market opportunity.

Despite logic, investors often allow the greed and fear of others to affect their decisions and react with blind emotion instead of calculated reason. In fact, emotions explain asset pricing bubbles.

Investor behaviour usually deviates from logic and reason as explained by Daniel Kahneman (2002) in his Nobel Prize winning thesis.

The prominent and renowned Financial Analysts Yeske and Buie said famously "Financial planning clients are as prone to behavioural bias as anyone, and we must work to mitigate these tendencies." Consequently, appropriate planning policies can play a powerful role in keeping clients committed to a consistent and disciplined course of action and in avoiding such biases. Ignoring or failing to grasp this concept can have a detrimental influence on achieving life goals.

We can start by examining some behavioural aspects of planning and investing. Differentiating between traditional or standard finance and behavioural finance and stressing the importance of understanding investor psychology. We then focus on how behavioural biases, emotions, and systematic cognitive errors can affect investment decisions. We conclude with a few observations about how understanding investor behaviour can help improve our decision-making processes.

## Mitigating this risk.

We need to incorporate the insights gained from behavioural finance when investing. We need to be increasingly aware that personality traits, demographic and socioeconomic factors, household characteristics, cognitive and emotional biases, and even religion can affect financial our decisions.

Having an effective plan for our family requires understanding investor psychology. Data on equities, are no match for human emotions. One of the best ways to invest in our futures is define our life goals and keep on track in all market scenarios.

We need to lay the groundwork of the plan during calm times.

That is, we should consider what individual investing strategies should be followed in the event of turbulent markets. This imposes a disciplined approach instead of an emotional reaction if that situation presents itself.

Understanding fundamental human tendencies can help recognize behaviours that may interfere with achieving our long-term goals. People typically do not have investment problems; instead, investments have people problems.

It happens to most of us at some time or another: You're at a cocktail party, and "the blowhard" happens your way bragging about his latest stock market move. You discover that he knows nothing about the company, is completely enamoured with it, and has invested 25% of his portfolio hoping he can double his money quickly.

Here are the four mistakes the resident blowhard has made that we want to avoid.

## Not Understanding the Investment

One of the world's most successful investors, Warren Buffet cautions against investing in companies whose business models you don't understand.

## Falling in Love with an Investment

Too often, when we see a company we've invested in do well, it's easy to fall in love with it and forget that we bought the stock as an investment. Always remember, you bought this stock to make money. If any of the fundamentals that prompted you to buy into the company change, consider selling the stock.

## Lack of Patience

Warren Buffett famously said that the art of investing is the transfer of wealth from the impatient to the patient.

A slow and steady approach to portfolio growth will yield greater returns in the long run. Expecting a portfolio to do something other than what it is designed to do is a recipe for disaster. This means you need to keep your expectations realistic regarding the timeline for portfolio growth and returns.

**Too Much Investment:** Turnover (aka churn) or jumping in and out of positions, is another return killer. The transaction costs can eat you alive—not to mention the short-term tax rates and the opportunity cost of missing out on the long-term gains of other sensible investments.

Although planning and being aware of the behavioral pitfalls, cannot prevent behavioral biases, it can reduce their influence on achieving our goals.

It is important to stress again and again, the best strategy is to invest aligned with our life goals, considering our needs, capacity, and tolerance to exposure to risk and determine an appropriate asset allocation strategy, and rebalance our portfolio on a yearly basis.

# Chapter Nine

## "The Expatriate's Survival Kit: Essential Awareness for Navigating New Territories"

As an expat, you may have more money than you did before and pay less tax than you did before (hence you could become a magnet to unethical people)

Coming into a large sum of money is a dream for most of us, but for those who experience it – whether after signing an amazing work contract overseas, or just paying less tax – the excitement of sudden additional wealth can give way to more complexity than you can imagine damaged personal relationships, poor financial decisions, psychological strain and dangerous behaviours.

There is an enormous emotional and intellectual burden that comes with a life-changing event. It seems that the reality of the dream is significantly more complex than the dream itself.

Expats who have experienced an event such as this, are surprised to find out that there is a great void between how they imagined they would feel and how they really feel.

First, there is often a puzzling challenge of new economic and legal issues to deal with, along with unfamiliar technical jargon. This can lead to a sense of anxiety.

One expat who moved overseas and was netting almost triple the money he had earned beforehand, said "I knew my work, and I knew my industry. But now, I don't even know what I don't know."

Regardless of what you do, many expats report having crazy fears about spending, investing, or running out of money. And frequently, the attempt to address these challenges and decide, creates, a sense of defeat.

It is also common that this can affect relationships as well. Sometimes jealousy, and uncertainty over how to deal with jealous behaviour, can damage even the closest relationships. This can lead to suspicion, loss of trust and social isolation.

## Why do we react sometimes this way?

The complexity of human emotions around accumulating wealth derives from several different sources. For many of us, the money messages transmitted by parents and grandparents are a primary influence on our spending decisions and financial habits for the rest of our lives.

Our parents talked about saving for education, the challenges of everyday life, budgeting holidays, watching hard earned income being spent.

One such person who has lived the expat life admits to driving his car further than he needs to so he can refuel at a gas station that charges a few pennies less – a habit inherited from his mother.

Cultural norms can be a major influence as well. Many people report an aversion to talking about money at a personal level, such as how much you have, how much you earn and how much you spend.

There also seems that the public have a deep fascination with stories about other people's money, particularly when things go wrong.

In addition to this as you grow wealthier your choices also grow and complicate things.

For example, TripAdvisor reports that there are 75 five-star hotels in central London alone and close to 200 in Greater London. How can anyone be sure that they have chosen the best one? Perhaps the vacation might have been more fun, more relaxing, or more romantic at a different five-star hotel. For some, the constant second-guessing associated with having too many options can turn the blessing of ample resources into a curse.

## Build A Tax Plan That Serves Your Short-Term and Long-Term Interests.

When it comes to tax planning, your mileage may vary. Everyone has a unique tax situation, and it is imperative to build a tax-efficient and tax-compliant plan for your money.

This tax plan should assist you in the short-term (income taxes), medium-term (capital gains taxes), and long-term (estate planning).

## Build A Plan That Focuses on Wealth Preservation

Risk and return are the yin-and-yang of building a portfolio. As you start making your money work for you, devote as much focus to capital preservation as you do to capital growth.

## Assume Your New Role as a Passive Investor

The hardest transition following a liquidity event may be the evolution from active business owner to a passive investor. However, having your money work hard for you is anything but passive. To ensure long-term capital preservation and growth, you must still be at the helm, conducting due diligence and making the decisions when to pull the trigger on different investment options.

This new role may let you utilize your existing talents: the same combination of work ethic, wits, and persistence that helped build a successful business will come in handy when making the tough decisions.

## As a Passive Investor, Leverage the Expertise and Experiences of Others

While there are many ways to make a fortune, there are just as many ways to lose one. Your success in previous ventures may be proof of great talents, but sometimes these talents do not translate into other fields.

For example, take private real estate. Real estate may be the world's oldest investment vehicle, but that doesn't mean it's all a matter of "buy it and forget it." Like any business venture, there is a steep learning curve that could take years of trial and error to master.

Why devote your scarcest resource (time) when you can devote it to opportunities better aligned with your core competencies? Leveraging the expertise of others (such as investing in private real estate funds) may be an option.

## Incorporate Alternative Investments as Part of Your Portfolio

Public equity investments such as stocks and bonds are the most popular vehicles to put your money to work. However, in a world rampant with high volatility and market swings it may be beneficial for you to consider alternative investment vehicles such as private real estate.

Private real estate investments have historically provided consistent, low volatility returns not correlated with the public markets. Such investments may help provide both long-term growth and capital preservation, providing potential sustainability of the proceeds from selling your business.

## Begin Assessing Alternative Investment Opportunities

Now that you have devised a tax planning strategy and a portfolio strategy, it's time to assess individual investments. While financial and tax advisors will play their part, you make the final call.

When you experience a liquidity event, the steps outlined above can serve as a guide to achieving your long-term goals.

## Beware Unethical Advisors

Most financial professionals are honest, skilled, and ethical. However, a few bad eggs can spoil the reputation of those thousands of upstanding professionals. Bernie Madoff the once highly regarded investment advisor turned Ponzi plan swindler, exemplifies the dark underbelly of the financial advisor field. At first, Madoff appeared to be the perfect financial professional for his clients. The rich and elite had no idea their stellar returns were funded by incoming Madoff investors.

If the wealthy elite can get snookered by a financial advisor, what's to protect the average individual from the same fate? Beware of financial advisor scams and learn how to protect yourself.

Beware of a Ponzi Scheme

A Ponzi scheme is an investment fraud that involves the payment of purported returns to existing investors from funds contributed by new investors. Ponzi scheme organizers often solicit new investors by promising to invest funds in opportunities claimed to generate high returns with little or no risk.

## Beware Affinity Fraud

Affinity fraud targets a particular group with its ploy, frequently in conjunction with a Ponzi scheme. This scam is effective because we tend to trust other members of our "tribe." The cohort group might share the same religion, cultural background, or geographic region. This affinity targeting makes gaining new participants in the scam easier because there is a built-in level of trust. To further con the participants, the scammer might belong to the group or pretend to be a member.

## Misrepresentation Scam

Misrepresentation of credentials is another way financial professionals can scam the unsuspecting public. The field of financial planning is ripe for malfeasance because there is not one credential or licensing requirement to practice.

The public may not be aware of the designations, ethics, or requirements for certification and thus may be receiving advice from someone with no education or experience or background in the field. It's quite easy for someone to hang up a certificate and start doling out advice. The scammer can then close shop and walk away with the proceeds.

## Unrealistic Returns

Promising or even guaranteeing higher than market returns for your investment is a common trick. The popular axiom, "if it's too good to be true, it probably is because it is too good to be true" is all too often so accurate. It is unlikely that an advisor can offer a client returns that are unavailable to the rest of the world. This scam preys upon the clients' greed and dreams of easy money. If an advisor offers or more often "guarantees" returns higher than 12-15%, it is likely a scam. For example, over the last 85 years, the U.S. stock market has averaged approximately 9.5%. This market return is not a "safe" return, but quite volatile, meaning there were many negative return years over the decades.

## Churning

Many stockbrokers have been charged with the churning. Since traditional stockbrokers are paid when their clients buy or sell a security, they can be motivated to make unnecessary stock trades to pad their own pockets. The churning scam involves the financial advisor making frequent buy and sell trades, which not only costs the customer in commissions but usually results in sub-optimal investment returns.

There are many other investment scams to beware of as well as additional varieties of the schemes mentioned above.

## How to Protect yourself

Verify the financial advisor's background. Find out if the advisor has received any disciplinary action or complaints.

Ask how the advisor is compensated. Is it by commission, assets under management, or a combination of payment structures? If the potential financial advisor is unclear or hedges when asked about fees, walk away. Ask for the advisor's ADV Part II document which explains the professional's services, fees, and strategies.

When discussing investment ideas and strategies, ask about the advantages and disadvantages of each recommendation. There are no perfect investments, and every financial product has a downside. If the advisor is unclear or you don't understand the investment, it may not be for you. Although, you may consider gathering a second opinion.

Do not give the financial advisor any power of attorney or ability to make trades without first consulting you. Require every financial action to be cleared with you first. Further, make certain you receive statements not only with the advisor's letterhead, but also from the custodian, or financial institution which holds your money and investments.

## Why should I want to only work with a fiduciary when I choose to seek advice?

What Is a Fiduciary Anyway?

A fiduciary is like a trustee, someone who is given and accepts the responsibility of managing assets for us. The primary duty of a fiduciary is to put our needs first and to give advice and recommendations that will benefit us. This duty protects us from conflicts of interest. For example, fiduciary duty prevents an advisor from making an investment with your money solely for a kickback commission. This standard includes providing guidance that is unbiased, is considered beneficial to you, and fees that are clear and up-front. This gives you confidence that your hard-earned money is in good hands.

## Why Should we work with a Fiduciary?

Let's look at the benefits of fiduciary rules in more detail.

## Transparency And Eliminating Conflicts of Interest

We spend hundreds of thousands of dollars in fees and commissions over our lifetime, and not all of it is warranted. Aside from our obvious goal of maximizing value for our money, working with a fiduciary will give us confidence that our advisor is working in our best interest rather than their own. As fiduciary rules become increasingly strict, our advisors will need to be up-front about how they will help us invest. This means no more too-good-to-be-true sales pitches with hidden fees and convoluted fine print. Advisors will need to be transparent about the various options available.

## We Get to Call the Shots

The bottom line is that by working with an advisor who is held to a fiduciary standard, one is empowered to make the best decisions. Clients have the power to ask questions and to demand the highest value for the service that advisors provide.

## Comprehensive Coordination

Independent, fiduciary advisors do so much more than just pick your investments. An experienced financial expert can be a realistic sounding board to help provide you with a litmus test when you have questions or face a big financial decision. Fiduciary advisors are required to create the most sensible plan for each client, no matter what. They'll give their true, professional opinion (even if it's not the answer you want to hear). They actively coordinate the accumulation, distribution, and transfer of your wealth, as well as between the estate, tax, and financial planning areas of your retirement plan. An advisor who looks at the big picture of your financial life can help you optimize income and mitigate taxes in retirement.

For example, this type of advisor helps you create a retirement income plan that strategizes when you take your withdrawals and what accounts you take them from first; not to mention, they also design a Social Security strategy that optimizes your benefits, minimizes Medicare confiscation, and addresses long-term care so you can feel confident that you're on the right track as you pursue your long-term goals. The objective advice of an independent fiduciary advisor can make an incredible impact on your financial situation in retirement.

## Do I Need a Fiduciary?

If you want to feel empowered to make the best decisions for yourself and your finances, the answer is yes.

# Chapter Ten

## "Mastering the Expat Finances: Strategies for Managing Your Financial Journey"

The purpose of Financial Management is to identify strategies and techniques to optimize short- and midterm cash flows, assets, and liabilities. The components of comprehensive financial planning cannot be dealt with in isolation from other components.

Wouldn't it be nice if there were a magic formula or simple trick that allowed you never to have to worry about money or manage your finances again?

While that may not be realistic, there are some simple things you can do right now to improve your situation. Try these steps for successfully managing your personal finances. If you stick to these tips, your financial problems may start to diminish, and you can start reaping the rewards of lower debt, saving for the future, and a solid credit score.

### Detail Your Financial Goals

Take some time to write specific, long-term financial goals. You may want to take a month-long trip somewhere, buy an investment property, or retire early. All of these goals will affect how you plan your finances. For example, early retirement is dependent on how well you save your money now and into what investments. Other goals, including home ownership, starting a family, moving, or changing careers, will all be affected by how you manage your finances.

Once you have written down your financial goals, prioritize them. This organizational process ensures that you are paying the most attention to the ones that are of the highest importance to you. You can also list them in the order you want to achieve them, but a long-term goal like saving for retirement requires you to work towards it while also working on your other goals.

Below are some tips on how to get clear on your financial goals:

Set long-term goals like ending debt, buying a home, or retiring early. These goals are separate from your short-term goals such as saving for a nice date night.

Set short-term goals, like following a budget, decreasing your spending, paying down, or not using your credit cards.

**Prioritize your goals to help you create a financial plan**. A financial plan is essential in helping you reach your financial goals. The plan should have multiple steps or milestones. A sample plan might include creating a monthly budget and spending plan, then getting out of debt.

Once you've accomplished all this and have followed through on your new plan for a few months, you may find that you have extra cash, and the money you free up from your debt payments can be used to reach your next round of goals.

Again, it's key to decide what priorities are most important to you. Keep steadily working toward your long term retirement goals, but also start to focus on the most important near-term goals you have set for yourself. Do you want to take an extravagant trip? Start investing? Buy a home or build your own business? These are all things to consider when deciding on your next step.

Your goals, along with an emergency fund, will help you stop making financial decisions based on fear and help you get control of your situation.

When creating a financial plan, remember these things:

Your budget is key to success. It is the tool that will give you the most control of your financial future. Your budget is the key to achieving the rest of your plan.

You should keep contributing to long-term goals, like saving for retirement, no matter what your financial plan stage is.

Building an emergency fund is another key factor in financial success and stress reduction.

## Make and Stick to a Budget

Your budget is one of the biggest tools that will help you succeed financially. It allows you to create a spending plan so you can allocate your money in a way that will help you to reach your goals.

You can make your budget as high-level or detailed as you want, as long as it helps you reach your ultimate goal of spending less than you earn, paying off any debts, padding your emergency fund, and saving for the future.

A budget will also help you decide how to spend your money over the coming months and years. Without the plan, you might spend cash on things that seem important now, but don't offer much in terms of enhancing your future. Many people get caught in this quagmire and get down on themselves for not reaching the financial milestones they want for their family and their own life.

Don't forget to celebrate small victories along the way. For example, congratulate yourself once you pay off your debt, or reward yourself when you stick to your plan for three months solid, or when you successfully pad out your emergency fund.

If you are married, you and your spouse need to work together on the budget. Working together makes it feels fair to both of you, and you both have the same level of commitment towards achieving it. This unity can go a long way towards helping you prevent money-related arguments. Below are some tips for married couples who want to create a budget together:

Consider switching to an envelope budgeting system that uses cash for spending areas that require more discipline.

Plan expenses in advance to avoid overspending.

## Pay off Debt.

Debt is a huge obstacle for many when it comes to reaching financial goals. That's why you should make eliminating it a priority. Set up a debt elimination plan to help you pay it off more quickly. For example, while making minimum payments on all of your debt accounts, pay any extra money towards one debt at a time. After paying off one debt account, move all the money you were paying on the first debt to the next debt and continue from there, creating a debt-paydown "snowball effect."[1]

Once you are totally out of debt, commit to staying out of debt. Leaving credit cards at home may be a wise strategy. Save up an emergency fund to cover unexpected items, so you aren't tempted to use a credit card to cover them.

Try this to help you pay off debt more quickly:

- Sell unused or unwanted items around your home to find extra money to add to your debt repayment plan.

- A second job can help speed up the process and can be necessary if you want to make fast or lasting changes to your situation.

- Look for areas in which you can cut your budget to increase the cash available for your debt payments.

## The Challenge of Living a Life of Security and Dignity in an unchartered world.

The COVID-19 pandemic and Ukraine war caused two years of dramatic economic and social disruption that have presented unique challenges. Tough times need tough people so the world can emerge stronger. That is even more true in the field of finance and investments, where there is much uncertainty and volatility. Market volatility – be it stock prices, interest rates or even liquidity – can and do create a lot of pressure.

Warren Buffett famously said that "Only when the tide goes out do you discover who's been swimming naked". There is a need for advisors with strong subject knowledge, a good grasp of current market realities and, above all, strong business ethics.

How to prevent **Identity Theft**

Preventing identity theft is important for anyone, including expats. Here are some steps you can take to protect yourself as an expat from identity theft:

Secure Your Personal Documents: Keep your important documents, such as your passport, visa, and identification cards, in a safe and secure place. Consider using a locked drawer or a safe deposit box.

Be Cautious with Personal Information: Be cautious about sharing personal information, especially online. Be mindful of what information you share on social media platforms and ensure your privacy settings are appropriately configured.

Use Strong Passwords: Create strong and unique passwords for your online accounts. Use a combination of upper- and lower-case letters, numbers, and symbols. Avoid using easily guessable information, such as your name or birthdate.

Enable Two-Factor Authentication: Whenever possible, enable two-factor authentication (2FA) for your online accounts. This adds an extra layer of security by requiring a second form of verification, such as a temporary code sent to your mobile device.

Secure Your Internet Connection: When using public Wi-Fi networks, avoid accessing sensitive information or logging into important accounts. Public Wi-Fi networks can be insecure, so consider using a virtual private network (VPN) to encrypt your internet connection.

Be Wary of Phishing Attempts: Be cautious of suspicious emails, messages, or phone calls asking for personal or financial information. Avoid clicking on links or downloading attachments from unknown sources. Legitimate organizations will not typically request sensitive information via email or over the phone.

Monitor Your Accounts Regularly: Keep a close eye on your bank accounts, credit cards, and other financial accounts. Review your statements regularly for any unauthorized transactions. Consider setting up alerts or notifications for unusual activity.

Shred Sensitive Documents: Dispose of any documents containing personal information, such as bank statements or utility bills, by shredding them before discarding. This prevents dumpster diving or other attempts to gather your personal information.

Protect Your Mail: If you're living in a location where mail security may be a concern, consider using a mailbox with a lock. Retrieve your mail promptly and notify the postal service if you suspect any mail tampering.

Regularly Check Your Credit Report: Monitor your credit report for any unauthorized accounts or suspicious activity. In many countries, you are entitled to a free credit report annually or at regular intervals.

Use Trusted Websites and Services: When conducting online transactions or sharing personal information, ensure that the websites and services you use are reputable and secure. Look for HTTPS encryption and a padlock icon in the browser's address bar.

Be Mindful of Your Surroundings: When entering your PIN at ATMs or making purchases, be cautious of your surroundings. Shield your PIN from prying eyes and beware of skimming devices that criminals may use to steal card information.

Be Vigilant with Financial Statements: Regularly review your financial statements, including bank statements, credit card bills, and investment account statements. Report any suspicious activity to your financial institution immediately.

Inform Relevant Parties: If you suspect that your identity has been compromised, contact your local law enforcement authorities, and inform your embassy or consulate. They can provide guidance on the appropriate steps to take.

By following these precautions, you can significantly reduce the risk of identity theft as an expat. Stay vigilant and take proactive measures to protect your personal information and financial well-being.

# Chapter Eleven

## From Crisis to Confidence: Embracing Risk Management as an Expat

---

**W**hat Is Risk?

Risk is defined in financial terms as the chance that an outcome or investment result will differ from our expected outcome or return. Risk includes the possibility of losing some or all our investment.

Risk is very difficult to Quantify and Financial Researchers over the years have tried to find mathematical ways to measure risk.

The study of "risk" in the financial world has been discussed for decades, and it has grown to encompass dozens of different opinions and methodologies. When it comes to understanding and measuring risk specifically within wealth management, recently things have really become complicated.

In his book "A Random Walk Down Wall Street" the renowned Princeton economist and professor Burton Malkiel said, "Risk is a most slippery and elusive concept. It's hard for academic economists let alone investors to agree on a definition and to understand what it means."

A Princeton Professor of Economics when discussing the issue of defining a risk profile for clients suggested that we may as well ask the client how many red blood cells he has in his system as in both cases he is aware of the concept but cannot comprehend the implications.

It is also clear that attempting to accumulate assets without exposure to some risk is futile and the whole investment community would find itself in an impossible situation.

It is customary for financial professionals aligned with compliance directives to build each client a "Risk Profile" and then purchase suitable investments aligned with the profile. However, you should question the value of this methodology.

The "Risk Profile" is an evaluation of an individual's willingness, capacity, and ability to take on risks. A risk profile theoretically therefore is important for determining a proper investment asset allocation for a portfolio.

Controversially, it is accepted that if an individual expresses a desire for the highest possible return —and is willing to endure large swings in the value of the account to achieve it—this person would have a high willingness to take on risk and is a risk seeker, however is it really clear to the investor that the risk the investor is taking is not achieving a high return over time with volatility in the process but actually taking on the risk that they will in high probability expose themselves to the possibility of losing all.

It is clear, that there are many challenges in the process, however most investment houses and banks try to align themselves with a process that is compliant with the regulatory directives that requires them to build a "Risk Profile" and then match suitable asset allocations and products.

## The evolution of Understanding Risk

In 1952 Harry Markovitz published his thesis that was named the "Modern Portfolio Theory" (MPT) on portfolio selection, arguing that portfolios should optimize expected return relative to volatility, with volatility measured as the variance of risk and return. He proposed the now ubiquitous efficient frontier. By the mid-1960s, this mean-variance model had become a mainstay within academic finance departments.

The modern portfolio theory argues that any given investment's risk and return characteristics should not be viewed alone but should be evaluated by how it affects the overall portfolio's risk and return. That is, an investor can construct a portfolio of multiple assets that will result in greater returns without a higher level of risk.

As an alternative, starting with a desired level of expected return, he said that an investor can construct a portfolio with the lowest possible risk that can produce that return.

Based on statistical measures such as variance and correlation, a single investment's performance is less important than how it impacts an entire portfolio.

Combining Markowitz's model with restrictive assumptions regarding investor rationality, information availability, and market trading structure, Bill Sharpe derived a model of capital Market equilibrium in the mid-1960s. Soon the capital asset pricing model (CAPM) became a central tenet of MPT.

## What happened?

MPT quickly became Mainstream for the quantitative-based analysts who dominated the investment industry, a simple theory like MPT that explained messy financial markets was very attractive. Now investors have a rigorous theory of markets and a rational approach to building investment portfolios.

But then the first shots were fired across MPT's bow in the late 1970s.

The initial CAPM (Capital Asset Pricing Model) empirical tests uncovered a negative return to beta relationship, the opposite of what was predicted.

Beta is a measure of a stock's volatility in relation to the overall market. The market, such as the S&P 500 Index, has a beta of 1.0, and individual stocks are ranked according to how much they deviate from the market. A stock that swings more than the market over time has a beta above 1.0. If a stock moves less than the market, the stock's beta is less than 1.0

Rather than reject CAPM, however, the discipline responded by searching for statistical problems in these tests.

Then in the early 1980s, Nobel Prize winner Robert Shiller argued that almost all volatility observed in the stock market, even on an annual basis, was noise rather than the result of changes in fundamentals. Since CAPM held that prices fully reflect all relevant information, volatility driven by anything other than fundamentals strikes at the very heart of the theory.

Shillers Noisy Market model created problems for Markowitz's portfolio optimization. If volatility is the result of emotional crowds, then emotion has been placed in the middle of risk management.

So rather than being a risk-return optimization, it is an emotion-return optimization.

Overall, it is possible and prudent to manage risks by understanding that we do not have control over what happens to our investments. Learning the risks that can apply to different scenarios and understanding what we are investing in and aligning the investments to our life goals is the key to succeeding in achieving our goals in the highest scenario.

## The Basics of Risk

Everyone is exposed to some type of risk every day—whether it's from driving, walking down the street, investing, capital planning, or something else. An investor's personality, lifestyle, and age are some of the top factors to consider for individual investment management and risk purposes. Each investor has a unique risk profilethat determines their willingness and ability to withstand risk. In general, as investment risks rise, investors expect higher returns to compensate for taking those risks, however as we mentioned before this is not a proven fact.

## Behavioral Economics and understanding risk.

Daniel Kahneman is a professor emeritus of psychology and public affairs at Princeton University. Despite having reportedly never taken a course in economics, he is widely regarded as a pioneer of modern behavioral economics. In 2002, he was awarded the Nobel Prize for his research on prospect theory, which deals with human judgment and decision-making.

## Risk Profiling

When profiling ourselves for risk exposure we should ask ourselves the following questions:

1. **Do I need to take a risk**: Now that we understand that there is risk in any decision, we make I need to understand what kind or returns I need to achieve to achieve my goals and what kind of risk I need to expose myself to achieve it.

2. **Can I afford to fail**? (My Risk Capacity): When assessing a goal, we must consider the consequence of failure. Risk consequence refers to the financial and emotional threats an investor faces if a goal is not achieved. For example, some

investors may consider that ensuring sufficient capital is available to pay for a grandchild's college education is a goal with an acceptable consequence of failure, whereas others might consider that not achieving this goal is unacceptable. Goal consequence, therefore, is a key element in determining how much portfolio risk is appropriate to recommend. The consequence of failing to meet an investor's goal is not specifically quantified within the risk-need factor. However, when combined with an investor's ability to take risk and our behavioral loss tolerance (defined in detail later in this report), the severity of failing to meet a goal should be accounted for using the financial advisor's judgment as to whether the advisor should "nudge" an investor toward a higher volatility.

3. **My need for Liquidity**: Need for liquidity is defined as an objective requirement or desire to hold cash for ongoing current or future expected expenses. During the capital accumulation phase of our lifespan, liquidity needs may be quite low—which would increase our ability to withstand market risk—whereas a liquidity need may be very high during the capital distribution phase of our lifespan—thus reducing our ability to incur investment risk.

4. **Goal Time Horizon**: Our goal time horizon is an input we can use to determine our ability to take risk. Conceptually, the goal time horizon is the period between when a goal is established and the date of that goal's achievement, which in some cases may exceed our remaining lifetime.

5. **My attitude towards risk**: Most professionals will focus on this as this is part of the directives of the regulators. Risk profiling by discussing attitude to risk refers to an investor's use of subjective and objective cognitive evaluations to describe our feelings regarding a real or potential course

of action. For example, we may prefer investing in certificates of deposit based on subjective probability estimates that indicate a minimal chance of losing money; another common scenario is that we may prefer to avoid certificates of deposit based on our evaluation showing that the after-tax and after-inflation returns associated with these assets result in problematic outcomes.

6. In nearly all cases, most of us prefer taking less risk. Stated another way, we may prefer low volatility investments while concurrently exhibiting a willingness to take financial risk so there is a paradox if we only discuss our attitude to risk without taking into consideration our goals, needs, capacity, liquidity and time horizons.

## Stress Testing and Stochastic Modelling

The use of scenario techniques enables stress testing (what if scenarios, for example what if the dollar loses 20% of its value, what if there is a crisis in the stock market etc) —in addition to realistic economic performance scenarios—to be factored into decision making. Scenario-based asset allocation can therefore be an effective tool for constructing stress-resilient portfolios.

While risk profiling and scenario management is very important the priority is to work on the individuality of investors and their specific life goals, dreams, values, and aspirations Using stochastic modelling for building an asset allocation.

In the last decade as the risk modelling and profiling families has evolved stochastic modelling has entered the arena as an important tool.

## What is stochastic modelling?

Stochastic modelling is used to help make investment decisions. This forecasts the probability of various outcomes under different conditions, using random variables.

Stochastic modelling presents data and predicts outcomes that account for certain levels of unpredictability or randomness. Planners, analysts, and portfolio managers use stochastic modelling to manage client assets and optimize portfolios.

The Stochastic analysis takes the data from the last ten years (for example) of a specific asset or asset class and explores the volatility of the asset in hundreds of billions of scenarios. The result is a map of possibilities that the asset should achieve over time and the probability of this happening.

The advantage of using this tool is that it is available, and when discussing risk with families, the adviser can add an additional dimension to the equation and can talk about probabilities of achieving a specific goal. In other words, if you define a goal such as retirement at age 70 and you need to accumulate assets of let's say one million dollars, stochastic planning will deliver the range of possible outcomes and define the probability of achieving the specific goal.

The disadvantage of the tool is that it is based on past results of each asset class, equity, or bond. Everyone is aware the past is no indication of the future.

For example, stochastic planning will not consider the present yield to maturity for sovereign bonds which were historically low and then in a matter of weeks rose to an over average high.

While all these tools are very important and the concept of taking responsibility when managing clients' financial destinies is a very important development, we need to improve on these methodologies to include the individuality of our investors and their specific life goals and align the asset allocation accordingly.

## How do banks create a "Risk Profile"?

It is customary to use a methodology of asking the potential investor questions. If this process is worthy, then you might wonder how many questions are sufficient? Is three enough or at least ten, or perhaps one hundred?

Dilemma No 1: Who writes the questions? Do they have the backing of academic research? Who decides what kind of questions should be asked? Is there any sequence to the questions?

Dilemma No 2: Who decides based on the answers received what the risk profile is? Let's say that you define the risk profile as "10 being willing to take on the most risk and 1 being the most risk averse", then who decides that, based on the questions asked, it would be fair to conclude that the individual should be categorized somewhere within this framework.

Dilemma No 3: Who decides what products or what portfolio should be matched to each risk profile? Let's say that you are categorized as a level 7 "Risk Profile" then who decides what funds, equities or bonds should be in the allocation?

Dilemma No 4: Can you really be categorized in a 1-10 system? Are all the families in category 5 in need of the same asset allocation? Do all have similar family circumstances, life goals, challenges, and dreams? If not how can this system work?

## The Perception of Risk

The regulatory requirements that a financial professional must prepare a "KYC" (Know Your Client) report, including building his/her/their risk profile, is a universal requirement among investment regulators around the world.

Yet when studying these directives, they reveal a disturbing lack of understanding of what exactly we want to achieve.

In part, this appears to be driven by the fact that regulators articulate the principle of "know your client's risk tolerance" but provide little guidance on how it should be done to ensure that it's right or even that they understand what they want to achieve. The problem stems from the reality that neither regulators, academics, nor advisors themselves, agree on exactly what key factors of a client's "risk profile" should be evaluated in the first place.

Lately there are significant developments in the basic understanding of the role of risk perception and misperceptions when discussing client behaviour, and how "risk composure" (the stability of a client's perceptions of risk) itself can vary from one family to the other. Of course, just because these factors can be identified doesn't make them easy to measure, especially when it comes to "subjective" abstract traits like risk.

It is important to recognize that different people see risk in different ways – The key point is that if perceptions are not aligned with reality, investors may engage in "surprising" behaviour that may seems inconsistent with their risk profile. For instance, an individual who is highly risk tolerant, but has the perception that a calamitous economic event will cause the market to crash to zero, might still want to sell everything and go to cash. Even though he/she is tolerant of risk, no one wants to own an investment going to zero! Some people may have better risk perceptions than others; in other words, some investors can keep their composure and maintain a consistent perception of the potential risks around them, while others have risk perceptions that are more likely to move wildly. And of course, perceptions of risk themselves also vary by the information that the individual has available to them – poor financial literacy and education can increase the likelihood of risk misperception, as can media coverage of scary/risky events (triggering fear and irrational conduct).

Notably, in this context, risk capacity is an objective measure (the dollars-and-cents mathematical analysis of the consequences of risky events), while risk tolerance (and risk perception) remains more subjective (an assessment of an abstract trait) but the most important factor is actually the need for exposure to risk that is a factor or analysing the family's life goals and understanding what risk is needed in order to achieve these goals.

## Portfolio Construction for Navigating a New World of Risk

Establishing an appropriate asset allocation and staying invested in the markets are fundamental to successful investing. But market volatility can unnerve the most seasoned of investors, causing them to abandon their plans and jeopardize their long-term investment goals.

In today's volatile environment, investors are increasingly seeking solutions that will maximize their returns while minimizing their risk exposure.

Alpha (Alpha ($\alpha$) is a term used in investing to describe an investment strategy's ability to beat the market, or its "edge. Alpha is thus also often referred to as "excess return" or "abnormal rate of return,") opportunities exist in every asset class, by they're not the only route to market-beating returns. What's more, the traditional approach to portfolio construction is outdated – no longer simply a matter of selecting stocks and bonds and determining their allocation – and it's time for investors to stop thinking in 'active versus passive' terms.

In today's developing market, there are so many new opportunities, as technology exposes more are more people to exciting asset classes that we were once the playing field for large institutions and ultra-high net worth families.

So, when planning for medium to long term investments where should we look?

## Optimising ESG investments in our portfolio

Sustainable investing has become one of the biggest trends in recent years. Once considered a specialist strategy, ESG (Environmental, Social and Governance) is now the new normal. Investors expect to generate sustainable returns across multi-asset portfolios. They also expect not just a portion of these investments but most of their portfolio, to positively impact on the community and the environment.

Where money flows, regulation follows. In the future the EU's Sustainable Finance Disclosure Regulation (SFDR), will put in place new reporting frameworks to help the sector tackle reporting gaps, creating a level playing field and greater transparency.

## The rise of Fintech

The impact of bank regulation, FATCA (The Foreign Account Tax Compliance Act (FATCA) requires all non-U.S. foreign financial institutions (FFIs) to search their records for customers with a connection to the U.S., including indications in records of birth or prior residency in the U.S., or the like, and to report such assets and identities of such persons to the US Treasury.

AML (Anti Money Laundering) directives has created a situation where we are even more frustrated with financial institutions who have traditionally been overcharging for services and then underdelivering.

This has created a void for young professional entrepreneurs to create alternative solutions for trading, managing money, lending and almost every function that was traditionally a monopoly of the banks. Some of the sector's largest asset managers have already begun launching innovation hubs and incubators, resulting in technology arms that can potentially be spun off as separate businesses in the fintech arena.

Having got through the first wave of fintech mania that successfully took on the giants in the industry, they have proven that technology can deliver long-term benefits.

## Taking the risk out of human capital

Digitization and automation have taken on new meaning.

Artificial Intelligence systems are now able to do amazing things and save organizations time and energy in doing cumbersome work on databases.

But rather than replacing humans, technology has addressed the vast volumes of data submerging people and processes. Firms are now empowered and able to address their human capital risk by making their employees' roles more valuable with greater focus on upskilling.

And with employees no longer needed to create and monitor highly customized spreadsheets, talent is once again invigorated. Access to technology means that we can access knowledge to understand our investments better and improve results.

## Do we need a professional to guide in managing our risks?

Families now go direct to market and bypass traditional financial constructs in favour of technology. In the future, direct risk management will have taken off, with Gen Z and millennial investors assisted by Artificial Intelligence will proving to be far savvier on risk management and investment strategies such as ESG and Private Equity.

In response, asset managers have introduced a range of new solutions to attract investors and expose them to asset classes they could never afford to be previously but with this, comes the challenge of working on new innovative structures and managing them efficiently.

At the same time, cryptocurrencies have also gained momentum with thousands of transactions daily. And while newer more stable digital currencies have come to market, since Bitcoin and Ethereum, there is a feeling that the future is efficient global currencies that allow companies and global families to trade globally without currency restrictions.

The journey into the future is starting here and now. We may still need to work with an advisor, but as new technologies improve, for example ChatGPT, we will have the tools and abilities if we want to run the show on our own.

# Chapter Twelve

## "From Expat to Investor: Building Wealth in the Global Market"

**W**hy have an Investment Management strategy?
An investment management strategy provides the framework for your investment decisions. It ensures that the decision-making process with respect to the management of your portfolio will be consistent, even when unexpected market fluctuations tempt distraction from your long-term strategy. Investment recommendations will always be made in concert with the guidelines that we agree upon and outline. The development of an effective investment management strategy creates the essential foundation to build your future.

### Understanding the Evolution of Investing

When talking about an investment portfolio, most people are not confused by the term. An investment portfolio is a collection of growth or income-producing assets that have been bought together to meet a financial goal.

However, if we went back 50 years or more in a time machine, no one would have the slightest clue what we were talking about.

It is amazing that something as fundamental as an asset allocation in a portfolio didn't exist until the late 1960s. The idea of investment portfolios has become so ingrained in society that we can't imagine a world without it, but it wasn't always this way.

I want to explore the evolution of the modern portfolio from its humble beginnings in an unremarkable, and largely ignored, doctoral thesis, all the way to its current dominance.

First, we need to define what an Investment Portfolio is: "An investment portfolio is a grouping of financial assets—such as stocks, bonds, commodities, currencies, alternatives and funds—that an investor purchases to produce income and meet his family's financial goals".

In the early 18th century, Daniel Bernoulli proposed that individuals maximize expected utility when they make decisions under uncertainty. This reasoning launched the rational model of human behavior that underpins many of today's theories in economics and finance, including modern portfolio theory (MPT). The mathematical models that sprang from these theories provide a veneer of orderliness while obscuring the behavioral messiness of real-world financial markets.

In 1952 Harry Markovitz changed the investment world by publishing his article on portfolio selection, arguing that portfolios should optimize expected return relative to volatility, with volatility measured as the variance of risk and return. He proposed the now ubiquitous efficient frontier. By the mid-1960s, this mean-variance model had become a mainstay within academic finance departments.

Harry Markovitz's research was given the name "Modern Portfolio Theory" or simply MPT.

Modern portfolio theory is a practical method for selecting investments to maximize their overall returns within an acceptable level of risk.

A key component of the MPT theory is diversification. Harry claimed that most investments are either high risk and high return or low risk and low return. He argued that investors could achieve their best results by choosing an optimal mix of the two based on an assessment of their individual tolerance to risk.

Modern portfolio theory argues that any given investment's risk and return characteristics should not be viewed alone but should be evaluated by how it affects the overall portfolio's risk and return. Thus, an investor can construct a portfolio of multiple assets that will result in greater returns without a higher level of risk.

As an alternative, starting with a desired level of expected return, the investor can construct a portfolio with the lowest possible risk that can produce that return.

Based on statistical measures such as variance and correlation, a single investment's performance is less important than how it impacts the entire portfolio.

The term variance refers to a statistical measurement of the spread between numbers in a data set. More specifically, variance measures how far each number in the set is from the mean and thus from every other number in the set. Variance is often depicted by this symbol: $\sigma^2$. It is used by both analysts and traders to determine volatility and market security. The square root of the variance is the standard deviation($\sigma$), which helps determine the consistency of an investment's returns over a period.

To explain this simply in order for us to understand how "spread out" values affect us we must understand how we can measure dispersion, we measure this usually by:

The range: the difference between the largest and smallest value in a dataset.

The interquartile range: the difference between the first quartile and the third quartile in a dataset (quartiles are simply values that split up a dataset into four equal parts).

The standard deviation: a way to measure the typical distance that values are from the mean.

The variance: the standard deviation squared.

Out of these four measures, the variance tends to be the one that is the hardest to understand intuitively.

The reason we use variance as opposed to standard deviation to describe volatility is to try and make the statistical measurement clear and easy to understand.

For example, you might want to understand how much variance in test scores can be explained by IQ and how much variance can be explained by hours studied.

If 36% of the variation is due to IQ and 64% is due to hours studied, that's easy to understand. But if we use the standard deviations of 6 and 8, that's much less intuitive and doesn't make much sense in the context of the problem.

Correlation, in the finance and investment industries, is a statistic that measures the degree to which two securities or asset classes move in relation to each other. Correlations are used in advanced portfolio management, computed as the correlation coefficient, which has a value that must fall between -1.0 and +1.0.

Combining Markowitz's model with assumptions regarding investor rationality, information availability, and market trading structure, Bill Sharpe derived a model of capital Market equilibrium in the mid-1960s. Soon the capital asset pricing model (CAPM) became a central tenet of MPT.

The Sharpe ratio (also known as the Sharpe index, the Sharpe measure, and the reward-to-variability ratio) strives to measure the performance of an investment such as a security or portfolio compared to a risk-free asset after adjusting for its risk. It is defined as the difference between the returns of the investment and the risk-free return. It strives to measure the additional amount of return that an investor will receive per unit of increase in risk.

Eugene Fama erected the final pillar of the MPT theory in the mid-1960s, in perhaps the most famous finance doctoral dissertation of that generation. Extending the concept of rational investors to its logical conclusion, Fama proposed the efficient market hypothesis (EMH), that financial market prices reflect all relevant information and thus generate excess returns (Alpha).

MPT quickly became the ascendant paradigm. For the quantitative-based analysts who dominated the investment industry, a simple theory like MPT that explained messy financial markets was very attractive. Now they had a rigorous theory of markets and a rational approach to building investment portfolios.

The first shots were fired across MPT's bow in the late 1970s.

The initial CAPM empirical tests uncovered a negative return to beta relationship, the opposite of what was predicted. Rather than reject CAPM, however, the discipline responded by searching for statistical problems in these tests.

## What is beta?

In finance, beta ($\beta$) is a measure of a security's or investment's volatility in relation to the overall market. It quantifies the systematic risk of an asset, indicating how it tends to move in response to fluctuations in the broader market.

Beta is typically calculated by comparing the historical price movements of an asset to the price movements of a benchmark index, such as the S&P 500. The benchmark index is assigned a beta of 1.0, and a security with a beta greater than 1.0 is considered more volatile than the market, while a security with a beta less than 1.0 is considered less volatile.

In the early 1980s, Nobel Prize winner Robert J Shiller argued that almost all volatility observed in the stock market, even on an annual basis, was noise rather than the result of changes in fundamentals. Since EMH held that prices fully reflect all relevant information, volatility driven by anything other than fundamentals strikes at the very heart of the MPT theory.

Shiller's Noisy Market model also created problems for Markowitz's portfolio optimization. If volatility is the result of emotional crowds, then emotion has been placed in the middle of the portfolio construction process. So rather than being a risk-return optimization, it is an emotion-return optimization. In summary, all pillars supporting EMH and MPT were toppled.

Next, Daniel Kahneman who is a professor emeritus of psychology and public affairs at Princeton University, despite never having reportedly taken a course in economics, emerged with the "behavioral economics theory" In 2002, he was awarded the Nobel Prize for his research on prospect theory, which deals with human judgment and decision-making.

Now decades later, there is little evidence to support MPT. It seems it is time to move on. There is an alternative way to view securities markets, their movements, and their participants: behavioral finance and the transition to ALM. (Asset Liability Management)

The new theories that are emerging from academic research is simple. The Key to bringing real value in the investment world is understanding clients and their life goals.

## The "Yale Model" arrives.

Swensen of Yale University joined the league of elite academics of the investment world.

Few academics can rival the late David Swensen, former head of the Yale Endowment. As Chief Investment Officer of this multi-billion-dollar fund, he delivered top performance over multiple decades, and his investing style influenced an entire industry. Swensen's innovative and rigorous approach to asset allocation and expanding its range was revered, with others rushing to replicate it. This approach became known as the "Yale Model", and revolutionized endowment investing.

## What is the Yale Model?

Swensen, understood that a portfolio's long life significantly enhanced its ability to search for yield beyond public markets. By eliminating the constraints of a reactive, short-term approach, Swensen delved into private assets, which afford greater access to management, and insight into their strategies as well as value drivers.

He realized that private assets that required rigorous research and have no active exchange, offered a premium to patient investors that could forgo the need for immediate liquidity.

Seeing higher yields in alternative assets such as real estate, private equity, and natural resources – he aggressively shifted the asset mix.

Today also because of the David Swenson the investment world looks at "Alternative Investing" as core assets of a portfolio.

# Chapter Thirteen

## "Unveiling Investment Opportunities: The Crucial Role of Due Diligence for Expats"

Due diligence is an investigation or review performed to confirm facts or details of an investment. In the financial world, due diligence requires an examination of financial records before entering into a proposed transaction with another party.

Here are some steps you should consider before investing. Performing this due diligence will allow you to gain essential information and vet any possible new investment.

The steps are organized so that with each new piece of information, you'll build upon what you previously learned. In the end, by following these steps, you'll gain a balanced view of the pros and cons of your investment.

### Managers Experience and Track Record

The first step is for you to form a mental picture or diagram of the proposed manager you're researching.

Active Portfolio Manager: Past performance does not guarantee future results but looking at track record is one way to gauge a manager's expertise. How has the manager fared in prior years?

Did they show responsible custodianship over investors' funds in the past? What does their portfolio say about their investment biases? How is their portfolio weighted?

Alternative Investment Manager: If you are investing in real assets the person you are working with is of utmost importance. Who is he/she? What is her/his experience? How long has she/he been involved in the business? Has he/she had bad experiences? As the project you are investing in becomes more complicated the due diligence required becomes more complicated and may involve understanding who is involved in the project (for example in initiation you have builders and professionals who must come together for a good outcome, any one of these could cause havoc in the business case and may even wipe out the whole investment.

## Revenue, Margin Trends

When you begin looking at the financial numbers related to the investment you're researching, it may be best to start with the revenue, profit, and margin trends.

You should also review profit margins to see if they are generally rising, falling, or remaining the same.

You should also look at the profit margins of similar investments to see if the profit margins presented are realistic.

## Understanding Trends and Sectors in Real Estate investments (for example)

The Covid-19 pandemic accelerated disruption in virtually every corner of the global economy— for example global real estate was no different. What was traditionally a slower-moving sector, driven primarily by demographics and local economics, during this period sat at the epicenter of profound changes in how people live, work, shop and communicate.

## Offices

More than two decades ago, the arrival of "dot coms" set in motion profound changes that have touched every industry, including real estate. Demand shifted from retail centers to warehouses and data centers, while more flexible work arrangements changed the dynamic for office space.

Real estate is reinventing itself to serve its original purpose—to facilitate commerce, store goods and provide shelter—but adapted for a digital age. While technology has shifted real estate demand from physical retail or office space to data centers, cell towers and logistics facilities, it will create property winners and losers. While I do not claim to be a prophet here are my assumptions on examples of winners and losers in the real estate arena

## Example of the winners in the long term:

Residential property should always be on the winners list as this is a basic need of humanity (shelter) and the sector should grow well into the future.

Healthcare related assets are also a basic need and as health developments prolong life and prolong life threatening diseases and disabilities, the need for care facilities will only increase.

**Student Accommodation and the demand for beds**: Any real estate asset class that involves selling beds should be in the winner's category. Student Accommodation experienced a shock during COVID and there was a massive transfer to home learning but as we emerge from this trauma students are flowing back to colleges and Universities in record numbers as the factor of social integration emerges as one of the main factors of importance in the learning experience.

## Short Term Winners

Data centers, cell towers and logistics facilities and specific infrastructure projects: These serve the development of economies and now are in demand, but the disadvantage may be that in the future they may become irrelevant as new technologies or needs change priorities.

## Example of losers in the long term:

**Office Space**: By rethinking how employees work, companies are reducing the amount of office space they need, driving lower costs and even better employee experience.

It seems that in this asset class, the results of the pandemic-driven shift to remote work have been better than expected. It seems that remote working is here to stay: More than one-third of employees in the financial and high-tech sectors will continue to work from home at least a few times a week. This could change their need for office space and consequently affect the demand and supply.

In addition, given that real estate has one of the lowest technology adoption rates among global industry categories, investing in real estate companies may have an embedded added value to their share price.

### ESG investing is here to stay.

ESG stands for Environmental, Social, and Governance, and it is a framework designed to be embedded into an organization's strategy that considers the needs and ways in which to generate value for all organizational stakeholders.

ESG corporate reporting can be used by stakeholders to assess the material sustainability-related risks and opportunities relevant to an organization. ESG investing refers to a set of standards for a company's behavior used by socially conscious investors to screen potential investments.

Environmental criteria consider how a company safeguards the environment, social criteria examine how it manages relationships with employees, suppliers, customers, and the communities where it operates, and governance deals with a company's leadership, executive pay, audits, internal controls, and shareholder rights. Successful companies are implementing ESG strategies that increase financial, societal, and environmental impact as well as ensure long-term competitiveness.

## Why Does ESG Investing Matter?

The future of our planet and people has become a priority among economies, governments, and communities. Social inequality, unethical company operations, carbon emission, deforestation, and climate change are just a few issues across the globe. More and more firms have started to realize the negative impact they have on the earth and are trying their level best to minimize it or turn it into a positive one.

We realize now that the world's largest businesses, governments and investors are committing to achieving carbon neutrality by 2050—and this has significant implications for global real estate.

While the growing focus on sustainability is a global trend, it is important to note that there are regional differences due to existing norms and new or expected regulations that mandate energy efficiency.

## Healthcare Facilities and Social Housing

Social housing investment trusts offer retail investors the opportunity to invest in a sector which has to this point largely attracted institutional investment. The listed structure breaks down barriers for everyday investors looking to invest in a good cause while providing a steady guaranteed income.

## Define Expectations

This step in the due diligence is a sort of "catch-all," and requires some extra digging. You'll want to find out what the consensus revenue and profit estimates are for the next two to ten years, long-term trends affecting the property sector (for example). News about a new product or service on the horizon may be what initially interested you in the investment. Now is the time to examine it more fully with the help of everything you've accumulated thus far.

## Understand the Risks

Setting this vital piece aside for the end makes sure that we're always emphasizing the risks inherent with investing. Make sure to understand both sector risks and specific risks. Consider liquidity risks. Are there outstanding legal or regulatory matters? Is the strategy eco-friendly? What kind of long-term risks could result from it embracing/not embracing green initiatives? You should always keep a healthy devil's advocate mindset, picturing worst-case scenarios and their potential outcomes on the strategy.

## The Bottom Line

Once you've completed these steps you should be able to evaluate an investment's future potential and how the strategy might fit into your portfolio aligned to your life goals. Inevitably, you'll have specifics that you will want to research further. However, following these guidelines should save you from missing something that could be vital to your decision.

Veteran investors will throw many more investment ideas (and cocktail napkins) into the trash bin than they will keep for further review, so never be afraid to start over with a fresh idea and a new strategy. There are literally tens of thousands of opportunities out there to choose from.

# Chapter Fourteen

## "Beyond Traditional: Exploring Alternative Investment Opportunities for Expats"

The last 30 years have seen steady growth and acceptance of alternative asset classes in public portfolios as investors seek diversified sources of income and return. These asset classes are sometimes called illiquid or private asset classes because one important characteristic is that they are not publicly listed in markets or no active dealer market exists.

Past success of these asset classes, continuous innovation, and the ongoing low interest rate environment are the main drivers of this growth.

One characteristic of alternatives is that these assets classes are far more difficult to implement than traditional assets. Except for commodities, there are no low-cost index funds.

They require higher levels of oversight and management than those offered in the public markets. Additionally, due to the closed-end nature of many of the investments, continuous search costs are necessary, thus requiring either sophisticated staff to build and maintain these portfolios or high outsourcing costs.

Hedge funds require a high degree of active management both at the fund level and the total portfolio level.

## How are investors adjusting their allocation to alternatives, and what are the results?

Historically the most aggressive users are University endowments, some with allocations as high as 60%. Yale University started this trend in the 1980s and is now over 75% invested in alternatives.

It is the new norm to see 40% to 60% allocations to alternatives in large endowments.

Global family offices are allocating an average 37% to a variety of alternatives according to a recent survey. Mega funds like large public pension plans and sovereign wealth funds typically allocate 15% to 25% to alternatives and are considering increasing their alternatives allocation.

When building an asset allocation for families to meet their life goals, we have target returns and these are very difficult to achieve in a world of volatility. Using alternative allocations such as investing in real estate we can make our life mor predictable.

Improving portfolio performance provides a comprehensive overview of the different asset classes investors we can integrate into our portfolios, for example – private equity, hedge funds, real estate, infrastructure, and commodities – and how to do so.

Families that add exposure to alternatives under the guidance of professional managers will be able to improve the risk/reward profile of their portfolios through superior returns and diversification benefits.

Because of illiquidity, many of these asset classes don't have actual transactions to assess short term performance. Instead, they rely on net-asset-values (NAVs) based on appraisals, which can distort performance. For long term performance, these asset classes rely on cash flows with the traditional measure being the internal rate of return (IRR). Other measures such as the Public Market Equivalent (PME) are gaining attention. Right now, it is still very difficult to obtain good measures of risk in these asset classes compared to traditional asset classes.

Another feature of alternatives is the almost exclusive reliance on professional management. (For example, investing in a real estate project we are reliant on the mangers of the project)

Commodities, however, are the only alternative asset class that can run passive strategies at low cost, but accessing an index fund that tracks alternatives is not really alternative investments are we are still exposed to market volatility.

For investing in Real assets, the management factor adds on an additional layer of risk.

The historic performance of alternatives has been in line with expectations with return and risk profiles that can help investors build better portfolios.

## What is the Market size of Alternative Investing?

To estimate the size of the alternative market we need to combine various types of data.

First, we look at the public equity and fixed income markets. As of June 2020, it is estimated that the size of the public equity market in USD is 53 trillion and the private fixed income market at and additional USD 62.9 trillion, which gives a total of about USD116 trillion of public assets of debt and equity.

Additionally, for December 2019 it is estimated that an additional USD 9.55 trillion are invested in direct real estate assets and about USD3.0 trillion is held in gold.

To this opportunity set, we can add the closed-end funds of private assets (private equity, private debt, infrastructure, and natural resources) of about USD4.8 trillion.

Thus, the sum of the public assets, direct real estate, and closed-end funds, which is approximately USD134 trillion.

We now need to add in hedge funds, and open-ended real estate and commodity funds. which we estimate to be about USD3 trillion and infrastructure funds USD 250 billion.

## Should I invest in Real Estate?

Real Estate behaves differently than most asset classes. It starts with the contractual nature of real estate, which is always a tangible asset (physical ownership of land or buildings).

This limits the potential volatility of real estate compared to equities and the probability of losing your money. The historical experience of Global real estate is quite good.

Unleveraged real estate traditionally has had equity like-returns in the long run but without volatility – admittedly distorted by the appraisal process, but this is getting better.

In the short future due to interest increases globally analysts don't expect stellar performance, but even with lower returns and possible stagnation, real estate clearly deserves strong consideration in portfolios.

The main advantage of real estate is its historically low correlation with equities – around 0.2 to 0.3 – and it has at times had its own distinct cycle. We can easily find periods where equities behave quite differently, namely the real estate bust of the 1980s and the tech bust of the early 2000s.

On the other hand, both real estate and equities had large declines around the Global Financial Crisis (GFC)od 2008 but real estate recovered must faster.

An additional feature of the private real estate market and its vehicle structure is that it allows the use of leverage to improve the return profile.

This leverage would be difficult for us as individual investors but can be effectively implemented and managed by professionals for collective plans.

## Property Asset Classes

Typical property types are offices, residential, and industrial. Another distinct feature of real estate is the different measures of valuation.

Real estate focuses on capitalization rates, which are more similar to a yield and price per square foot, for example. Real estate's illiquid nature makes all buying and selling a negotiated process. It reinforces the long-term view of investing.

Investors even in the most liquid vehicles (core funds) should expect that it may take several quarters to sell properties and redeem the fund's holdings.

The industry is evolving, and managers are looking at the secondary market for more liquidity options.

## Examples of Real Estate Asset Classes

### Supported Housing: The Green Agenda Takes roots.

The term "Supported Housing" refers to housing for the disabled provided by the central Government or a housing association.

This is a relatively new type of property investment that is both ethical and profitable and has become available for investors who would like to diversify their portfolios. The social housing markets offer advantages for medium and high budget investors.

The supported housing market had always been available to large institutions such as hedge funds and pension funds that take advantage of the government-backed leases. In the last few years though, the private sector through collective schemes (funds) have started to delve into this market, making the market available to mass affluent investors.

## Why is the social housing market advantageous for families?

The market entry minimum now can be as low as one hundred thousand GBP and the minimum government-backed lease is fifteen years. This Guarantees income linked to the cost of Living (CPI) that could even outlive us while retaining our capital to sell later of transfer to the next generation.

Investing in the social housing market fund could be a fine opportunity to start building an investment portfolio based on one of the most resilient assets in the market.

## The Residential Market

Rising interest rates have cooled the housing market.

As we enter times of a moderate recession, high inflation and rising interest rates are putting downward pressure on growth.

As a result, the environment will be more challenging for property, with higher debt costs, you can expect lower investment volumes.

This trend should be short lived, with the green shots of recovery already evident. After this period real estate investment markets will emerge from a period of uncertainty, pricing should stabilize, and activity should return.

For all assets you can expect a continued flight to quality, and real estate that does not match investor and occupiers' environmental goals will be increasingly marginalized.

It seems though that this could be a time of opportunity as it is now a buyers' market and not a seller's market. Assets will be sold in the next few years at a significant discount.

## Single-family rentals could remain an investing sweet spot.

Institutional investors have gotten a lot of the credit, or blame, for helping to drive up home prices, and a lot of that activity has gone toward building portfolios of single-family rentals (SFRs) for Generation Y & Z. In fact, rentals focused on these generations are on the rise, and it's reasonable to expect most of that to become investment opportunities with reliable returns.

## Multifamily in the US should stay strong.

Primarily in fast-growing Sun Belt markets like Atlanta; Phoenix; Orlando, Florida; Denver; and Austin, Texas for the same reason. Young professionals moving around the country need a roof over their heads and are buying/renting Multifamily properties.

## Office real estate will continue to sputter.

The assumption that after COVID we would see a rally for office real estate never happened. High Tech and Financial companies have discovered the home working concept that is loved mutually by employers and employees. It is common now for employees to sign contracts that specify how many days a week they will work from homa end how many in the office.

## Industrial real estate will present diverse growth opportunities.

Industrial real estate -- especially that large chunk of it devoted to logistics -- has been and will continue to be perhaps as hot as any segment of commercial real estate easily accessible to everyday investors. The dynamics driving the surge, including virtual shopping and e-commerce and the supply chain issues that are encouraging the growth of "just in case" instead of "just in time" use of warehouses, are going to hang around indefinitely.

## Will Alternative Investments Improve Investor Outcomes?

With today's markets reaching all-time volatility and inflation poking its head out, it has become more difficult for advisors and portfolio managers to diversify portfolios and find new opportunities for higher yields in the liquid market. The good news is that with continued innovation and better access to new asset classes available for the masses, there are more ways to diversify portfolios, streamline workflows, and deliver better performance.

The answer to the above question is based on disciplined exposure. The careful and informed use of alternative investments in a diversified portfolio can help you reduce risk, lower volatility, and improve returns over the long-term, enhancing your ability to your investment goals.

## The Challenge of Liquidity in Alternative Investing

As alternative investing gathered increased attention and popularity in recent years, focus has emerged on the question of liquidity in these investments.

It is imperative to understand these issues before investing in alternatives.

Interest in this "patient" approach has especially intensified after the financial crisis of 2008, as investors realized the importance of risk mitigation by investing in assets that are not correlated to markets.

Despite this, there are still some who shy away from alternatives altogether because these investments are less liquid (harder to buy and sell) when compared to their public stock and bond counterparts.

In addition to being a major deterrent to portfolio inclusion, illiquidity has presented many challenges to investors new to increasing allocations to alternative investments.

## Challenges of Illiquid Alternative Investments

Traditional investments such as public stocks and bonds are frequently traded at high levels of volume. By contrast, alternatives have varying degrees of trade-ability and sometimes can take upwards of a few years for an investment to be realized responsibly. The longer lockup periods of alternative investments and a lack of secondary markets result in a reduced ability to address cash flow requirements, quickly react to new information, enter, and exit investments, and consequentially, rebalance portfolios on a frequent basis. As a result, investors with shorter time horizons and greater liquidity needs may find it difficult, even undesirable, to incorporate alternatives.

The extended time it takes to realize investment returns also makes it more difficult to manage a consistent allocation to alternatives. After all, it is all very well knowing that time is up on a particular investment but selling it at a profit can be so much harder.

## Liquid Alternative Investments

Liquid alternative investments are mutual funds, for example REITS (Real Estate Investment Trusts –these are available Globally or exchange-traded funds (known as ETFs). Some ETFs aim to provide investors with diversification and downside protection through exposure to alternatives.

These products' selling point is that they are liquid, meaning that they can be bought and sold often, unlike traditional alternatives which offer monthly, quarterly, or less often liquidity. These REITS or ETFs often come with lower minimum investments than a typical alternative investment fund, and investors don't have to pass net-worth or income requirements to invest.

Liquid alternatives aim to counteract the drawbacks of alternative investments by providing investors with exposure to alternative investments through products that can be redeemed daily, just like a mutual fund.

As defined earlier, an alternative investment refers to almost any asset that is not a stock or a bond. Examples include fine art, private equity, commodities, real estate, private debt and hedge funds.

A drawback of any of these investments, however, is their lack of liquidity. Even if the private market is in its best times, it still will take considerably more time and effort to sell an alternative investment, and there may be lock-up periods so the REIT or the ETF can be an alternative for those who want exposure to alternatives without the restrictions of alternative liquidity.

However, some critics even here argue that the liquidity of so-called liquid alternatives will not hold up in more trying market conditions, most of the capital invested in liquid alternatives were established post 2008 financial crisis so only now they are being tested. It is advised to take note of the fees for these funds which usually are a bit higher than the standard equity or bond.

It is important to note that in the 2022-2023 crisis the Global REIT sector has been very volatile with some of the REITS loosing even 40% of their value but we need to understand that the underlying asset in the REIT is still real estate and for instance the UK REIT Cevitas lost over 50% of its value in the market in 2023 but recovered once the institutional investors made a private offer to buy the shares at double their traded value that was still in their opinion at a market discount.

For families struggling to invest and diversify, liquid alternatives can be a valuable innovation because they provide us with access to this important asset class.

## Benefits of Illiquid Alternative Investments

Despite the perceived challenges of investing in alternatives, these assets have the potential to enhance returns. In fact, returns are known to generally increase with degree of illiquidity, somewhere in the region of more than 3% annually.

For many investors, this "illiquidity premium" is more than suffi-cient compensation for less liquidity. A portfolio that incorporates an asset allocation to alternatives has the additional benefits of potentially diversifying risk exposures and cushioning market volatility. As alternatives are incorporated, a wider investment opportunity net is cast and a balancing effect on a portfolio is achieved.

## Should we focus on creating returns or creating income in the investment world?

Research reveals that clients are moving their core assets from liquid strategies to real assets that create income to prepare themselves for retirement.

The face of retirement has changed radically in recent decades. People are living longer. Pensions linked to final salaries are increasingly rare. Add to this market volatility, as well as questions surrounding the long-term financial health of Social Security and similar schemes, and it's no wonder many people feel anxious about funding their golden years.

They are making the change as they are looking for sustainable "retirement income" that resembles a traditional pension plan.

For example, a family with 500,000 USD can annuitize their money in an insurance company. They will probably get a guarantee from the insurance company to pay them a guaranteed lifetime annuity of 2000 USD a month but if they die after the annuity starts their beneficiaries with get nothing.

Alternatively, if they invest the same money in real estate and get rental income that is equal to six percent they will have after tax approximately the same but if they die their beneficiaries will receive the full 500,000 USD value of the property (and this is if the property has not grown in value).

The other alternative is to invest the money in the market and expose the family to volatility.

It is possible to provide a guaranteed stream of income that lasts a lifetime, and the asset will retain its value and will not be affected by the inevitable ups and downs of the markets?

If this is something, you identify with them "income investing" may be relevant for you.

Income investing is the practice of designing a portfolio of investments that will give you an income that you can live on. Investments could include real estate, debt, private equity, stocks, mutual funds, and bonds. It's crucial to consider which types of assets will enable you to meet your passive-income goals and investing philosophy while understanding the risks that can affect an income investing portfolio.

## What Is Income Investing?

The art of good income investing is gathering a collection of assets such as real estate, debt, private equity, stocks, mutual funds, and bonds, that will generate the highest possible annual income at the lowest possible risk. Most of this income is paid out to the investor so they can use it in their everyday lives to buy clothes, pay bills, take vacations, help the kids, and live a life of security without worrying about where the money is coming from.

Naturally, income investing is popular with those at or nearing retirement. When you are retired, you need to depend on a steady flow of income to replace the income you once had when you were working. Today, with a defined benefit going the way of the dinosaur and defined contribution holders being spooked by fluctuating balances as investments go up and down, there has been a resurgence of interest in income investing.

## What is defined Benefits and why are they now extinct?

A defined benefit plan offers guaranteed retirement income for employees. Defined benefit pension schemes offered security and retirement certainty for recipients.

The first defined benefit schemes emerged in Germany at the end of the nineteenth Century.

## Who invented Pensions?

In 1881 Otto von Bismarck, the conservative minister president of Prussia, presented a radical idea to the Reichstag: government-run financial support for older members of society. In other words, retirement. The idea was radical because back then, people simply did not retire. If you lived, you worked—probably manual labor—or, if you were wealthier, managed a business or an estate.

But von Bismarck was under pressure, from socialist opponents, to do better by the people in his country, and so he argued to the Reichstag that "those who are disabled from work by age and invalidity have a well-grounded claim to care from the state." It would take eight years, but by the end of the decade, the German government would create a retirement system for the over 70s.

This was unlikely at the time. Life expectancy in Germany at that time was about 40 and only a few percent of the workforce managed to get to age 70. Those who did reach the golden age could expect an average life span of an additional three to four years.

The workforce had to pay for this as an additional tax, so the government made a profit from the venture, but this changed over time.

After WW2 with the introduction of mass production of antibiotics along with access to clean water and nutritious food our live expectancy soared and by 2020 was over 80 in developed nations. The probability of reaching age 70 also changed drastically and more than 90% of those born will arrive at age 70 and those who do can expect to live on average over twenty more years.

## How Times Have Changed for Defined-Benefit Plans

Up until the 1980s, defined benefit pensions were the most popular retirement plan offered to employers. Today, less than 15% of workers have access to one.

From the employee's perspective, the beauty of the defined-benefit plan is that the employer helps fund the plan while the employee reaps the rewards upon retirement.

Not only do employees get to keep and spend all the money they earn in their pay checks, but they can also easily predict how much money they will receive each month during retirement because pay-outs from a defined-benefit plan are usually based on the worker's salary before retirement.

Of course, there are always two sides to every story. The Government, insurers or companies providing this service must provide the assets to guarantee this enormous liability. In fact, the pension funds liabilities in some of the world's largest employers were larger that the whole business (for example British Airways).

Funding for these plans came from corporate earnings or government budgets, and this had a direct impact on future generations or company stability. A drag on profits can weaken a company's ability to compete. So, switching to a defined-contribution plan such as a 401(k) in the US, which is mainly funded by employee contributions, saves a significant amount of money.

## What is a Defined Contribution Plan?

A defined contribution, or money purchase, pension scheme is the most common type of workplace pension these days. It is built up through your own contributions, those of your employer and tax relief from the government.

Defined contribution schemes will provide you with an accumulated sum when you come to retire that you can use to secure a pension income through buying a product called an annuity or opting for income drawdown. You can also take the lot as a lump sum - but may face a hefty tax bill.

Most company pension schemes now define the contribution.

## What is an annuity and what is drawdown?

The main difference between an annuity and drawdown is that an annuity guarantees the same payment for a fixed term while drawdown allows you to access your pension at any time and draw as much money as you need.

Learning about this type of retirement plan can help you determine how your pension works or whether it's suitable for you to implement.

## Defining a target income

To find the monthly income you need to create, you need to calculate a target withdrawal rate, which is how much income you want to pull out from your investments each year.

The rule of thumb in income investing is if you never want to run out of money, you should take no more than 5% of your balance out each year for income. This is commonly referred to on Wall Street as the 5% rule. This allows for inflation.

Put another way, if you manage to save $3,500,000 you should be able to make monthly withdrawals of $15,000 without ever running out of money.

By the time you retire, you'll probably own your own home and have very little debt. Absent any major medical emergencies, the number you come to should suffice.

Your target withdrawal can be calculated by:

Documenting for yourself your income, your expenses, your assets and liabilities, cash flows and defining your life goal.

## What are life Goals?

Life goals are defined as the desired states that you seek to obtain, maintain, or avoid. When we set life goals, we need to envision, plan for, and commit to achieving those desired results.

Because our lives include many different parts, life goals can be broad, including things like money we will require to improve our lives (buying or upgrading the house for example), retirement income you will need when you stop working, money you want to leave for your beneficiaries and more.

Setting life goals is an important part of what it means to be alive and achieving them can feel rewarding, give a sense of security and confidence in our future, or even generate a greater sense of purpose and meaning.

## What are the next steps?

Building an asset allocation with as much diversification as the strategy will allow.

Stress tests the allocation using "what if scenarios".

Build a tax strategy.

Build a strategy for the transfer of your estate to the next generations.

## Key Investments for Your Income Investing Portfolio

When you build your income creating portfolio, you are going to have three major "buckets" of potential investments. These include:

**Real estate**: You can own rental properties outright or invest through real estate funds or investment trusts (REITs). Real estate has its own tax rules, and some people are more comfortable because real estate offers some protection against high inflation and income they can control.

**Private Debt** Private debt is the debt held by or extended to private companies, households, and individuals. It is not available via publicly traded markets. It involves private, non-bank loans that generate returns via interest payments that we could live off. Private debt funds are investors that make or buy these loans on behalf of clients. Since the Global Financial Crisis in 2008, private debt has received increased attention and growth for a variety of reasons. These have included the low interest rate environment that existed for over ten years, elevated equity valuations that seemed ready for a correction, the diversification benefits and higher yield potential offered by private debt to create income for families. The case for private debt appears to be strong for families with long-term investment horizons and high-risk tolerances.

**Private Equity**: Investors seek out private equity (PE) funds that invest in companies that are not traded in order to earn returns that are better than what can be achieved in public equity markets.

1. Dividend-paying stocks: Both common stocks and preferred stock (stock that entitles the holder to a fixed dividend, whose payment takes priority over that of ordinary share) Companies that pay dividends pay a portion of annual profit to shareholders based on the number of shares they own. This can create part of the cash flow we need for our plan.

2. Bonds: You have many choices when it comes to bonds. You can own government bonds, agency bonds, municipal bonds, savings bonds, or others. It is worth it to note that in recent history bonds were trading at the lowest levels ever and in most developed countries government bonds were trading at negative returns (that means that you give the government for example one hundred and the Government guarantees to give you back less than that. This phenomenon exists when interest rates are low, and the price of money is cheap. Governments lower interest rates to make it cheaper to borrow. This tends to encourage spending and investment. This leads to economic growth but may also cause inflationary pressures.

## Can we make a full-time income from investing?

It's possible to make enough of your investments to cover your costs of living, but this doesn't happen overnight. It requires years of careful and disciplined investing and patiently allowing your wealth to grow. Once you do have enough invested to earn a full salary's worth in annual returns, you must be careful not to withdraw more than what your investments earn each year. Remember the 5% rule.

## What is Passive income?

Passive income is income generated from someone other than an employer or a contractor. It can be generated by earning interest on savings, renting out a space, or purchasing dividend-paying stocks, and so on.

Passive income is usually defined as an influx of income paid out with little effort required of the individual receiving the passive income to increase their revenue stream. Examples of passive income can include income from the rental of a real estate property and any business activity in which the earnings owner does not participate materially during the year.

The US-based IRS defines passive income for tax purposes as income from income sources that are not a "business" or "occupation", such as rental income, royalty income, dividend and similar.

## Planning passive income and self-management

In recent years, the creation of passive income for the family has become one of the most talked about and important topics in the financial world.

In a world without guaranteed benefits, where each of us is responsible for our own destiny, the question is "How do we generate for ourselves passive income that is an alternative to our permanent work, creating income that is not dependent on us and in fact allows us in stages to move forward on two tracks at the same time (passive and active income).

The first track in which we continue to work (perhaps in a partial format) and generate a passive supplementary income, but at the same time we have an additional and permanent source of income every month.

## Why should creating passive income be a priority?

New York is renowned to have some of the hardest-working citizens in the world. They work many hours, but what seems to be a safe and stable income can turn out to be fragile once an economic or health crisis begins. This is where generating passive income becomes essential.

In short, passive income is important because it creates stability, security, and freedom in your financial life. Additionally, since passive income is not limited by your time and effort, it can have a positive, and significant, effect on your ability to build wealth.

# Chapter Fifteen

## The "Law of Supply and Demand" and our Portfolio

The law of supply and demand is a theory that explains the interaction between the sellers of a resource and the buyers of that resource. The theory defines the relationship between the price of a given product and the willingness of people to either buy or sell it.

Generally, as price increases, people are willing to supply more and demand less and vice versa when the price falls.

Understanding supply/demand dynamics gives important insights into the future of our portfolio.

### What happened after COVID?

The pandemic caused an almost immediate consumption shock, resulting from the forced shutdown of entire consumer service industries.

On the flip side, there was a rise in household savings. In a typical recession, savings rates rise by a few percentage points and remain elevated for several years during recovery.

This meant that COVID-19 recession was dominated by the collapse in consumer spending and the rise in savings, making the consumer more important than ever as a trigger for investment decisions and achieving economic recovery.

Then post COVID the public woke up after hibernating and started to require material goods, go on holidays for a more comfortable and efficient lifestyle.

However, global manufacturing and delivery systems were not ready for this surge in demand. Demand was accelerating much faster than production.

Then add to this the havoc of the war in Ukraine.

## Supply Chains & Transporting of Goods.

Transportation systems were also not able to meet demand. There were not enough truckers, trains, cargo containers, containers, and warehouse space etc.

Continued supply-chain disruptions lead to sticky core inflation, particularly in food and energy. This could lead to further interest rate hikes, raising the risk of debt distress, a prolonged economic downturn, and a vicious cycle for fiscal planning.

With the COVID-19 crisis, fundamental changes in consumer behavior, supply chains, and routes to market are knocking companies off balance. Responding to the pandemic has under-scored the need for leaders to accelerate the adoption of agile ways of working and value chain transformation to help outmaneuver uncertainty.

All this will have an impact on the markets and create significant volatility.

## Supply and Demand in Housing

The supply of residential housing (especially after the 2008 US Housing Crisis) has not kept pace with increased demand – mostly from new family formation and added immigration in the OECD.

The UK has one of the highest population growths among developed nations. They need housing. Even the current levels of buildings are insufficient to meet the need often due to labor and material shortages, cost of land and taxes, government zoning regulations and community opposition.

This "affordability crisis" problem is extending globally, young family's strain to be able to buy a home as prices surged in the last ten years. The Office for National Statistics in the UK reports that the average hose price rose from 150,000 GBP in 2006 to 256,000 GBP in 2022.

Driving the debate over affordable housing is the recognition that it is a necessary part of modern societies. Everyone should have the opportunity to be able to live in a decent home – which they can afford – in a sustainable community.

Affordable homes provide social stability, enabling families to 'put down their roots' and begin to look for, or hold down, employment in their local area. They support a spending boost in the local economy. And in a settled environment, children can be sent to local schools, and this will make learning and, in turn, social advancement more likely.

## Supply and Demand in the Energy Market

Demand for energy has recovered faster than supply. Environmental concerns target decrease/ elimination of fossil fuels; this supply decrease is not fully met by more alternative (clean) energy. As the cost of borrowing rises the cost of replacing infrastructure is delaying political reform in green energy.

Production growth of traditional energy is outsourced to OPEC, a monopoly which is using the opportunity to control supply, and due to this, all energy prices rose significantly fueling inflation in the short term.

## Supply and Demand in the Labour Market

The supply of labor has declined largely due to increased early retirement in the 55+ group.

This is due to their investment wealth, housing wealth and a comfortable early retirement experience during the initial COVID layoff.

The result is that more people are exiting the workplace than entering it. This means less taxpayers and more expenses.

## What does this mean for us?

If in the past, we could rely on our governments to look after us in this new reality it is safe to say that we need to look after ourselves and not rely on anyone.

We need to understand how demand and supply will affect our futures and prepare accordingly.

## Inflation and our Investments

My Father-in-Law who was a real estate trader used to tell me regarding housing "It's all about location, location, location". This is a cliché calling the desirability of a property and it dates all the way back to real estate magnate Harold Samuel (founder of Land Securities, the largest publicly quoted landowner in the UK) who said this in 1926.

I will borrow this concept and state that the entire market and economy today revolves around "inflation, inflation, inflation"!

## The four drivers of inflation now are:

1. Supply chain disruptions

2. Excess capital paid into the system.

3. Excess savings that accumulated during the pandemic

4. Energy prices (and other commodities) increasing because of the war in Ukraine.

It seems that the first three will resolve themselves in due time and the last is supply-side inflation, which if not controlled correctly can turn to demand-side inflation.

This is an important differentiator as the largest fear would be that we will return to the inflation realities of the eighties. Between then and now energy prices have decreased from double digits down to single digits in our annual spending budgets.

The same thing is the case for food, and instead most of our spending is made on discretionary items like vacations and eating out. These items are easier to rein in during inflationary times.

Unemployment is reaching historic lows, which should be a good thing, except that this drives up wages which becomes inflationary. When inflation increases, interest rates increase to try to combat them, which in turn pulls down valuations on stocks and bonds.

But Politics is hindering the battle with inflation and Government spending is leading the way most notably the 1.2 $ Trillion Infrastructure Bill in the US signed in 2021 and the 1.7 trillion $ Budget passed in December 2021.

These kinds of fiscal policies which will last for years can undermine the attempts by central banks to curb inflation by curbing demand as Government spending has the opposite effect.

In the UK and Europe, the Governments have spent billions subsidizing energy bills while the economic slowdown has reduced tax revenue leading to mega deficits.

Understanding these trends are crucial to us and it means that more than ever it is important to plan and adopt our investments to the new realities.

Understanding inflations impact on our investments

Exploring investments to hedge against inflation.

Having a financial plan in place that equates for inflation.

Sticking to your long-term financial goals

While inflation is a cause for concern for everyone, it is important to have a financial plan in place. Financial planning can help you reach your goals and avoid costly mistakes. For example, if you are thinking about buying a house but don't know how much money you should be saving each month to pay the mortgage, it may be worth taking some time to sit down and come up with appropriate savings targets.

The good news is that Inflation should moderate over time, but I (along with others) don't see it getting back to the Government target in the US, the UK or Europe of 2% anytime soon. However, the longer high inflation persists, the stickier it gets and that is what affects interest rates.

So, what should our strategy be now to protect ourselves against this challenge? A few ideas:

## 1. Reallocate Money into Stocks

If inflation is high, it's generally a problem for the bond market, but it could be an opportunity for the stock market.

Buying preferred stocks is another possibility. These liquid issues will pay a higher yield than most types of bonds and may not decline in price as much as bonds when inflation appears.

Utility stocks represent a third choice, where stock prices rise and fall in a somewhat predictable fashion through the economic cycle as well as paying steady dividends.

## 2. Diversify Internationally

Investors tend to lean towards local stocks, but the practice can be costly over the long term, especially during times of inflation. Increasing international exposure can be a good strategy to hedge against inflation.

There are several major economies in the world that do not rise and fall in tandem with each other, such as the US, Italy, Japan, Australia, and South Korea. Adding stocks from these or other similar countries can help to hedge your portfolio against domestic economic cycles.

## 3. Consider Residential Real Estate (especially with CPI inflation linked rental agreements)

There are many advantages to investing in real estate. This asset class has intrinsic value and provides consistent income through dividends. It often acts as a good inflation hedge since there will always be a demand for homes, regardless of the economic climate, and because as inflation rises, so do property values, and therefore the amount a landlord can charge for rent.

Because real estate is a tangible asset, however, it's illiquid. An alternative to consider is Real estate Investment Funds, which are more liquid investments and can be bought and sold relatively easily in the markets. REITs are companies that own and operate portfolios of commercial, residential, and industrial properties. Providing income through rents and leases, they often pay higher yields than bonds. Another key advantage is that their prices probably won't be as affected when rates start to rise, because their operating costs are going to remain largely unchanged.

## The battle with Inflation – A case for real assets

As we said before we are experiencing our highest inflation levels in over 40 years and despite drastic measures globally and it is expected that inflation will remain elevated for some time. Many portfolios are allocated for an environment where inflation was non-existent and accommodative policies helped foster robust economic growth and a strong equity market. But as conditions change to point towards slowing growth along with higher inflation, there is growing concern, and we want to protect our investment portfolios.

### First, we need to Understand what real assets are:

Real assets include real estate, infrastructure, commodities, and resource equities—These may offer an effective solution amid inflation risks.

### Inflation is here to stay – no matter whatever central banks say.

A major shift in the drivers of this business cycle points to enduring inflation and a prolonged environment favourable for real assets for long term allocations.

The global economy's rapid recovery from Covid has been characterized by inflationary forces (wage/price pressures) and insufficient aggregate supply to keep up with an over-stimulated private sector. This convergence of supply and demand pressures is jointly driving inflation higher.

Add to this equation the Russia–Ukraine war continues and creates the likelihood that supply disruptions will endure.

Inflation, therefore, it seems, is likely to stay well above the previous cycle average.

### Positioning portfolios for long-term inflation risk.

What unifies real assets more than any other attribute is that their returns have historically benefited from inflation surprises. In other words, this means real assets have tended to outperform during periods of rising and unexpected inflation, contrasting with the modest or negative inflation sensitivity of stocks and bonds. The economic drivers of real assets are often directly or indirectly tied to inflationary trends; this linkage historically has resulted in outsized returns when inflation exceeds expectations. An allocation to real assets may therefore help to preserve future purchasing power, potentially offsetting the vulnerability to unexpected inflation that is historically common to traditional portfolios of stocks and bonds.

## Why real assets?

Real assets are the structures and raw materials that economies rely on to function and be productive. That includes the properties where we live, work and shop; the infrastructure that provides power and water and enables transportation and communications; and the basic natural resources, such as food and energy, that sustain societies.

A diversified blend of real assets—including real estate, infrastructure, commodities, and natural resource should help enhance a portfolio in three keyways:

Positive inflation sensitivity to help mitigate the potentially damaging effects of accelerating inflation.

## Diversification

Every investor is aware of the importance of diversification in every asset allocation.

The goal of diversification is investing in assets that have negative correlations in different economic and market environments, so when one asset zigs, the expectation is that another will zag. Real assets' distinct economic sensitivities tend to differentiate them from traditional risk assets such as stocks and bonds and should not be correlated to markets.

## Why Diversify into Real Assets?

Priced attractively and with resilience in the face of inflation, portfolio diversification and historically attractive returns through an economic cycle are reasons an allocation to real assets in a diversified portfolio makes sense in most economic regimes. Potentially adding to the asset class appeal are attractive relative valuations.

Our lives today are characterized by repeated and unprecedented surprises, this could impact our families' destinies so now is the time to align our investment strategy with our life goals and introduce asset classes that will help on the journey.

## Understanding Inflation and Interest Rates

The international investor must understand interest rates, inflation and the play-off between the two.

The Central Bank directs the Ministry of Finance to promote maximum employment and stable prices. Most countries target an annual inflation of 2% as consistent with the stable prices portion of this dual mandate.

The Central Bank targets a positive rate of inflation, defined as a sustained rise in the overall price level for goods and services, because a sustained decline in prices, known as deflation, can be even more harmful to the economy. The positive level of inflation and interest rates also provides the central bank with the flexibility to lower rates in response to an economic slowdown.

## How Changes in Interest Rates should affect Inflation

When a central bank responds to elevated inflation risks by raising its benchmark interest rate it effectively increases the level of money available to the public in a close to risk-free environment (deposits), limiting the money supply available for businesses to grow or for mortgages.

Conversely, when a central bank reduces its target interest rate it effectively increases the money supply available for businesses to grow or for mortgages.

By increasing borrowing costs, rising interest rates also should discourage consumer and business spending, especially on housing, retail shopping and capital equipment. Rising interest rates also tend to weigh on prices, reversing the wealth effect for individuals and making banks more cautious in lending decisions.

Finally, rising interest rates signal the likelihood that the central bank will continue to tighten monetary policy further tamping down inflation expectations.

## So, what is the challenge?

First, we need to understand that economy is a social science and not an exact one. It is a game of experimenting and seeing if the theory works, then correcting and trying again. There are no guarantees that the theory will work as the regulator expects and even if the theory worked in the past, every event is different so the reaction to the event may have different outcomes than expected.

Add onto this that policymakers often respond to changes that are needed with a lag, and their policy changes, in turn, take time to affect the trends.

Because of these lags, policymakers must try to anticipate future inflation trends when deciding on rate levels in the present. Yet the regulators' adherence to its inflation target can only be gauged with backward-looking inflation statistics. These can range widely amid economic shocks that can sometimes prove transitory and other times less so.

To sum it up, if making monetary policy is like driving a car, then the car is one that has an unreliable speedometer, a foggy windshield, and a tendency to respond unpredictably and with a delay to the accelerator or the brake.

Central banks trying to anticipate inflation trends risk could be making a policy error by needlessly stoking inflation with rates that are too low, or stifling growth by raising them. We also have no real proof that the outcome will be aligned with the strategy or if the outcome is aligned with the strategy that it happened because of the regulators policy.

Interest Rates as a tool to leverage or control inflation.

In the years following the 2008 global financial crisis, the focus of bank regulation shifted to ensure long-term solvency. Interest rates and inflation tend to move in the same direction but with lags, policymakers try to manipulate it to estimate future inflation trends, and the interest rates they set take time to fully affect the economy. The theory is that higher rates are needed to bring rising inflation under control, while slowing economic growth often lowers the inflation rate and may prompt rate cuts in the future.

## Why Interest rates effect all of us

Interest rates affect the decisions we make about our money. Some of these are obvious – think about how much more money you would stick in your savings account if it paid 15% interest and not 5%. How much less money would you put into stocks if you could get 15% in a simple deposit account? On the flip side, you might take out a new credit card at 3%, but you probably wouldn't borrow at 30% unless you absolutely needed to.

There are less obvious impacts, too. For **entrepreneurs** and bankers, interest rates affect calculations about future profitability. For instance, it's easy to enter the capital markets and finance a new project when interest rates are at historic lows, but the same project might not be a money maker in the long term if expected interest payments double. This, in turn, affects which products and services are offered in the economy, which jobs become available and how investments are structured.

Since interest rates affect how much a new bank loan costs, less money is circulating in the economy. There is no uniform or single natural rate to determine an interest rate.

## Capital Preservation is the Key

Ironically, even economic recovery creates the need for caution in the markets.

For you know it may be "A Time for Caution" as it seems maturing economises and expected rising interest rates could require a more cautious investment strategy.

As we approach retirement, we may want to change our strategy from Growth to Preservation.

## What Is Preservation of Capital?

Preservation of capital is a conservative investment strategy where the primary goal is to prevent loss in a portfolio. This strategy necessitates investment in safe investments, such as Treasury bills, Real Estate, structured notes with Capital Guarantees and certificates of deposit.

## Understanding Preservation of Capital

The key to understanding the preservation of capital lies in understanding needs and constructing a strategy based not only on aspirations but also on the capacity to bear risk. It is crucial to comprehend the implications if investments were to lose value in the short or medium term.

Investors should diversify their funds across different types of investments that align with their investment objectives. These objectives and portfolio strategies are influenced by various factors, such as age, family responsibilities, education, and annual income.

Preservation of capital is a fundamental principle in financial management that emphasizes the protection and conservation of invested funds. While the pursuit of growth and profitability is vital, preserving capital plays a crucial role in ensuring long-term financial stability and the ability to seize opportunities. This article highlights the significance of capital preservation and its implications for individuals and organizations.

Risk Mitigation: Preserving capital helps mitigate the potential risks associated with investments. Financial markets are inherently volatile, and unforeseen events can lead to sudden downturns. By prioritizing capital preservation, investors can safeguard their assets against market fluctuations and minimize the impact of unforeseen events, such as economic recessions or industry-specific downturns. Capital preservation provides a buffer that allows individuals and organizations to weather storms and remain financially secure.

Stability and Liquidity: Capital preservation contributes to financial stability, enabling individuals and businesses to meet their short-term obligations and maintain a solid financial footing. By preserving capital, one can create a safety net for emergencies or unexpected expenses, ensuring liquidity and reducing the need for high interest borrowing or selling assets at unfavourable prices. This stability allows individuals to withstand economic downturns and organizations to navigate challenging business environments without compromising their long-term objectives.

Flexibility and Opportunity: Capital preservation offers individuals and organizations the flexibility to seize opportunities when they arise. By preserving capital, individuals can accumulate resources to invest in new ventures, expand their businesses, or pursue strategic acquisitions. Preserved capital can act as a catalyst for growth, providing the necessary funds to capitalize on emerging trends or breakthrough technologies. The ability to leverage preserved capital for future opportunities creates a competitive advantage and enhances overall financial resilience.

In a dynamic and unpredictable financial landscape, the importance of capital preservation cannot be overstated. By prioritizing the preservation of capital, individuals and organizations can mitigate risk, maintain stability, and capitalize on future opportunities. By safeguarding the foundation for growth, capital preservation becomes an indispensable component of a sound financial strategy.

## "Money Matters: Essential Tools for Managing Finances as an Expat"

Focusing on financial management of the family is crucial for several reasons:

Economic Stability: Effective financial management helps maintain economic stability within the family. It ensures that there is enough money to cover essential expenses, such as housing, food, education, and healthcare. By managing finances well, families can avoid financial crises, debt, and the stress that comes with them.

Goal Achievement: Financial management enables families to work towards their short-term and long-term goals. Whether it's saving for a down payment on a house, funding children's education, or planning for retirement, sound financial management provides the means to achieve these objectives.

Emergency Preparedness: Life is unpredictable, and unexpected expenses can arise at any time, such as medical emergencies, car repairs, or job loss. By practicing financial management, families can build emergency funds to handle such situations without disrupting their overall financial stability.

Debt Reduction and Avoidance: Proper financial management helps families reduce and avoid unnecessary debt. By budgeting, tracking expenses, and making informed financial decisions, families can avoid overspending, high-interest loans, and credit card debt. This leads to improved financial well-being in the long run.

Improved Communication: When families focus on financial management, it necessitates open and honest communication about money matters. Regular discussions about budgeting, financial goals, and spending priorities promote transparency, teamwork, and understanding among family members.

Financial Education: Managing family finances offers an opportunity for everyone to learn about money management, budgeting, saving, and investing. Teaching children about financial responsibility from an early age can instil good habits and prepare them for their own financial futures.

**Future Planning**: Financial management involves planning, such as retirement savings, estate planning, and insurance coverage. By proactively addressing these aspects, families can safeguard their financial well-being and ensure a comfortable future for themselves and their loved ones.

Overall, focusing on financial management empowers families to take control of their financial situation, reduce stress, achieve their goals, and build a foundation for long-term financial security.

## Creating a sustainable future for your family by managing assets and liabilities

A monthly mortgage or monthly living costs are common examples of a liability that a consumer pays for from current cash inflows. Each month, the family must have sufficient assets to pay their liabilities.

In today's fast-paced and ever-changing world, families face numerous challenges in securing a sustainable future. A crucial aspect of achieving long-term stability lies in effectively managing assets and liabilities.

This essay explores the significance of asset and liability management for families and emphasizes the importance of adopting sustainable practices. By understanding the intricacies of financial planning, investing wisely, and balancing debts, families can pave the way for a prosperous and secure future.

Asset management plays a pivotal role in creating a sustainable future for families. Assets encompass a wide range of resources, including financial investments, properties, and personal possessions.

Proper management of these assets ensures their preservation and growth over time. Families should adopt strategies such as diversifying investments, aligning with sustainable ventures, and planning for long-term goals. By investing in socially responsible funds or green energy projects, families can contribute to a sustainable future while also earning returns. Additionally, proactive financial planning, including retirement savings, education funds, and emergency funds, helps secure a stable future for both immediate and extended family members.

Conversely, managing liabilities is equally critical for families aiming for long-term sustainability. Liabilities consist of debts, loans, mortgages, and other financial obligations. High-interest debts, such as credit card balances, can hinder financial stability and limit opportunities for growth.

Families should prioritize debt reduction strategies, such as budgeting, debt consolidation, and negotiating lower interest rates. Effective management of liabilities not only minimizes financial stress but also frees up resources for asset accumulation and investments. Adopting responsible borrowing practices, such as only taking on debts that align with long-term goals and avoiding unnecessary consumer debt, can greatly benefit families in the quest for sustainability.

Creating a sustainable future for families requires a holistic approach that extends beyond financial management. It involves embracing environmentally conscious practices and fostering a culture of sustainability within the household. By reducing energy consumption, implementing recycling initiatives, and adopting sustainable lifestyles, families can contribute to a greener future for generations to come. Educating family members about the importance of sustainability and encouraging responsible habits from an early age can have a lasting impact on their choices and behaviours.

In conclusion, managing assets and liabilities is crucial for creating a sustainable future for families. By effectively managing assets through diversification, socially responsible investing, and proactive financial planning, families can ensure long-term stability and growth.

Simultaneously, responsible management of liabilities, including debt reduction and prudent borrowing practices, minimizes financial burdens and enables families to invest in their future. Furthermore, embracing sustainable practices and instilling a culture of environmental responsibility within the household paves the way for a greener and more sustainable future.

By balancing assets and liabilities while embracing sustainability, families can navigate the challenges of the modern world and secure a prosperous future for themselves and future generations.

## What Are Assets and what are Liabilities?

An asset is any investment or resource that could be used to generate cash flow, reduce expenses, or provide future economic benefits. Assets contain economic value and can benefit a family's future planning or raise the family's net worth.

When it comes to family financial management, understanding the concepts of assets and liabilities is crucial. Assets represent the valuable resources a family possesses, while liabilities encompass their financial obligations. This essay aims to define and explore the significance of assets and liabilities within the context of family finances.

Assets are the tangible and intangible resources that families own and control. Tangible assets include properties, vehicles, and personal possessions such as jewellery or electronics. These assets can appreciate or depreciate over time and may generate income or be sold for monetary value when needed. Intangible assets, on the other hand, include investments, savings accounts, stocks, and bonds. These financial instruments offer opportunities for growth and can contribute to long-term wealth accumulation. Assets serve as a means of security and provide families with the ability to meet future financial goals, such as funding education, retirement, or emergencies.

Liabilities, in contrast, are the financial obligations that families owe to others. They include debts, loans, mortgages, credit card balances, and any other monetary liabilities. Liabilities can arise from various sources, such as borrowing for education, purchasing a home, or financing a vehicle. It is important for families to manage their liabilities carefully to avoid excessive debt burdens and financial strain. While some liabilities may be necessary and contribute to long-term goals, such as a mortgage for a home, families should aim to minimize high-interest debts, such as credit card balances, that can hinder financial stability and growth.

Assets and liabilities are fundamental components of family financial management. Assets represent the valuable resources that families own, providing them with security and the means to achieve their financial goals. On the other hand, liabilities encompass the financial obligations families owe to others, and careful management is essential to prevent excessive debt burdens. By understanding and effectively managing assets and liabilities, families can work towards achieving financial stability and a prosperous future.

You can calculate a family's equity, solvency, or financial health by subtracting its liabilities—meaning outstanding debts or accounts payable—from the value of its total assets. This is referred to as a family's "Net Value".

## Who is responsible for your investment outcomes? The Investment Manager or the market?

Investing in the financial markets can be a complex endeavour, and achieving favourable investment outcomes is a goal shared by all investors. However, the question of responsibility for investment outcomes arises: is it primarily the investment manager or the market that bears the responsibility? This essay aims to explore the dynamics between investment managers and the market, discussing their respective roles and influences on investment outcomes.

Investment managers play a vital role in the investment process. They are entrusted with making informed decisions on behalf of their clients, based on their expertise, research, and analysis. Investment managers are responsible for formulating investment strategies, selecting appropriate investment instruments, and managing portfolios. They are expected to exercise due diligence, perform thorough research, and employ risk management techniques to maximize returns while minimizing risks.

Investment managers are also responsible for monitoring market conditions, identifying trends, and adjusting investment strategies accordingly. They strive to generate positive investment outcomes by leveraging their knowledge and experience in navigating the complexities of the financial markets. However, it is important to note that investment managers are not infallible, and their decisions are subject to various factors, including market volatility, economic conditions, and unforeseen events.

The market, comprising the collective actions of buyers and sellers, plays a significant role in investment outcomes. Market dynamics, such as supply and demand, economic indicators, geopolitical events, and investor sentiment, influence the performance of investment instruments. The market can experience fluctuations, periods of growth, or downturns, impacting the value of investments. These market forces are beyond the control of individual investment managers.

Investors must recognize that markets are inherently unpredictable and subject to volatility. Market movements can be influenced by factors beyond anyone's control, such as global economic trends, political events, or natural disasters. While investment managers strive to make sound investment decisions, the market's performance can significantly impact investment outcomes, even when investment managers have made prudent choices.

It is essential to understand that investment outcomes are a result of the interplay between investment managers and the market. Investment managers are responsible for conducting thorough research, analysis, and risk management, which can contribute to favourable outcomes. However, they operate within the framework of the market, where external factors can influence investment performance.

Investors also bear a level of responsibility for their investment outcomes. It is crucial for investors to set clear investment objectives, communicate them to their investment managers, and maintain open lines of communication. Investors should also conduct their own due diligence and understand the risks associated with their investments. By actively engaging in the investment process, investors can make informed decisions and align their expectations with market realities.

Investment outcomes are influenced by a combination of factors, with both investment managers and the market playing significant roles. Investment managers bear the responsibility of formulating strategies, making informed decisions, and managing portfolios. However, they operate within the framework of the market, which is subject to external forces and fluctuations.

Investors also have a responsibility to set clear objectives, communicate effectively, and stay informed about their investments. Recognizing the shared responsibility between investment managers and the market is essential for understanding the dynamics that contribute to investment outcomes. By embracing a collaborative approach and maintaining realistic expectations, investors can navigate the complexities of the market and work towards achieving their investment goals.

## The secret in the methodology and not in the asset.

When it comes to achieving success in any field, including investments, many people believe that the key lies in finding the right asset. However, a closer examination reveals that the real secret to success lies in the methodology employed rather than the specific asset chosen. This essay explores the significance of methodology and highlights how it can lead to favourable outcomes in various endeavours.

While assets undoubtedly play a role in investment performance, the methodology used to analyse, select, and manage those assets is what truly determines success. A robust and well-defined methodology provides a systematic approach to decision-making, minimizing the reliance on luck or chance. It includes thorough research, analysis of historical data, consideration of risk factors, and the implementation of appropriate risk management strategies.

A sound methodology allows investors to identify opportunities, navigate market volatility, and make informed decisions based on data and analysis rather than emotions or market trends.

The efficacy of a methodology can be observed across various fields. In sports, for example, successful athletes and teams often attribute their achievements to disciplined training, strategic planning, and adherence to a proven methodology. Similarly, in business, entrepreneurs who follow structured processes, conduct market research, and adapt their strategies based on market dynamics tend to achieve sustainable growth.

The secret to success does not solely lie in the asset chosen, but rather in the methodology applied. A well-developed methodology empowers individuals in various domains to make informed decisions, mitigate risks, and achieve favourable outcomes. By focusing on refining and implementing a robust methodology, individuals can unlock the true potential of their endeavours and increase their chances of long-term success.

## Asset Liability Matching for families.

Asset liability management (ALM) is a crucial financial strategy that families can adopt to effectively plan and achieve their life goals. ALM involves managing the balance between assets (what you own) and liabilities (what you owe) to optimize financial stability and success.

By adopting an ALM approach, families can align their financial resources with their long-term objectives, such as buying a home, funding education, saving for retirement, and leaving a lasting legacy.

**Goal Alignment**: Asset liability management allows families to align their assets and liabilities with their specific life goals. By identifying their objectives, families can create a roadmap that guides their financial decisions and ensures that resources are allocated appropriately. For instance, if the goal is to purchase a home, families can focus on reducing liabilities, such as credit card debt, while simultaneously increasing assets, such as savings and investments, to accumulate a down payment.

**Financial Stability**: Implementing an ALM strategy promotes financial stability by minimizing risks and uncertainties. Families can assess their income, expenses, and debt obligations to identify areas where adjustments can be made. By managing their liabilities effectively, families can reduce financial stress, improve cash flow, and build an emergency fund, creating a safety net for unexpected expenses and emergencies.

**Long-Term Wealth Creation**: Asset liability management encourages families to adopt a long-term perspective on wealth creation. By carefully managing their assets, such as investments and retirement accounts, families can benefit from compounding growth over time. Simultaneously, they can strategically manage their liabilities, ensuring that debts are handled responsibly and do not hinder wealth accumulation.

This approach enables families to maximize their financial resources, ultimately achieving long-term goals, such as retiring comfortably or leaving a substantial inheritance for future generations.

**Risk Mitigation**: ALM enables families to mitigate financial risks by diversifying their assets and reducing liabilities. Diversification spreads risk across different asset classes, minimizing the impact of market fluctuations and economic downturns. Additionally, effective liability management helps families avoid excessive debt burdens and high-interest obligations, protecting them from financial hardships and potential defaults.

**Legacy Planning**: Asset liability management plays a pivotal role in legacy planning. By managing their assets and liabilities effectively, families can ensure the smooth transfer of wealth to future generations. Proper estate planning, including the creation of wills, trusts, and charitable contributions, helps families protect and distribute their assets according to their wishes, leaving a lasting legacy that supports their values and goals.

Asset liability management is a powerful financial strategy that empowers families to achieve their life goals. By aligning assets and liabilities, families can effectively plan for major milestones, enhance financial stability, create long-term wealth, mitigate risks, and leave a meaningful legacy.

Adopting an ALM approach enables families to make informed financial decisions, optimize their resources, and navigate the path towards their desired future.

## Options for Expat Families

Expat families have several investment options available to them. The choice of investment will depend on various factors such as their financial goals, risk tolerance, investment horizon, and tax implications.

Here are some investment options commonly considered by expat families:

**Stock Market**: Investing in the stock market provides an opportunity to participate in the growth of publicly traded companies. Expats can invest in individual stocks or opt for diversified exposure through mutual funds or exchange-traded funds (ETFs). It's important to conduct thorough research or consult with a financial advisor before investing in individual stocks.

**Bonds**: Bonds are debt instruments issued by governments, municipalities, or corporations. They offer fixed income and are considered lower risk compared to stocks. Expats can invest in government bonds, corporate bonds, or bond funds.

Real Estate: Investing in real estate can provide a stable income stream and potential capital appreciation.

Expats can consider purchasing rental properties, commercial properties, or invest in real estate investment trusts (REITs). It's essential to understand the local real estate market and regulations before making any investments.

**Mutual Funds and ETFs**: Mutual funds and ETFs offer diversification by investing in a portfolio of securities such as stocks, bonds, or a combination of both. They are managed by professionals and provide an easy way to gain exposure to different asset classes and markets.

**Retirement Accounts**: Expats may have access to retirement accounts like Individual Retirement Accounts (IRAs) or employer-sponsored plans. These accounts offer tax advantages and long-term savings benefits. It's crucial to understand the tax implications both in the expat's current country of residence and their home country.

**Index Funds:** Index funds are passively managed funds that aim to replicate the performance of a specific market index, such as the S&P 500. They offer broad market exposure and generally have lower fees compared to actively managed funds.

**Education Savings**: If expat families have children, they may consider investing in education savings plans or college savings accounts. These accounts provide tax advantages and can help save for future educational expenses.

**Alternative Investments**: Expats with higher risk tolerance and a longer investment horizon may explore alternative investments like private equity, hedge funds, venture capital, or commodities. These investments often require higher minimum investments and are generally more complex and illiquid.

It's important for expat families to consider their specific circumstances, seek professional advice, and understand the tax implications in both their current country of residence and their home country before making any investment.

## Active or Passive Investing?

As a member of the baby boomer generation, I grew up with a rotary dial phone in the house, I recall when we needed phones and computers, and they had nothing to do with each other. Phones were just communication devices, while computers were gateways to limitless knowledge and entertainment. Nowadays, that distinction has dissolved. For many consumers, phones are their personal computers.

The world of investing too has evolved and diluted away the distinction between active and passive investing. In the current landscape, characteristics implied by such traditional, standardized labels may not be sufficient to describe many of today's investment approaches.

## Active Investing

Active investing, as its name implies, involved a hands-on approach to investing. The goal of active money management is to beat the stock market's average returns and take full advantage of short-term price fluctuations using research and analysis to pinpoint when to pivot into or out of a particular stock, bond or any asset. A portfolio manager usually oversees a team of analysts who look at quantitative factors, then gaze into their crystal balls to try to determine where and when that price will change.

Active investing requires confidence that whoever is investing in the portfolio will know exactly the right time to buy or sell. Successful active investment requires being right more often than wrong. Over the years this has proved to be almost an impossible task.

## Passive Investing

Passive investing and active investing are two distinct approaches that individuals employ to manage their investment portfolios. While both strategies have their merits, it is important to understand the key differences between passive and active investing to make informed decisions.

Passive Investors: Passive investors follow a "buy and hold" strategy, aiming to replicate the performance of a specific market index or benchmark. They build diversified portfolios by investing in index funds or exchange-traded funds (ETFs). The primary characteristics of passive investing include:

Minimal Intervention: Passive investors do not actively trade securities. Instead, they maintain a long-term investment horizon and resist frequent buying and selling decisions based on short-term market fluctuations.

Lower Costs: Passive investing typically involves lower fees and expenses compared to active investing. Since passive investors focus on replicating an index, they do not incur costs associated with extensive research or active management.

Market Exposure: Passive investors believe in the efficiency of markets and aim to capture the overall market returns. They accept that it is challenging to consistently outperform the market and instead seek to match its performance.

Both passive and active investing strategies have their own advantages and drawbacks. Passive investing offers simplicity, lower costs, and broad market exposure, while active investing allows for potential outperformance and tailored portfolio management.

The choice between these two approaches depends on an individual's financial goals, risk tolerance, time commitment, and investment expertise. Some investors may prefer the ease and cost-effectiveness of passive investing, while others may be inclined to actively manage their portfolios to seek greater returns. Ultimately, it is crucial for investors to carefully evaluate their objectives and preferences before deciding which strategy aligns best with their financial goals.

However, a sailboat without an engine must still be actively manipulated to keep wind in its sail. Indexes are not perpetual motion machines free of maintenance, but require active management through additions, deletions, and reweighting.

Also blurring the line between active and passive is the fact that some investors may use index funds to pursue an active investment approach. For example, the largest index the S&P 500 has the highest average daily trade volume of any US-listed securities in 2021, at $31 billion, according to Bloomberg. It is reasonable to assume a portion of that trading activity represented asset allocation changes motivated by market viewpoints, rather than buy-and-hold position accumulation.

## Investing in Private Equity

How do companies grow? In the past they would typically have relied on private capital, talent, experience, and the banks. If they survived this first stage, and still had great potential, they could consider an initial public offering (IPO) on the stock market, and then after they are well established, they could also turn to the bond market as the source of greater funds for expansion.

Those things still exist, but increasingly, the capital behind growth around the world is a product of private equity funds and not public markets. In private equity offerings, deep pools of money are used to make direct deals, in what companies see as a more cost effective and flexible approach for providing the resources needed for growth.

## What is private equity?

Investopedia defines Private Equity as "An alternative form of private financing, away from public markets, in which funds and investors directly invest in companies or engage in buyouts of such companies. Private equity firms make money by charging management and performance fees from investors in a fund".

It's not new, It's the way J.P. Morgan, the private banker, worked in shaping the US steel industry. In the decades after World War II, private banking was overshadowed by Global Stock Exchanges that provided an access to liquidity, which helped make equities widely held among global investors, while traditional banks were the main source for startup loans.

What is happening now? Traditionally private equity was reserved for ultra-high net worth families (the very rich) or institutional investors that had the resources to put large amounts in one tranche, but now private equity is entering the mainstream, fuelled by technology that allows crowdfunding or investment funds that can register on exchanges with minimal cost (the Cost of an IPO can be over one Million USD without a guarantee of success and launching a private equity fund would cost less than 5% of this.

## Why do companies go down this route?

Selling equity over borrowing – What seems logically fair? Getting into more debt (if they already have), borrowing more, paying more compound interest month after month and a horrendous late fee penalty if they miss the monthly instalment Or, offering a certain percent stake of your company in a private equity deal?

In this scenario, no pledging personal assets, no monthly payments, and no compound interest. Instead, companies can reduce the debt ratio (if any) and stabilise their balance sheets.

Cash Cushion: Whether they are trying to bring their talent or ideas to the market for the first time or expanding and scaling, they need funds at every stage of the business. Innovation, R&D, supply chains, marketing, getting, and keeping skilled talent, and everything that supports business growth demands cash resources, doesn't it? Not to mention the uncertain situation like the pandemic that turned around the situation overnight, throwing some companies into the dark hole questioning how they will even pay the salary, rent, bills, and overheads and protect themselves from sinking?

**Leadership**: Technology is advancing at lightning speed. And consumers are expecting an enriched, smoother, upgraded, and modernised experience at every level. Big giant corporations with deep fat pockets are continuously innovating and advancing their technology at every artificial intelligence, digitization, virtual reality and the internet. Private Equity allows companies to compete.

**Success**: Sometimes businesses are so close to the tree that they can't see the forest. The truth is the market is so fiercely competitive that if you are not 100% committed to success, your competition will eat you for lunch without a burp. PE funds want the business to grow because it's in their interest. They will support the business at the forefront.

How big is the private equity market today?

Assets in global private markets now top $10 trillion nearly five times as much as in 2007. Public markets are still far bigger but have grown more slowly, roughly doubling. In the US, companies that have stayed private have raised more money than those whose securities trade in public markets every year since 2009, according to a Morgan Stanley report. In debt markets, private credit represents a fraction of the financing provided by banks or publicly traded bonds but doubled globally over the last five years to $1.2 trillion.

## What is the Driver of Private Equity Funds?

According to Deloitte research, private equity investment growth has been driven by the public who have never had the ability to invest in this asset class. It has the potential to expose clients to initiation and be richly rewarded for successful performance. Investors should approach private equity with a clear-eyed, honest appraisal of both the risks and rewards it entails.

In summary: we live in an exciting new world and are swimming in uncharted waters, never have so many had access at the fastest growing stage of companies to investment and private equity is exposing more and more people every day to this exciting asset class. The market has grown by 500% in 15 years, it could grow another 500% in the next five years.

## Revenue Royalty Structures for Private Equity Funds

The first private equity funds were created in the 1950s. However, there were few such formal structures, and they were mostly marketed to institutional investors rather than to individual investors. A series of regulatory changes in the US and Europe enabled private investors to effectively access the funds but mostly these were very wealthy individuals. These favourable regulatory events together with the evolution of the limited partnership resulted in a spectacular growth of the private equity industry.

A hypothetical investment of USD 100 invested in five different financial instruments on 1 January 1980 and assuming reinvestment of all proceeds provides a clear return comparison across asset classes. Private equity clearly shows the highest returns with an ending value of USD 27,024, equating to an annual time-weighted return of 15.0% - an outperformance of 5.5% and 4.3% over the MSCI World and S&P 500 indices, respectively.

However, as opposed to public equity investments where the investor is immediately fully invested, private equity managers usually call committed capital from their investors over time as they find investment opportunities and distribute principal and gains as investments are exited. For this reason, the timing and size of cash flows is more important than in traditional asset classes. Private equity practitioners do not typically report time-weighted returns but analyse and report performance in a money-weighted performance metric, the internal rate of return (IRR). The money-weighted mechanic of the IRR better reflects the timing and size of the underlying cash flows.

## What Is a Royalty?

A royalty is a legally binding payment made to an individual or company for the ongoing use of their assets, including copyrighted works, franchises and natural resources. An example of royalties would be payments received by musicians when their original songs are played on the radio or television, used in movies, performed at concerts, bars, and restaurants, or consumed via streaming services. In most cases, royalties are revenue generators specifically designed to compensate the owners of songs or property when they license out their assets for another party's use.

## Examples of Royalty Deals in Private Equity

Royalty deals in private equity refer to agreements where an investor provides capital to a company in exchange for a percentage of the company's future revenue or profits. This arrangement allows the investor to receive a consistent return on their investment without having an ownership stake in the company. Here are a few examples of royalty deals in private equity.

**Technology Licensing Royalty Deal**: A private equity firm invests in a tech startup that has developed a groundbreaking software product. In return for their investment, the private equity firm negotiates a royalty agreement where they receive a percentage of the startup's revenue generated from licensing the software to other companies.

**Franchise Royalty Deal**: A private equity firm provides funding to a successful franchise business that wants to expand its operations. In exchange for their investment, the private equity firm secures a royalty arrangement, where they receive a portion of the franchise's ongoing royalty fees collected from franchisees.

**Entertainment Royalty Deal**: A private equity firm invests in a film production company. As part of the investment, the private equity firm structures a royalty agreement that entitles them to a percentage of the film's box office revenue or ancillary revenue streams, such as DVD sales, streaming, and licensing.

**Healthcare Royalty Deal**: A private equity firm provides capital to a pharmaceutical company that has developed a promising drug. In return for their investment, the private equity firm negotiates a royalty agreement, where they receive a portion of the drug's sales revenue over a specified period.

**Energy Royalty Deal**: A private equity firm invests in an oil and gas exploration company. As part of the investment, the private equity firm structures a royalty agreement that entitles them to a percentage of the company's future production revenue from oil and gas wells.

It's important to note that the specifics of royalty deals can vary widely depending on the nature of the industry, the company's stage of development, and the terms negotiated between the private equity firm and the company seeking funding. Top of Form

## Our Future – Creating Passive Income?

Investing has long been recognized as a powerful tool for wealth accumulation and financial freedom. However, the future of investing is rapidly evolving, and one concept that holds great promise is the creation of passive income. Passive income refers to earnings generated with minimal effort or active involvement, allowing individuals to generate wealth while enjoying the freedom to pursue other interests.

In ground-breaking research conducted by global investment giant Blackrock it is revealed that families all over the world are focusing on investing with the goal of creating sustainable passive income and not only the search for returns.

So, you have a steady income flow from working 9 to 5 and that's great.

But families globally are rethinking their strategy, as deep down they want much more, more independence from a pay check, more freedom, more flexibility, and you should act on this.

**The Rise of Passive Income:** In recent years, the traditional notion of investing has undergone a significant transformation. Passive income has emerged as a key focus for investors seeking to diversify their revenue streams and build long-term wealth. This shift can be attributed to several factors, including technological advancements, changing societal norms, and the desire for financial independence.

Technological advancements have played a crucial role in enabling passive income opportunities. Online platforms and digital marketplaces have opened doors to various investment options such as peer-to-peer lending, real estate crowdfunding, and automated investment platforms. These innovations have democratized investing, making it accessible to a broader audience and facilitating the generation of passive income.

Furthermore, the changing dynamics of the workforce and the desire for flexibility have fuelled the rise of passive income. The traditional 9-to-5 job is no longer the sole path to financial stability. With the gig economy, remote work, and freelance opportunities on the rise, individuals are actively seeking alternative income sources that provide flexibility and freedom.

**Strategies for Creating Passive Income**: Creating passive income requires a thoughtful and strategic approach. Here are some popular strategies that are likely to shape the future of investing:

**Dividend Investing**: Dividend stocks have long been a staple for income-focused investors. Companies that distribute a portion of their earnings as dividends provide shareholders with a recurring income stream. As investors seek stable and reliable returns, dividend investing is expected to gain further prominence.

**Real Estate Investment**: Real estate has always been a favoured investment avenue for generating passive income. However, the emergence of real estate crowdfunding platforms has made it easier for individuals to invest in properties and receive regular rental income without the burden of property management.

**Peer-to-Peer Lending**: Peer-to-peer lending platforms connect borrowers directly with lenders, cutting out traditional financial intermediaries. By lending money to borrowers in need, investors can earn interest income without the involvement of banks. This form of investing offers attractive returns and diversification.

**Digital Products and Intellectual Property**: In the digital age, creating and selling digital products, such as e-books, online courses, or software, can provide a scalable and passive income stream.

**Embracing Technological Advancements**: The future of investing and passive income will be intertwined with technological advancements. Artificial intelligence, blockchain, and automation will revolutionize investment strategies and enhance the potential for generating passive income.

Robo-advisors, powered by artificial intelligence, have already gained traction in the investment industry. These digital platforms provide personalized investment advice and automatically manage portfolios, reducing costs and maximizing returns.

Blockchain technology, with its transparency and security features, has the potential to disrupt traditional investment processes. Smart contracts and decentralized finance (DeFi) platforms can automate investment transactions, eliminate intermediaries, and provide investors with greater control over their assets.

Automation will also play a crucial role in shaping the future of passive income. From automated dividend reinvestment plans to algorithmic trading systems, investors will be able to streamline and optimize their investment strategies, allowing their money to work for them more efficiently.

## Our World has Changed.

The world has changed. In 1875 Bismarck in Germany invented the "retirement age" and created the "pension system" based on the fact that the young working population could finance the retirement of those who arrived at the defined retirement age (70) and they could enjoy the few years that they had left, with financial security guaranteed by the working masses or the government.

Those were the days of the industrial revolution, people mostly worked their whole lives with one employer, life expectancy was low. only a few percent of the population were dependent on the working mass and those who had "made it" could expect a life expectancy from 65 of three to five years.

The reality today is certainly different, today over ninety-five percent of the population will reach Bismarck's retirement age of sixty-five, and they can expect to live on average twenty-five to thirty additional years.

The working mass is shrinking due to families worldwide creating fewer and less children, and the new working force, which is substantially smaller, cannot finance any more the retired public who could be soon more than them.

Governments all over the world understand that they can no longer afford to finance the future of their citizens so instead of raising the retirement age from sixty-five to let's say eighty or eight five, they have just transferred the responsibility to their citizens.

The move from defined benefits (A defined-benefit plan guarantees a specific benefit or payout upon retirement for the duration of the workers life) to defined Contribution (A defined-contribution plan is a retirement plan that's typically tax-deferred, in which employees contribute a defined amount or a percentage of their pay checks to an account that is intended to fund their retirements.

The employees' company will, at times, match a portion of employee contributions as an added benefit. These plans usually place restrictions that control when and how each employee can withdraw from these accounts without penalties) is de facto transferring the responsibility from Governments or employers to the public.

It took some time for the public to digest the new reality, most thought that the Government or their employers had not abandoned them but just changed the system in their best interests, but slowly they realized that when they arrive at the age when they need to finance their futures from what they have accumulated, there is just not enough, and it is too late to adapt.

The younger generation is beginning to understand that they need not only to accumulate assets but to create passive income that will replace them when they cannot work anymore and guarantee them the life they are used to living with dignity and security.

Passive income can help families "fill in the gaps" and create security for the day that the nine to five job is over.

The earlier you start thinking and acting on this the better, it is fine to have passive income even when you are still working.

So, whether you are investing in real estate, debt, dividend paying equities or creating a passive business strategy you should start taking your first steps today. As the saying goes "Even a trek of a thousand miles starts with the first step".

## Case Study: "Outcome Investment Orientation Methodology"

Outcome Investment Orientation Methodology is an investment approach that focuses on achieving specific outcomes or goals rather than merely seeking to maximize returns. This methodology considers the broader impact and results of investments, considering both financial and non-financial factors.

The key principle of the Outcome Investment Orientation Methodology is aligning investment decisions with desired outcomes. It involves a structured process that begins with clearly defining the desired outcomes or goals that we want to achieve. These outcomes can vary widely and may include objectives such as long-term financial security, transferring assets to our beneficiaries or even short-term goals such as acquiring a home.

Once the outcomes are defined, the methodology involves identifying investment opportunities that have the potential to contribute to those specific outcomes. This requires thorough research and analysis to evaluate the potential impact and effectiveness of different investments in achieving the desired outcomes.

The Outcome Investment Orientation Methodology also emphasizes ongoing monitoring and measurement of investment performance against the defined outcomes. This allows investors to assess whether their investments are making progress toward their desired goals. It involves tracking both financial metrics, such as returns and risk indicators, as well as non-financial metrics (if this is a priority for us) related to the desired outcomes, such as carbon emissions reduction or community development.

One of the key benefits of this methodology is that it provides a more holistic approach to investing. It recognizes that financial returns are not the only measure of investment success and places importance on broader societal or environmental impacts. By aligning investments with desired outcomes, investors can contribute to positive change in areas that matter to them while still aiming for financial growth.

The Outcome Investment Orientation Methodology is closely related to the concept of impact investing, which seeks to generate positive social or environmental impact alongside financial returns. However, the methodology is broader in scope as it encompasses a range of desired outcomes, not limited to impact considerations alone.

The Outcome Investment Orientation Methodology represents a shift in investment mindset towards a more outcome-focused approach. It acknowledges that investment decisions can have far-reaching consequences and aims to align investments with desired outcomes, enabling investors to make a positive impact while pursuing their financial objectives.

# Case Study Client X

The client is a dual US and British Citizen

She is 52 years old; she lost her husband to cancer in 2007. She has a son and a daughter.

Her son 22, is in the process of moving to Nottingham to study theatre. He is independent and mostly self sufficient.

Her daughter 16, is advancing to the 11th grade in school.

Her priorities are the welfare of her children and living a life of security.

## Her main goals and objectives are:

1. To secure a sustainable cash flow that will finance her lifestyle.

2. To optimize her estate and pass it on in an orderly and tax efficient manner.

## Financial Management:

It is recommended that she prepare a budget based on her current expenses. She has estimated that expenses of GBP 23,000 a month.

Her estate today is estimated at GBP 7.6 million. This could sustain her for life. She also has income from social security in the US as she worked in the US for more than 10 years.

She needs to create a withdrawal strategy based on tax efficiency and sustainability.

## Assets and Asset Management

Most of her assets are in cash as she has liquidized some assets in the US. She has a portfolio of GBP 1,159,000 (in an IRA account managed by Wells Fargo in the states).

She has a home in north London (worth 2GBP).

## Tax Planning

She does not pay tax on income in the US as she has an exemption as an expat for the first 11,000 USD.

She has a tax consultant in the US who does her tax returns.

When planning she needs to explore potential taxes and liabilities in the UK and build a strategy to mitigate taxes.

## Risk Management

She has a significant exposure to US Dollars. As she lives in the UK, she must take this into account.

Long term care: in the event of long-term care, she has income from her insurance policy and passive income of GBP 23,000 monthly.

## Retirement Planning

Her goal is to create passive income that can sustain for life.

## Estate Planning

She must look at the wills prepared in the States and in the UK.

There is a need to define all expected taxes to be paid on the estate and a strategy for optimizing the transfer of these assets.

## Assets

| | Passive Income in GBP per month | GBP |
|---|---|---|
| Home | | 2,000,000 |
| Sale of Property | On the market | 1,584,000 |
| Cash in the US | | 1,059,000 |
| IRA Account | 3600 | 591,500 |
| 25th Street | 7875 | 2,590,000 |
| Clarkson Street | | 210,000 |
| Total | 10,475* | 7,994,000 |

Net Income after tax: $9,427 a month

Net Worth Client X: $7,794,000

Assets to Invest: GBP 2,600,000

Income Required: GBP 23,000 less GBP 9427 = GBP 13,573

**Strategy** There is a need to create sustainable income from the $2.6 M.

To create an additional GBP 13,573 at a benchmark return of 6% net (in 75% probability) she needs to allocate to income creating investments.

There are various income-generating investment options available for individuals looking to create a passive income stream. Here are a few examples:

**Dividend Stocks:** Dividend stocks are shares of companies that distribute a portion of their earnings to shareholders as dividends. By investing in dividend-paying stocks, investors can earn regular income in the form of dividends. Dividend stocks are particularly popular among income-focused investors due to their potential for consistent cash flow.

**Real Estate Investment Trusts** (REITs): REITs are investment vehicles that own and manage income-generating real estate properties, such as residential complexes, office buildings, or shopping malls. By investing in REITs, individuals can gain exposure to the real estate market and earn regular income from rental payments or property sales.

**Bond Funds**: Bond funds pool money from multiple investors to invest in a diversified portfolio of bonds. Bonds are fixed-income securities issued by governments, municipalities, or corporations. By investing in bond funds, individuals can earn regular interest payments, making them a reliable source of income.

**Peer-to-Peer Lending:** Peer-to-peer lending platforms connect borrowers directly with lenders, allowing individuals to lend money to borrowers in exchange for interest payments. By participating in peer-to-peer lending, investors can earn interest income while diversifying their investment portfolio.

**Rental Properties:** Owning and renting out residential or commercial properties can be a lucrative investment strategy. Rental properties generate income through monthly rental payments from tenants, providing a consistent cash flow stream. However, it's important to consider the responsibilities and risks associated with property management.

**High-Yield Savings Accounts:** While not traditionally considered an investment, high-yield savings accounts offer individuals a way to earn passive income with minimal risk. These accounts typically offer higher interest rates than regular savings accounts, allowing individuals to earn a modest income on their savings.

**Dividend-focused Exchange-Traded Funds (ETFs):** Dividend-focused ETFs invest in a portfolio of dividend-paying stocks, providing investors with exposure to a diversified set of companies. By investing in dividend-focused ETFs, individuals can earn regular income from the dividends distributed by the underlying stocks.

It's important to note that these investment options carry varying degrees of risk, and individuals should carefully assess their financial goals, risk tolerance, and investment time horizon before making any investment decisions. Consulting with a financial advisor can also provide valuable guidance in selecting income-generating investments that align with one's specific needs and objectives.

## Why do we need to understand behavioral finance Behavioral Finance?

Understanding behavioural finance is essential for investors and financial professionals because it provides valuable insights into the psychological and emotional factors that influence financial decision-making. Behavioural finance combines principles from psychology, economics, and finance to study how individuals make financial choices and the cognitive biases that can impact those decisions. Here are several reasons why understanding behavioural finance is crucial:

**Overcoming Biases**: Behavioural finance helps individuals identify and overcome cognitive biases that can hinder rational decision-making. Common biases, such as overconfidence, loss aversion, and herd mentality, can lead to irrational investment decisions and suboptimal outcomes. By understanding these biases, investors can make more informed and rational choices, leading to better financial outcomes.

**Managing Emotions**: Emotions play a significant role in financial decision-making. Behavioural finance helps individuals recognize and manage emotions like fear, greed, and panic, which can drive impulsive or irrational investment behaviours. By understanding how emotions can influence decisions, investors can maintain a long-term perspective, avoid emotional trading, and make decisions based on sound financial principles.

**Improving Risk Management**: Behavioural finance sheds light on how individuals perceive and respond to risk. It highlights the tendency for individuals to be risk-averse when faced with gains and risk-seeking when faced with losses, known as the "prospect theory." Understanding these risk perceptions can help investors make more balanced risk assessments and develop appropriate risk management strategies.

**Explaining Market Anomalies**: Behavioral finance provides insights into market anomalies that cannot be fully explained by traditional finance theories, such as the efficient market hypothesis. Phenomena like market bubbles, herding behaviour, and irrational pricing can be better understood through behavioral finance, as it considers the impact of psychological and emotional factors on market dynamics.

**Enhancing Investor Education**: Behavioral finance has implications for investor education. By incorporating behavioral finance principles into financial literacy programs, individuals can become more aware of their biases and learn to make better financial decisions. This knowledge can empower investors to navigate market volatility, resist impulsive behaviours, and develop disciplined investment strategies.

**Personalizing Financial Advice**: Understanding behavioral finance allows financial professionals to provide more personalized advice to clients. By considering clients' behavioral biases, risk tolerances, and individual goals, financial advisors can tailor recommendations that align with clients' unique needs and preferences. This personalized approach can improve client satisfaction and increase the likelihood of achieving financial objectives.

**Long-Term Investing Perspective**: Behavioral finance emphasizes the importance of long-term investing and the benefits of disciplined, patient strategies. It encourages individuals to avoid short-term market fluctuations and focus on long-term wealth accumulation. By understanding the behavioral biases that can lead to short-term thinking, investors can adopt a more strategic and patient approach to investing.

## The Advantage of illiquidity in Behavioral Finance

Illiquidity has the additional benefit of promoting rational investment behaviour by insulating an investment portfolio from irrational investor behaviour. The longer lockup periods that characterize alternative assets can benefit investors by reducing behavioural risk.

As seen in the public markets, continuous pricing on investments can have the adverse effect of framing irrational results. As market volatility is tempered through allocations to alternative investments, so too is the likelihood that an investor will succumb to fear-based selling. All too often during market corrections, investors consistently stray from the course and sell at the wrong time, increasing the potential for losses and damaging returns. The illiquid nature of certain alternatives can temper these impulsive reactions.

## Is liquidity the king?

The importance of liquidity appears to be debatable.

An investor with a long enough time horizon can benefit greatly from incorporating alternative illiquid investments and ensuring that the range of allocations over a certain time is acceptable. However, investors should also consider their risk profiles, need to access capital over a given time, and spending requirements in evaluating the trade-off between liquidity and potentially enhanced returns.

Liquidity is often considered a critical factor in financial markets and investment strategies, earning the phrase "liquidity is king."

Liquidity refers to the ease with which an asset can be bought or sold in the market without causing significant price changes. Here are a few reasons why liquidity holds such importance:

**Flexibility and Efficiency**: High liquidity allows investors to quickly enter or exit positions, providing flexibility and agility in responding to market conditions or changing investment objectives. It facilitates efficient portfolio management and enables investors to capitalize on opportunities or mitigate risks promptly.

**Price Discovery**: Liquidity contributes to accurate price discovery in financial markets. When there are numerous buyers and sellers actively participating, prices tend to reflect the true value of an asset. Liquidity ensures that transactions occur at fair and competitive prices, enhancing market efficiency.

**Lower Transaction Costs**: Liquidity reduces transaction costs, including bid-ask spreads, brokerage fees, and other expenses associated with buying or selling assets. In liquid markets, the spread between the buying and selling prices is narrower, minimizing the impact of transaction costs on investment returns.

**Risk Management**: Liquidity plays a vital role in risk management. Investors value the ability to convert assets into cash quickly, especially during times of financial stress or economic downturns. High liquidity provides a cushion against unexpected liquidity needs, allowing investors to address emergencies or meet financial obligations without significant losses.

**Investor Confidence and Market Stability:** Liquidity inspires investor confidence and contributes to overall market stability. When investors know that they can easily buy or sell assets when desired, it fosters trust and encourages participation in the market. Robust liquidity enhances market depth, reduces price volatility, and mitigates the potential for market manipulation.

While liquidity holds significant importance, it is crucial to note that focusing solely on liquidity can have drawbacks. Investors should also consider other factors, such as asset quality, diversification, and long-term performance. Additionally, excessively chasing liquidity can lead to reduced returns or missed opportunities in less liquid but potentially profitable investments.

Liquidity is indeed important in financial markets. It provides flexibility, enhances price discovery, lowers transaction costs, facilitates risk management, and promotes investor confidence. However, investors should strike a balance between liquidity and other investment considerations to develop a well-rounded and effective investment strategy.

ESG and Cause related Investments Strategies for expats.

ESG (Environmental, Social, and Governance) and cause-related investment strategies have gained significant traction in recent years, as individuals seek to align their investments with their values and contribute to positive social and environmental impact. Expatriates, or expats, who are living and working abroad, can also adopt these strategies to support sustainable and socially responsible investments.

ESG investing involves considering environmental, social, and governance factors alongside financial performance when making investment decisions. Expats can embrace ESG investing by following these steps:

**Research ESG Practices:** Learn about ESG best practices in the host country. This includes understanding the local environmental regulations, labor standards, diversity and inclusion practices, and corporate governance frameworks. Consider companies or funds that prioritize these factors.

**Collaborate with Local Experts:** Seek advice from local investment advisors or experts who have a deep understanding of the ESG landscape in the host country. They can help identify investment opportunities aligned with ESG principles while considering local nuances and regulations.

**Engage with Companies:** As an expat, you can engage with companies to advocate for improved ESG practices. This can involve attending shareholder meetings, participating in proxy voting, or joining investor coalitions that push for positive change.

**Invest in ESG Funds:** Consider investing in ESG-focused mutual funds, exchange-traded funds (ETFs), or impact investment funds. These investment vehicles allocate capital to companies or projects that demonstrate strong ESG performance. Conduct thorough research to ensure the fund aligns with your values and meets your investment objectives.

**Cause-Related Investing for Expats:** Cause-related investing allows individuals to support specific causes or issues through their investment decisions. Expats can adopt cause-related investment strategies by:

**Identifying Causes:** Determine the causes or social issues that you are passionate about supporting. It could range from renewable energy and clean technologies to education, healthcare, or poverty alleviation.

**Seek Investment Opportunities:** Look for investment opportunities that directly support those causes. For instance, consider investing in companies developing renewable energy solutions, healthcare providers, or microfinance institutions that promote financial inclusion.

**Explore Philanthropic Investing:** Consider philanthropic investments that provide both social impact and potential financial returns. Social impact bonds, for example, allow investors to support projects with social objectives, such as reducing recidivism rates or improving educational outcomes, while potentially earning a financial return if the project achieves its goals.

**Collaborate with Impact Investment Organizations:** Partner with impact investment organizations that connect investors with projects aligned with specific causes. These organizations have networks of social enterprises, nonprofits, and projects seeking funding to create positive change.

**Evaluating Investment Performance and Impact:** Expats engaged in ESG and cause-related investing should evaluate both the financial performance and impact of their investments. Consider the following:

**Financial Performance:** Regularly review the financial performance of your investments. Compare returns against relevant benchmarks and assess whether your investments are meeting your financial goals. Diversification remains important, and it is essential to balance risk and return.

**Impact Measurement:** Assess the impact of your investments on the chosen causes. Look for metrics and reporting frameworks that measure social and environmental impact, such as the United Nations Sustainable Development Goals (SDGs). This evaluation helps ensure that your investments are making a positive difference.

**Reporting and Transparency:** Seek investments that provide transparent reporting on both financial performance and impact metrics. This allows you to track progress, hold companies accountable, and communicate the impact of your investments to others.

ESG and cause-related investment strategies offer expats the opportunity to align values with investments.

## What is the difference between Cause related Investing and ESG?

Cause-related investing and ESG (Environmental, Social, and Governance) investing are related but distinct approaches to incorporating non-financial factors into investment decision-making. Here's a breakdown of the two concepts:

**Cause-Related Investing:** Cause-related investing involves making investment decisions based on specific social or environmental causes or issues that we are passionate about supporting.

The primary focus is on generating a positive impact on a particular cause through investments. We could actively seek out investment opportunities that align with their chosen cause and support organizations or projects addressing that cause.

For example, if we are passionate about renewable energy, we may specifically invest in companies developing solar or wind energy technologies or funds that prioritize investments in the clean energy sector.

The objective is to channel financial resources towards initiatives that directly contribute to a chosen cause while potentially seeking a financial return.

**ESG Investing:** ESG investing takes a broader approach by considering environmental, social, and governance factors when evaluating investment opportunities. It seeks to incorporate sustainability and ethical considerations alongside financial analysis. ESG factors encompass a range of criteria, including a company's environmental impact, social responsibility practices, employee relations, corporate governance, and more.

ESG investing aims to identify companies or funds that exhibit strong ESG performance, demonstrating responsible and sustainable business practices. This approach acknowledges that companies with robust ESG practices may be better positioned for long-term success and may present lower risk profiles.

While ESG investing can indirectly support causes through investments in companies with positive social or environmental impacts, it is not explicitly focused on targeting specific causes. The emphasis is on considering a broad set of ESG factors and selecting investments that align with those principles.

Cause-related investing focuses on supporting specific causes or issues through investments, while ESG investing takes a broader approach, considering environmental, social, and governance factors when making investment decisions. Both approaches reflect a growing desire among families to align their investments with their values and make a positive impact beyond financial returns.

## Is the future of investing green?

The future of investing is undeniably leaning towards "green" or sustainable investing. Green investing refers to investment strategies that prioritize environmental sustainability, climate change mitigation, and the transition to a low-carbon economy. Several factors contribute to the growing prominence of green investing:

**Climate Change and Environmental Concerns:** The increasing awareness of climate change and its potential impacts on the planet has led to a heightened focus on environmental sustainability.

Governments, corporations, and individuals are recognizing the urgency to address climate-related issues such as carbon emissions, resource depletion, and biodiversity loss. Green investing aligns with these concerns by directing capital towards companies and projects that are actively working towards a more sustainable future.

**Policy and Regulation:** Governments worldwide are implementing policies and regulations to accelerate the transition to a low-carbon economy. This includes setting emission reduction targets, promoting renewable energy, and enacting environmental regulations. Such initiatives create favourable conditions for green investing, as companies adhering to sustainability practices tend to benefit from supportive policies and face lower regulatory risks.

**Market Demand and Investor Preferences:** Investors are increasingly demanding investment options that align with their values and address environmental challenges. This includes individuals, institutions, and even large asset managers.

The younger generation is more focused on sustainable investing, with studies indicating that millennials and Gen Z are more likely to invest in companies with strong environmental and social performance. As investor preferences shift, financial institutions are responding by offering a range of green investment products to cater to this demand.

**Financial Performance:** Contrary to earlier perceptions that sustainable investing sacrifices financial returns, growing evidence suggests that integrating environmental, social, and governance factors can lead to competitive financial performance. Numerous studies have shown that companies with strong sustainability practices tend to be more resilient, better managed, and positioned for long-term success. This recognition has attracted more investors who are seeking to achieve both financial returns and positive impact through their investments.

**Innovation and Technological Advances:** The shift towards a green economy has spurred significant innovation and technological advancements. The development of renewable energy technologies, energy-efficient solutions, and sustainable infrastructure has created new investment opportunities. As the costs of renewable energy continue to decline, these sectors become increasingly attractive to investors looking for growth potential and a transition away from fossil fuels.

**Disclosure and Reporting Standards:** There is a growing push for standardized environmental and social disclosure requirements. Organizations such as the Task Force on Climate-related Financial Disclosures (TCFD) and Global Reporting Initiative (GRI) are promoting transparency and accountability in reporting environmental risks and sustainability performance. This increased transparency provides investors with the necessary information to assess the environmental impact and sustainability practices of potential investments.

It is important to note that green investing is not limited to renewable energy or clean technology sectors. It encompasses a broader spectrum of industries, including sustainable agriculture, water management, waste management, and green building solutions, among others.

The future of investing is indeed green. Climate change concerns, supportive policies, investor demand, positive financial performance, innovation, and reporting standards have all converged to drive the growth of green investing. As sustainable practices become integral to corporate strategies and global efforts to address environmental challenges intensify, green investing will continue to gain momentum, providing investors with opportunities to align their financial goals with their values for a more sustainable future.

## The Clean Energy Initiative

In a presentation by leading investment analysts, it was pointed out that market attention has now focused almost exclusively on broad economic concerns such as inflation, interest rates, recession risk, however he says investors should also consider the imminent passage of the new US "Inflation Reduction Act" (IRA) of which one major component creates the largest clean energy policy and financial initiative in national history.

Clean energy projects (solar farms, offshore wind turbines, etc.) are massive and expensive projects which require major upfront capital investment that is paid back slowly over time as their energy flows to utilities.

Raising the initial funding is a limiting factor. For example, in Canada, start-up projects are awarded long term (20 – 30 year) electricity purchase agreements, whose guaranteed revenues can be used to finance the capital project. In the US, the start-up projects are awarded various attractive tax credits which can benefit the project developers directly or be resold to financial buyers.

The IRA project is committing nearly $369 Billion in a variety of tax credits and direct investments intended to ensure energy security, reduce carbon emissions, and deploy low carbon technologies. Not only is the amount of tax credits increased, but the sector will also benefit from simplification of the tax credit calculations as well as confirmation of availability of these benefits for a decade.

This longer period of confirmed benefits is superior to the current practice of providing short term (and politically vulnerable) tax extensions which did not build investor confidence for these long-life of the capital assets.

Increasing confidence that the clean energy initiatives will be approved is bringing vast new opportunities for the development in the sector regardless of prevailing economic conditions, and interest rates. The clean energy sector is now, after several months of disinterest, catching the attention of investors. Their PE valuations are now expanding, and their market prices are increasingly reflecting their intrinsic value.

Morgan Stanley in their Wealth Management Insight points out, that the signs of growing interest in clean energy are easy to spot, solar panels line rooftops, wind turbines dot open plains, and electric cars cruise our highways.

Less apparent, but equally important, are the economics at the centre of this story: The costs to produce wind and solar energy have dropped markedly in the past decade, and demand has increased as electric utilities begin to phase out fossil fuels.

The costs to produce wind and solar energy have dropped markedly in the past decade, and demand has increased.

## How can investors position portfolios for a global shift toward renewables?

Investors can position their portfolios for a global shift toward renewables by considering the following strategies:

**Research and Identify Renewable Energy Opportunities:** Conduct thorough research on renewable energy companies, technologies, and projects. Look for companies engaged in renewable energy generation, equipment manufacturing, energy storage, and infrastructure development. Identify regions and countries that are actively transitioning to renewable energy sources.

**Invest in Renewable Energy Stocks and Funds:** Consider investing in individual stocks of renewable energy companies or exchange-traded funds (ETFs) that focus on the renewable energy sector. These investments provide exposure to the growth potential of renewable energy and can diversify a portfolio.

**Assess Renewable Energy Infrastructure:** Evaluate opportunities in renewable energy infrastructure, such as solar and wind farms, hydroelectric plants, and transmission networks. Infrastructure investments can provide stable income streams and long-term growth potential.

**Monitor Policy and Regulatory Developments:** Stay informed about government policies, incentives, and regulations related to renewable energy. Changes in regulations, subsidies, or tax credits can significantly impact the growth and profitability of renewable energy investments. Consider investing in regions where governments are actively supporting the transition to renewables.

Evaluate Technology and Innovation: Assess companies involved in renewable energy research and development, as well as those driving technological innovations in the sector. Advancements in energy storage, smart grid solutions, and clean technology can present investment opportunities.

**Consider ESG Investing:** Environmental, Social, and Governance (ESG) factors are increasingly important to investors. Incorporate ESG criteria into the investment process by considering companies with strong sustainability practices and commitment to reducing their carbon footprint.

**Diversify Across Renewable Energy Sub-Sectors:** Diversify investments across different sub-sectors within renewable energy, such as solar, wind, hydro, geothermal, and biomass. This diversification can mitigate risk and capture opportunities in various segments of the renewable energy market.

**Engage in Impact Investing:** Consider impact investing, which focuses on generating positive environmental and social impact alongside financial returns. Look for opportunities to invest in renewable energy projects that directly contribute to a cleaner and more sustainable future.

## The Shift Toward Renewables Is Accelerating and may be the next investment opportunity

Innovation in the energy sector is nothing new—energy consumption has changed throughout history. Most recently in the U.S., that's been demonstrated in the decline of coal consumption and muted oil demand, while renewable sources such as wind, solar, geothermal and hydropower have grown their shares of the pie.

Globally, Morgan Stanley strategists expect the shift toward renewables to accelerate in the years ahead, with renewable energy likely to represent over 28% of global consumption by 2050, up from 15% in 2018, based on U.S. Energy Information Administration (EIA) forecasts.

Meera Pundit from J P Morgan adds: "Investing in renewable energy is not just about solar and wind. Of equal importance is investing in storage, transport, and electrification, which is underway". These are the investments we will focus on in the next few years.

Progress on mitigating climate change hinges on cleaner energy as 73% of global greenhouse gas emissions come from energy usage in industry, buildings, and transport. This means the continued expansion of renewable energy and investment in the ecosystem around clean energy which includes storage, transportation, and grid modernization.

Currently about 5% of energy globally comes from solar and wind power. However, for the world to meet its ambitious net zero carbon emissions targets, that share needs to grow to 60% by 2050. Getting there over the next three decades could require $100 trillion in clean energy investment.

Although solar and wind power once felt like a pipe dream, subsidies, innovation, and investment have helped reduce break even costs by 90% and 72% respectively since 2009. These advances have made renewable energy not just about sustainability, but also increasingly about affordability, and most recently about reducing geopolitical vulnerability as well.

Expats should follow this dramatic development as it may prove to be the future of our families and an interesting avenue for investing.

## Warning Signs that your investment is in trouble

After investing we should always be on the lookout for what we decide to do, failing. Learn to determine the warning signs that a company or an investment is in trouble or headed for serious financial difficulties.

## Dwindling Cash or Losses

Companies that lose money quarter after quarter burn through their cash fast. It would be advised to review the company's balance sheet and its cash flow statement to determine how the cash is being spent. Also, compare the current cash flows and cash holdings with the same period in the prior year to determine if there's a trend.

If the company is burning through cash because of increases in investing activities, it might mean the company is investing in its future. However, if on the cash flow statement, the company is consuming cash in its operating activities as shown by a negative cash from operations, it should be much more of a concern. Also, watch for large increases in cash because the company has sold long-term assets which are reflected as cash inflows from investing activities. If they had done this, they might have sold a revenue generating asset for short-term cash injections, but future cash flows could be weaker.

Companies should also have retained earnings (RE), which is the money left over after earning a profit for a period. Effectively, RE is the savings account for corporations that accumulate profits over time to be used to reinvest back into the company, issue dividends, or buy back stock. If RE is not increasing or nonexistent, in the absence of dividends and buybacks, the company is either not profitable or barely getting by.

## Interest Payments

A company's income statement will show what it pays to service its debt. Can the company keep losing money and still have enough left to make the payments? Do the current revenue increases generate enough income to service the company's debt?

There are metrics and ratios that measure a company's ability to cover its debt obligations.

The interest coverage ratio for instance, indicates how well a company's earnings can cover its interest expenses. Analysts typically look for a ratio greater than 1.5x.

The current ratio (or cash ratio) is another calculation that aids in determining a company's ability to pay short-term debt obligations. It is calculated by dividing current assets by current liabilities. A ratio higher than one indicates that a company will have a high chance of being able to pay off its debt, whereas a ratio of less than one indicates that a company will not be able to pay off what it owes. The acid-test ratio can also be used.

The acid test ratio, also known as the quick ratio or liquid ratio, is a financial metric used to assess a company's short-term liquidity and ability to meet its immediate obligations. It is a more stringent measure of liquidity than the current ratio, as it excludes inventory from the calculation.

The acid test ratio is calculated by dividing a company's quick assets by its current liabilities. Quick assets are those that can be readily converted into cash within a short period, typically within

90 days. They include cash, cash equivalents, short-term investments, and accounts receivable.

## Switching Auditors

All public companies must have their books audited by an outside accounting firm. And while it is not uncommon for companies to switch firms from time to time, abrupt dismissal of an auditor or accounting firm for no apparent reason should raise red flags. It is usually a sign that there is a disagreement over how to book revenue or a conflict with members of the management team. Neither is a good sign.

Also, review the auditor's report which is included in the company's annual report (the 10-K in the US). Auditors are required to provide a report which concludes whether the information was presented fairly, and accurately describes the company's financial status, at least to the best of their knowledge. However, if an auditor questions whether the company has the ability to continue "as a going concern" or notes some other discrepancy in accounting practices, specifically how it books revenue, that should also serve as a serious warning sign.

## Dividend Cut

Companies that reduce, or eliminate, their payments to shareholders are not necessarily on the verge of bankruptcy. However, when companies experience tough times, dividends are usually one of the first items to go. Management is not likely to cut a dividend unless it's necessary since any cut is likely to send the company's stock price down significantly. As a result, view any dividend cuts or the elimination of a dividend as a sign that difficult times lie ahead.

It's important to consider other supporting evidence in determining whether a dividend cut is signaling dark times for a company. Namely, watch for declining or variable profitability, the dividend yield when compared to other companies in the same industry, and negative free cash flow.

## Management Defections

Typically, when things are heading seriously downhill for a company, senior members of the management team leave to take a job at a different company. In the meantime, current employees with less seniority will take the senior executives' places. If management defections are steady, it's seldom good news.

## Unauthorized Trading of Securities

Smart money investors, meaning institutional and executive holders of the stock, typically dump their shares ahead of a bankruptcy filing or really difficult times. Be on the lookout for insider selling.

However, during the normal course of business, some funds may sell stock from time to time. Essentially, you should pay attention to unusually large or frequent transactions, particularly those that occur in or around the time negative news is released.

## Selling Flagship Products

If you were going through some tough times, you would probably tap your savings. And when you went through that, you would probably consider selling some of your assets to raise money. But you wouldn't sell your personal mementos unless you really had to. Well, the same logic applies to a company. So, if you see the company selling off a major division or product line to raise cash, watch out!

## Cuts in Perks

Companies will seek to make deep cuts in their health benefits, pension plans or other perks during difficult times. Deep and sudden cuts, particularly when they take place in conjunction with any of the other above-mentioned issues, are a sign that trouble may lie ahead.

## Warning signs when Investing in Real Assets or Real Asset Funds

### Promise of high returns

The most common of all investment warning signs is the promise of returns that are too good to be true. In fact, promising returns that are any higher than bond yields or current interest rates is a red flag. High pressure sales tactics or promises of returns that will make you rich are a sure sign of an investment scam.

All investments carry some level of risk – which means you may lose some money. That means returns cannot be guaranteed or promised. Only a government can guarantee returns and there are even limits to that. Legitimate asset management companies explain their strategies and may have a benchmark that they aim to beat.

The fund's prospectus explains the strategy and shows the fund's returns. This is the realistic way to present an investment product.

### Moving the goal posts

Another sign of bad investments is that goals or benchmarks get moved when they are missed. This can happen when an investment recommendation fails to perform. Rather than acknowledging a bad call, the fund manager moves the goal posts by setting a new benchmark. Companies also do this when they repeatedly change strategy.

### Delayed redemptions

If withdrawals from any financial product provider take longer than is reasonable, or promised, there may be a problem. This is very common with forex brokers or asset managers. It's also a potential sign of a Ponzi scheme that uses new customer funds to pay redemptions. Redemptions from a fund may be suspended during periods of unprecedented market volatility. But they should not be suspended under normal market conditions.

It is important to stress that funds investing in real assets and having a run on their liquidity must delay redemptions to protect the shareholders and sell assets responsibly.

## No third party is involved in the administration of assets.

Legitimate asset management companies typically involve a third-party administrator or custodian in controlling assets. This means the manager does not have complete control of the client's assets to prevent investment fraud. Third party compliance and auditors provide another safeguard against fraud.

This doesn't mean the fund manager can't make bad investments, but the alarm may be raised if risk limits are breached. If a company has a single bank account and no external service providers, the likelihood of customer funds disappearing is much higher.

## Lack of liquidity

Typically, there are two ways for an investor to exit an investment. In the case of hedge funds, mutual funds and segregated accounts, a redemption request is made. The fund manager then sells securities and returns the cash to the investor. This situation is straightforward and there should be no problems. In the case of listed instruments, including ETFs and company stock, the investment is sold in the open market. Provided there is an active market for security this will not be a problem either.

Challenges arise when there is no active market for the investment. This can occur with very small, listed investments. But it's more likely to occur with OTC (over the counter) shares, derivatives, and structured products. If there is no buyer, you will not be able to sell the investment. A sure sign of bad investments are OTC products where the seller is the only market maker or promises to buy the investment back when you want to sell it. Typically, you will receive a terrible price or pay a hefty commission when you exit.

Reaching your investment objectives can take patience and hard work. A few bad investments that could have been avoided can make the process that much more difficult. By looking out for the investment warning signs and red flags listed in this article you can make things much easier and avoid a lot of stress.

## Common Mistakes when Investing

Making mistakes when Investing is just part of being human — this is also known as behavioral economics — We aren't always rational, and the decisions we make can therefore flawed.

## Why do we buy too late — and then sell too soon?

Why do companies with stock symbols that come earlier in the alphabet have a small but measurable advantage over those that come later?

Why do we refuse to withdraw money from savings accounts, even when we are drowning in debt?

Mistakes are common when investing, but some can be easily avoided if you can recognize them, but the worst mistake is failing to set up a long-term plan, allowing emotion and fear to influence decisions, and not diversifying a portfolio.

Other mistakes include falling in love with a stock for the wrong reasons and trying to time the market or not understanding the investment we are making.

## Additional Mistakes to avoid:

1. **Falling in Love with a Strategy or an Equity.** Too often, when we see a company or a strategy we've invested in do well, it's easy to fall in love with it and forget that we bought this as an investment. Always remember, you bought this strategy to make money. If any of the fundamentals that prompted you to buy into the strategy change, consider

selling it and changing to a new strategy that is aligned with market reality.

2. **Lack of Patience:** I suggest a slow and steady approach with the expectation that this will yield greater returns in the long run. Expecting a portfolio to do something other than what it is designed to do is a recipe for disaster. This means you need to keep your expectations realistic about the timeline for portfolio growth and returns.

3. **Buying and selling as a strategy:** Jumping in and out of positions, is another return killer, transaction costs can eat you alive—not to mention the short-term tax rates and missing out on the long-term gains of sensible investments.

4. **Attempting to Time the Market:** Attempting this kills returns. Timing the market is extremely difficult. Research shows that most of our portfolio growth is made by choosing strategies aligned with our life goals and not trying to time markets.

5. **Waiting to Get Even:** Getting even is just another way to ensure you lose any profit you might have accumulated. It means that you are waiting to sell an equity or strategy loser until it gets back to its original cost basis. This is a "cognitive error." By failing to realize a loss, investors are losing in two ways. First, they avoid selling a bad investment, which may continue to lose until it's worthless. Second, there's the opportunity cost of the better use of those investment finances.

6. **Failing to diversify:** Nobel Prize winner Prof Harry Markovitz said "Diversifying sufficiently among uncor-related risks can reduce portfolio risk toward zero." As a rule of thumb, do not allocate more than 5% to 10% to any one investment.

7. **Letting Your Emotions Rule:** Perhaps the number one killer of investment return is emotion. The concept that fears and greed rule the market is true. Investors should not let fear or greed control their decisions. Instead, they should focus on the bigger picture. An investor ruled by emotion may see a negative return and then panic and sell, when in fact they probably would have been better off holding the investment for the long term. In fact, patient investors may benefit from the irrational decisions of other investors.

## How to Avoid Mistakes

Below are strategies advised to avoid these mistakes:

1. **Develop a Financial Plan:** Determine what your life goals are, and how much to invest to get there. Remember why you are investing your own money, and you will be inspired to achieve life goals as opposed to making a profit and you may find it easier to determine the right allocation for your portfolio. Do not expect your portfolio to make you rich overnight. A consistent, long-term investment strategy over time is what will get you where you want to be and live the life you dream off.

2. **Monitor the Plan:** As your income grows, you may want to align your goals with the improved lifestyle you have achieved. Monitor your investments. At the end of every year, review your investments and their performance. Determine whether your strategy should stay the same or change based on where you are in life.

3. **Allocate Money to pamper yourself:** We all get tempted by the need to pamper ourselves. It's the nature of the human condition. So, instead of fighting it, go with it. Set aside "pampering money." You should limit this amount to no more than 5% of your liquid assets, and it should be money that you can afford to spend.

4. **Do not use retirement money:** The day will come that you can no longer create income and you will need your retirement accumulation to provide you with the alternative to working income. This is essential to understand. Contribute to retirement religiously, invest it in long term safe strategies and never touch it no matter what the seemed opportunity.

Mistakes are just part of the investing process. Knowing what they are, when you're committing them, and how to avoid them will help you succeed in life. To avoid committing the mistakes above, develop a plan, and stick with it. If you must do something risky, set aside money that you are fully prepared to lose and will not have an impact on your lifestyle.

# Chapter Sixteen

## Taxation Across Borders: Understanding the Expatriate Tax Landscape

The principles of tax planning form an integral part of any wealth-building strategy. The overall objective is to structure clients' affairs to legally minimize the amount of tax they must pay. They can accomplish this by adhering to what we call the 4D's of taxation: deduct, defer, diminish, and divide.

- Deduct – maximize all tax deductions and credits.

- Defer – Defer paying tax if possible. A tax dollar deferred is often a dollar saved.

- Diminish – Position investments in investment vehicles, which attract the least amount of tax, having full regard for your risk tolerance and asset allocation strategy.

- Divide – Split income among family members to the maximum degree possible while considering other personal objectives.

### What Are Taxes?

Taxes are mandatory contributions levied on individuals or corporations by a government entity—whether local, regional, or national. Tax revenues finance government activities, including public works and services such as roads and schools, or programs such as Social Security and Healthcare.

Taxes help fund public works and services—and to build and maintain the infrastructure used in a country—a government usually taxes its individual and corporate residents.

Globally, income taxes are applied to forms of money received.

This could be income earned from salary, capital gains from investment appreciation, dividends or interest received as additional income, purchase taxes for example on the acquisition of a car or on energy costs and so on.

Usually, a tax requires a percentage of the taxpayer's earnings or money to be taken and remitted to the government. Payment of taxes at rates levied by the government is compulsory, and evasion—the deliberate failure to pay one's full tax liabilities—is punishable by law.

On the other hand, tax planning —action taken to lessen tax liability and maximize after-tax income—is perfectly legal.

## Tax Dilemmas for expats

People moving across borders (expats) may have to pay taxes and make tax declarations in two or more countries. This is often the case for:

- People living in one country and working in another (cross-border commuters or frontier workers)

- People who have moved abroad to live and work.

- Retired people abroad.

Each country has the right to impose its own tax rules and regulations, and some have come to agreements as to how to impose taxes on their citizens or workers in different scenarios.

## Tax Treaties

Understanding Tax treaties.

When dealing with multi jurisdiction issues, understand the tax treaties between countries.

## What Is a Tax Treaty?

A tax treaty is a bilateral (two-party) agreement made by two countries to resolve issues involving double taxation of passive and active income of each of their respective citizens. Income tax treaties generally determine the amount of tax that a country can apply to a taxpayer's income, capital, estate, or wealth.

An income tax treaty is also called a Double Tax Agreement (DTA)

Some countries are seen as being tax shelters. Generally, a tax shelter is a country or a place with low or no corporate taxes that allow foreign investors to set up businesses there.

Tax shelters typically do not establish tax treaties.

## How does a Tax Treaty Work?

When a person moves to a new country and has income or assets in his original place of abode or an individual or business invests in a foreign country, the issue of which country should tax the investor's earnings will arise. Both countries–the source country and the residence country–may enter into a tax treaty to agree on which country should tax investment income to prevent double taxation.

The source country is the country that hosts the investment or the asset. The residence country is the investor's country of residence.

To avoidthis, tax treaties may follow one of two models:

The Organization for Economic Co-operation and Development (OECD) Model or the United Nations(UN) Model Convention.

## OECD Tax Treaty Model

The OECD is a group of 37 countries who have come together to promote world trade and economic progress.

The OECD Tax Convention on Income and on Capital is more favorable to capital-exporting countries than capital-importing countries. It requires the source country to give up some or all its tax on certain categories of income earned by residents of the other treaty country.

The two involved countries will benefit from such an agreement if the flow of trade and investment between the two countries is reasonably equal, and the residence country taxes any income exempted by the source country.

Examples of countries who are members in this Tax Convention are:

United States: The United States has signed bilateral tax treaties based on the OECD Model Tax Convention with numerous countries. These treaties provide guidelines for the allocation of taxing rights, facilitate the exchange of information between tax authorities, and promote investment and trade by reducing double taxation.

Germany: Germany has entered tax treaties with various countries based on the OECD Model Tax Convention. These treaties help prevent double taxation, provide mechanisms for dispute resolution, and promote economic cooperation by establishing favorable tax treatment for cross-border transactions.

Japan: Japan has signed tax treaties with several countries, including those based on the OECD Model Tax Convention. These treaties promote international investment, facilitate the exchange of information for tax purposes, and provide mechanisms to resolve tax disputes between countries.

United Kingdom: The United Kingdom has an extensive network of tax treaties based on the OECD Model Tax Convention. These treaties ensure that businesses and individuals are not subject to double taxation, provide mechanisms for resolving disputes, and help foster economic cooperation by offering tax incentives for cross-border transactions.

Canada: Canada has signed tax treaties with numerous countries based on the OECD Model Tax Convention. These treaties help avoid double taxation, provide rules for determining the allocation of taxing rights, and promote economic integration and investment by establishing favourable tax treatment.

Australia: Australia has a network of tax treaties based on the OECD Model Tax Convention. These treaties help prevent double taxation, facilitate the exchange of information between tax authorities, and promote cross-border trade and investment by offering tax relief and incentives.

France: France has entered tax treaties with various countries, including those based on the OECD Model Tax Convention. These treaties aim to prevent double taxation, promote economic cooperation, and provide mechanisms for resolving tax disputes between countries.

It's important to note that while these countries benefit from the OECD Tax Convention, the specific benefits and provisions may vary depending on the individual tax treaty signed between each country and its treaty partners.

## UN Tax Treaty Model

The second tax treaty model is formally referred to as the United Nations Model Double Taxation Convention between Developed and Developing Countries.

A treaty that follows the UN's model gives favorable taxing rights to foreign countries of investment. Typically, this taxing system benefits developing countries who receive inward investment. It gives the source country increased taxing rights over the business income of non-residents compared to the OECD Model.

One of the most important aspects of a tax treaty is the treaty's policy on withholding taxes because it determines how much tax is to be paid on any income earned (interest and dividends) from securities owned by a non-resident.

For example, if a tax treaty between country A and country B determines that their withholding tax on dividends is 10%, then country A will tax such payments going to country B at a rate of 10%, and vice versa.

For example, The U.S. has more than 200 tax treaties with other tax jurisdictions, that help to reduce—or eliminate—the tax paid by residents of foreign countries. These reduced rates and exemptions vary among countries and specific items of income.

Under these same treaties, residents or citizens of the U.S. are taxed at a reduced rate, or are exempt from foreign taxes, on certain items of income they receive from sources within foreign countries. Tax treaties are said to be reciprocal because they apply in both treaty countries.

Income tax treaties typically include a clause, referred to as a "saving clause," that is intended to prevent residents of a jurisdiction from taking advantage of certain parts of the tax treaty to avoid taxation of a domestic source of income.

For individuals that are residents of countries that do not have tax treaties between the source and resident jurisdiction, any source of income that is earned within the source is taxed in the same way and at the regular rates in each jurisdiction.

Examples of countries that do not have a tax treaty with the US are for example:

Cuba: The United States does not have a tax treaty with Cuba. There are no formal tax agreements between the two countries to address issues of double taxation or provide guidelines for cross-border tax matters.

Libya: The United States does not have a tax treaty with Libya. Due to political instability and limited relations between the two countries, there is no formal tax agreement governing tax matters and preventing double taxation.

Examples of countries that do not have a tax treaty with the UK.

Eritrea: The United Kingdom does not have a tax treaty with Eritrea. There is no formal tax agreement between the two countries to regulate tax matters or address issues of double taxation.

South Sudan: The United Kingdom does not have a tax treaty with South Sudan. Due to limited diplomatic relations and other factors, there is no formal tax treaty in place between the two countries.

Bhutan: The United Kingdom does not have a tax treaty with Bhutan. As of my knowledge cutoff, there is no bilateral tax agreement to address taxation or prevent double taxation between the two countries.

## What is a Tax Ruling?

If there is uncertainty regarding the tax treaty or the question of withholding taxes the Tax Commissioner of one of the jurisdictions can issue a ruling. Taxpayers who rely on tax rulings receive specific rights. They receive protection, so even when the Commissioner alters a ruling, it can't increase the taxpayer's obligation.

However, tax rulings are difficult to attain. They can take months to complete because the tax commissioners try to avoid legal bindings. There are some cases where the commissioner may not issue a ruling at all.

## What is a Tax Commissioner?

A tax commissioner is a government official or executive who oversees and manages the administration of tax laws and regulations within a particular jurisdiction. The specific responsibilities and authority of a tax commissioner can vary depending on the country and the level of government (federal, state, or local).

Generally, the role of a tax commissioner involves the following:

Tax Administration: The tax commissioner is responsible for the overall administration and enforcement of tax laws. This includes ensuring compliance with tax regulations, collecting taxes, and managing tax-related processes such as filing tax returns, assessing tax liabilities, and issuing tax refunds.

Policy Development: Tax commissioners may play a role in developing and recommending tax policies and legislative changes to the government or relevant legislative bodies. They provide expertise and advice on tax matters, assess the impact of proposed tax reforms, and help shape tax policy decisions.

Taxpayer Services: Tax commissioners often oversee taxpayer services, providing assistance and support to taxpayers regarding tax-related queries, concerns, and disputes. They may establish taxpayer education programs, facilitate the resolution of tax disputes, and provide guidance on tax obligations and compliance.

Budgeting and Financial Management: Tax commissioners are typically responsible for managing the budget and financial resources of the tax administration agency. They allocate funds for various tax-related activities, ensure efficient use of resources, and monitor the financial performance of the agency.

Collaboration and Coordination: Tax commissioners often collaborate with other government agencies, tax authorities, and international organizations to exchange information, improve tax administration practices, and combat tax evasion and avoidance. They may participate in international tax forums and contribute to discussions on global tax standards and cooperation.

### The alternative is a Tax opinion.

An opinion is not a legally binding statement. An opinion is just a way for your accounting firm or tax expert to guide you and to avoid litigation if you are audited, and the commissioner does not agree with the opinion.

Unlike rulings, opinions only take a few weeks to receive.

### Considerations when choosing Tax Jurisdictions to reside in for expats.

How can you legally benefit from your tax residence? One way is to become a fiscal resident abroad where you can enjoy some tax allowances and incentives.

However, it is not easy to make a choice and make sure that the choice is the right one. To get what you expect to achieve, you need to know how to choose the right jurisdiction for tax purposes and estimate its benefits, requirements, procedures, and possible challenges.

While many countries grant tax resident status to qualifying applicants, only a handful of jurisdictions offer genuinely benign tax regimes (zero or low rates of certain taxes). Many governments have designed special programs that make it easier for foreigners to obtain the status of fiscal residents plus the tax privileges that come with it.

The mere fact of someone residing in a jurisdiction (permanently or temporarily) or holding their citizenship does not automatically mean that a person will receive the status of a tax resident there.

In addition, there is always the risk that a person could qualify as a tax resident under the tax residence rules of more than one country.

The residence status can be chosen by individuals for tax purposes and a variety of other legitimate reasons, including the intentions to launch a business, work overseas, have better access to international education, or the desire to move to a country with political stability.

Tax residence is assigned to a person meeting certain criteria set by the host jurisdiction. The criteria and rules for granting residence for tax purposes are different across jurisdictions. Besides, the criteria for residence in double taxation treaties are often different from those of domestic law. However, there are also some commonalities.

Conventional schemes are based on standard requirements for every eligible applicant.

- To have a documented real, permanent physical residence address in some rented or owned property (and not just a PO box or in-care-of address) in the host jurisdiction

- To have resided in the host country for more than 183 days during the fiscal year (days of entry/exit are considered days of stay in the host jurisdiction; periods of stay for the sole purpose of education/medical treatment are often not included in the period of stay for purposes of determining fiscal residency status)

- To have vital interests in the host jurisdiction (ownership of the local property and/or business, development of professional activities, membership in clubs/charities, etc.)

- To pay fiscal duties to the treasury of the relevant country.

- Country-specific schemes involve reference to a variety of other factors, such as the requirements.

- To submit some evidence of the applicant's willingness to contribute certain amounts to the economy of the host state (this can be an investment or donation to some national project)

- To pay a one-time flat tax.

## Comparison of Countries Tax Rates

Here are some general tax comparisons for some global countries as an example. Tax rates and regulations can change over time, so it's essential to consult official sources or tax professionals for the most up-to-date information.

United States: Personal Income Tax: The U.S. has a progressive federal income tax system, with tax rates ranging from 10% to 37% for individuals.

Corporate Tax: The federal corporate tax rate is 21%.

Sales Tax: Sales tax rates vary by state, ranging from 0% to over 10%. Some states also impose local sales taxes.

**Canada**: Canada has a progressive federal income tax system, with tax rates ranging from 15% to 33% for individuals.

Corporate Tax: The federal corporate tax rate is generally 15%, but it can vary depending on factors such as the size and type of business.

Goods and Services Tax (GST): The federal GST rate is 5%. Some provinces have harmonized their sales taxes with the GST to create a Harmonized Sales Tax (HST) with higher rates.

**United Kingdom**: Personal Income Tax: The UK has a progressive income tax system, with tax rates ranging from 20% to 45% for individuals.

Corporate Tax: The current corporate tax rate is 19% but is expected to increase to 25% in the future.

Value Added Tax (VAT): The standard VAT rate in the UK is 20%.

**Germany**: Personal Income Tax: Germany has a progressive income tax system, with tax rates ranging from 14% to 45% for individuals.

Corporate Tax: The corporate tax rate in Germany is approximately 30%, including a 15% corporate income tax and a 5.5% solidarity surcharge.

Value Added Tax (VAT): The standard VAT rate in Germany is 19%.

**Spain Personal Income Tax**: Spain has a progressive income tax system, with tax rates ranging from 19% to 47% for individuals.

Corporate Tax: The general corporate tax rate in Spain is 25%.

Value Added Tax (VAT): The standard VAT rate in Spain is 21%.

**Portugal**: Personal Income Tax: Portugal has a progressive income tax system, with tax rates ranging from 14.5% to 48% for individuals.

Corporate Tax: The corporate tax rate in Portugal is 21%.

Value Added Tax (VAT): The standard VAT rate in Portugal is 23%.

**Gibraltar**: Personal Income Tax: Gibraltar operates a territorial tax system with no personal income tax on worldwide income for residents.

Corporate Tax: The corporate tax rate in Gibraltar is generally 10%.

Value Added Tax (VAT): Gibraltar does not impose VAT.

**Australia**: Personal Income Tax: Australia has a progressive income tax system, with tax rates ranging from 0% to 45% for individuals.

Corporate Tax: The corporate tax rate for companies with turnover under AUD 50 million is 25%. For larger companies, it is 30%.

Goods and Services Tax (GST): The standard GST rate in Australia is 10%.

**British Virgin Islands (BVI)**: Personal Income Tax: BVI does not levy personal income tax on worldwide income. Corporate Tax: BVI has no corporate income tax for most companies. However, certain regulated entities may be subject to specific taxes.

No Value Added Tax: BVI does not impose VAT.

These are just simplified summaries, and there may be additional taxes & exemptions.

## How to Choose the Jurisdiction

Some taxpayers have long dreamed of a utopia in which ordinary people would legally avoid paying income tax and save their earnings in full – down to the cent, penny, or shilling. To most people living in high-tax jurisdictions, including, for example, the

United States of America and Australia, such a possibility seems too good to be true, and in their case, the idea of changing tax residency could seem to be irrational. However, such an opportunity is quite feasible and legally justified in some jurisdictions with zero/very low taxes often called tax havens or countries that offer tax incentives for expats.

The first tax Haven reported was in Ancient Greece, but tax academics identify what we know as tax havens as being a modern phenomenon.

In the 1880s, New Jersey was in financial difficulty and the Governor, Leon Abbett backed a plan by a New York lawyer, Mr. Dill, which created a more liberal regime for establishing corporate structures, including the availability "off-the-shelf companies" (but not non-resident companies).

Delaware followed in 1898, based on lobbying from other New York lawyers. Because of the restrictive incorporation regime in the Anglo-Saxon world, New Jersey and Delaware were successful, and though not explicitly tax havens, many future tax havens would copy their "liberal" incorporation regimes.

The modern concept of a tax haven is generally accepted to have emerged at an uncertain point in the immediate aftermath of WW1.

Bermuda sometimes claims to have been the first tax haven based upon the creation of legislation in 1935. However, most tax academics identify the Zurich-Zug-Liechtenstein triangle as the first "tax haven hub" created during the mid-1920s. Liechtenstein's 1924 Civil Code created the "infamous" Anstalt corporate vehicle, while Zurich and Zug developed brass plate companies.

A tax academic identifies two of the three major groups of tax havens, as emerging during this period:

1. British Empire-based tax havens. The 1929 court case of Egyptian Delta Land and Investment Co. Ltd. V. Todd in Britain created the "non-resident corporation" and recognized a British-registered company with no business activities in Britain as not liable to British taxation. Another tax academic noted the creation of such "non-resident" companies was "a loophole which, in a sense, made Britain a tax haven". The ruling applied to the British Empire, including Bermuda, Barbados, and the Cayman Islands.

2. European-based tax havens. The Zurich-Zug-Liechtenstein triangle expanded and was joined by Luxembourg in 1929 when they created tax-free holding companies. However, in 1934, as a reaction to the global depression, the Swiss Banking Act of 1934 put bank secrecy under Swiss criminal law. Secrecy and privacy would become an important and distinctive part of European-based tax havens, in comparison with other tax havens.

3. Post World War II offshore financial centers. Currency controls enacted post World War II led to the creation of the Eurodollar market and the rise in offshore financial centers (OFCs). Many of these OFCs were traditional tax havens from the Post World War I phase, including the Caymans and Bermuda, however new centers such as Hong Kong and Singapore began to emerge.

4. London's position for OFCs was secured when a 1957 ruling that transactions executed by British banks on behalf of a lender and borrower who were not located in the UK, were not to be officially viewed as having taken place in the UK for regulatory or tax purposes, even though the transaction was only ever recorded as taking place in London. The rise of OFCs would continue so that by 2008, the Cayman Islands would be the 4th largest financial center in the world, while

Singapore and Hong Kong had become major Regional Financial Centers (RFCs). By 2010, tax academics would consider OFCs to be synonymous with tax havens, and that most of their services involved taxation.

5. Emerging economy-based tax havens. As well as the dramatic rise in OFCs, from the late 1960s onwards, new tax havens began to emerge to service developing and emerging markets, The first Pacific tax haven was Norfolk Island (1966), a self-governing external territory of Australia. It was followed by Vanuatu (1970–71), the Cook Islands (1981), Tonga (1984), Samoa (1988), the Marshall Islands (1990), and Nauru (1994). All these havens introduced familiar legislation modeled on the successful British Empire and European tax havens, including near-zero taxation for exempt companies, and non-residential companies, Swiss-style bank secrecy laws, trust company's laws, offshore insurance laws, flags of convenience for shipping fleets and aircraft leasing, and beneficial regulations for new online services (such as gambling and pornography).

6. Corporate-focused tax havens. In 1981, the US IRS published the Gordon Report on the use of tax havens by US taxpayers, which highlighted the use of tax havens by US corporations.

## What is tax inversion?

A tax inversion, also known as corporate inversion, is a strategy employed by multinational companies to reduce their tax liabilities by relocating their legal headquarters to a country with a more favorable tax environment. It involves a company based in one country acquiring or merging with a company in another country with lower tax rates, thereby shifting its tax domicile to the lower-tax jurisdiction.

The primary motivation behind a tax inversion is to take advantage of the differences in tax laws between countries. By relocating to a country with lower corporate tax rates or more favorable tax regulations, a company can potentially lower its overall tax burden and increase its after-tax profits.

Tax inversions typically occur when a company based in a high-tax country acquires a smaller company in a low-tax country and reincorporates the merged entity in the low-tax jurisdiction. This allows the newly formed company to benefit from the lower tax rates applicable in the new country.

There are several potential benefits for companies engaging in tax inversions, including:

Reduced Tax Liability: By relocating to a country with lower tax rates, companies can significantly decrease their corporate tax expenses, resulting in higher profits.

Access to Overseas Cash: Some companies have accumulated substantial amounts of cash in foreign subsidiaries. By investing, they can repatriate these funds without incurring high tax costs, as the lower-tax jurisdiction may have more favorable rules for bringing overseas profits back home.

Improved Competitiveness: Lowering tax burdens can enhance a company's competitiveness in the global market by freeing up funds for investment, research and development, or other growth initiatives.

Tax inversions, however, have attracted criticism due to concerns about tax fairness and revenue loss for high-tax jurisdictions. Critics argue that these strategies can erode the tax base of the home country, burdening other taxpayers and potentially reducing funding for public services and infrastructure.

To address these concerns, many countries have implemented measures to discourage or limit the benefits of tax inversions. These include stricter regulations, anti-inversion legislation, and measures to prevent profit shifting and tax avoidance.

It is important to note that tax inversions are complex transactions that involve legal, financial, and regulatory considerations. Companies considering such strategies should seek professional advice and carefully evaluate the legal and reputational risks, as well as the potential impact on their stakeholders and the broader tax environment.

## Are Tax Havens Tax Fraud?

The fiscal policies of these havens are often conceived as elaborate frauds plotted by large corporations and the rich.

However, tax havens themselves are not synonymous with tax fraud. Tax havens are jurisdictions that offer favorable tax regulations and financial secrecy to attract businesses and individuals seeking to minimize their tax obligations. These jurisdictions often have low or zero tax rates, lenient tax laws, and strict banking secrecy rules.

While tax havens can be used for legitimate tax planning purposes, they can also facilitate tax evasion and aggressive tax avoidance practices. Tax evasion is illegal and involves deliberately concealing income or assets to avoid paying taxes owed. On the other hand, tax avoidance refers to legal strategies that exploit loopholes in tax laws to minimize tax liabilities.

Tax fraud, specifically, refers to the intentional act of evading taxes by providing false information or engaging in fraudulent schemes to deceive tax authorities. It involves deliberate misrepresentation or manipulation of financial information to unlawfully reduce tax liabilities.

While some individuals and businesses may use tax havens for legitimate tax planning purposes, others may exploit the secrecy and favorable tax environment to engage in tax fraud. They may hide income, assets, or transactions from tax authorities, misrepresent the nature of transactions, or engage in other illegal activities to evade taxes.

It is important to distinguish between the concept of tax havens, which primarily refers to jurisdictions with favorable tax regulations, and tax fraud, which involves illegal activities to evade taxes. Not all individuals or businesses utilizing tax havens are engaged in tax fraud, but the opacity and lenient regulations associated with tax havens can create an environment conducive to fraudulent activities if proper oversight and enforcement measures are lacking.

Governments and international bodies are increasingly focused on combating tax evasion and aggressive tax avoidance facilitated by tax havens. Efforts such as international tax transparency initiatives, exchange of financial information, and stricter regulations aim to address these issues and promote greater tax fairness and compliance.

While tax havens themselves are not tax fraud, the secretive nature and lenient tax regulations of these jurisdictions can enable individuals and businesses to engage in tax evasion and aggressive tax avoidance practices. The distinction lies in the legality of the actions taken within the tax haven, with tax fraud involving intentional deception and illegal activities to evade taxes.

## Why swap Tax residency?

Every year, tens of thousands of high-net-worth individuals in search of favorable fiscal solutions resort to other tax residencies. There are different reasons for that.

A lot of people swap tax residency because they are repulsed by the ongoing discussions of politicians in their home jurisdictions about the virtues of increasing taxes.

Many individuals are unwilling to accept the loss of their right to privacy while the tightening control over personal data (including financial information) of individuals becomes more and more pronounced under the OECD's proposed Automatic Tax Information Exchange (see below) and other tools.

Having recognized this trend, some jurisdictions are shifting into the low-tax category, abandoning the taxation of fiscal residents on their incomes. This is how they try to attract the foreign investment/human capital needed to stimulate the economy.

In other words, many countries today offer a path to financial freedom and allow their residents to keep their earnings. The benefits of such an approach outweigh the gains from the personal income tax. Low-tax jurisdictions offer minimal rates or no tax on wealth, capital gains, gifts, inheritance. All one must do to enjoy such perks is to analyze the facts and make the right choice of tax residency.

## How to Choose the Jurisdiction by Assessing the Maximum Possible Benefit for you.

Dozens of states nowadays lure foreigners with zero income tax and other fiscal incentives. But to obtain the relevant benefits, it is not usually enough just to choose the tax residency of a particular jurisdiction and express a desire to get the appropriate status.

One will have to venture a full-scale relocation for long-term residence, meet the standard criteria set for tax purposes by OECD. In this case, you can choose tax residency from the following list of countries that do not charge personal income tax:

**Antigua** is a Caribbean nation with attractive immigration rules and liberal fiscal laws. By choosing the tax residency in Antigua and moving to the islands for most of the year, you can legally avoid paying personal income tax on worldwide income.

**Bahamas** is one of the most popular tourist destinations on the planet. The jurisdiction does not tax individuals on income/capital gains. The islands are heavily reliant on the financial sector and tourism.

**Bahrain**. Among the Gulf states, Bahrain is probably the most favorable place for nomadic professionals. However, it is extremely difficult for outsiders to obtain Bahraini citizenship for permanent legal residence.

**Bermuda** is a popular tax haven, known as a luxury vacation spot for the wealthy due to the extremely high cost of goods/services. Generates income from tourism and the financial sector.

**British Virgin Islands** is an island nation located in the Caribbean known for its picturesque beaches and vibrant nightlife. The popularity of the tourist industry allows the government not to tax residents. Only after twenty years of residency can one apply for permanent residency.

**Brunei** is a small country with the highest per capita incomes due to its huge oil reserves. Most of Brunei's wealth is concentrated in the hands of the Sultan and his associates. It is under a dictatorship, with very limited personal, social, and economic freedoms. It is virtually impossible to obtain permanent residency/citizenship.

**Cayman Islands** is a British Overseas Territory enjoying tax-free jurisdiction status due to tourism and a thriving financial sector, attracting high net worth expats. Such a status makes the jurisdiction one of the most expensive places to live in.

**Kuwait.** Kuwait's economy relies primarily on oil, which allows it to exempt all incomes from personal income tax. Despite the presence of many migrants, it is difficult to obtain a Kuwaiti residence permit. For example, a sponsorship visa from an employer would be required. Such a system has been heavily criticized as a means of incentivizing forced labor. In the case of digital nomads whose business does not need to be tied to ia location, it is simply impossible to obtain a long-term visa under the current legislation.

**Maldives**. This is a small island nation known for its expensive resorts. Although a short vacation trip to the islands may not seem too expensive, a permanent residence in the Maldives will cost a pretty penny. Only Sunni Muslims may become permanent residents of this island jurisdiction. Citizenship is not available even to foreign Muslims. The islands are subject to the negative effects of global warming and suffer from huge debts.

**Monaco** is an interesting option for tax residency. One of the best resort destinations in the world. Located on the French Riviera, Monaco is known for luxury casinos and the Formula One circuit. The absence of personal income tax is overshadowed by exorbitant real estate prices, as well as the high prices for goods and services.

**Nauru**. This island jurisdiction was once one of the richest in the world because of its active phosphate mining industry. However, the depletion of fertilizer reserves has turned this jurisdiction into a declining economy. Today its territory is used by Australia as a temporary detention center for asylum seekers. There is nothing attractive about the island, and the lack of taxes is practically the only advantage.

**Oman**. A Middle East country rich in oil. Oman is rapidly developing its tourism and shipping industry. The government is working hard to attract highly skilled migrants to fill the vacancies.

**Pitcairn**. The Pitcairn Islands are a British overseas territory with a tiny population. Located in the middle of the Pacific Ocean, the jurisdiction is known as the most isolated sovereign state. Its economy is based on fishing. Immigration procedures are extremely easy, but residents have nothing to engage themselves in on the islands, and you must get there by ship.

**Qatar.** Vast reserves of fossil hydrocarbons have allowed Qataris to achieve the highest per capita income, making the taxation of individuals unnecessary. Visa and immigration rules are quite strict.

**St. Barts**. Saint Barthelemy, a French-speaking Caribbean Island commonly known as St. Barts is an overseas collectivity of France in the Caribbean known for luxury tourism. The cost of living is much higher compared to other Caribbean Island jurisdictions. It is not difficult to obtain a residence permit if the candidate is a citizen of the European Union. During the first five years of residence the new resident is subject to a 30% personal income tax, and then it will be possible to live tax-free on the island.

**St. Kitts and Nevis** is a Caribbean tourist country with no resident income tax. It is located near Antigua and offers liberal immigration laws (see below).

**Turks and Caicos Islands** have the status of a British Overseas Territory. It is heavily dependent on tourism and financial services. Immigration laws are not overly strict and require applicants to demonstrate financial independence.

**United Arab Emirates**. The UAE is a group of emirates including Dubai and Abu Dhabi. The jurisdiction has huge oil and gas reserves. Besides, it is seeking to diversify the economy through the development of tourism, construction and financial services sectors. In particular, Dubai today is known for impressive megaprojects, from skyscrapers to artificial islands. The country receives a huge number of migrants sponsored by employers. It is possible to get a residence permit by opening a company in the UAE.

**Vanuatu** is an island nation with zero income tax, relying on tourism and the financial sector. The disadvantage is its rather low level of infrastructure development compared to other tropical resort destinations. The geographical location is far from optimal: it is quite difficult to get to the islands.

**Vatican City** is a very specific state. It is impossible to obtain Vatican residency status without being a high-ranking member of the Catholic Church. With its micro-state status, the Vatican generates its income mainly from donations from religious organizations, pilgrimage and religious tourism, and investments. There are no taxes at all.

**Wallis and Futuna**. These islands are French Overseas Territories. This circumstance allows EU citizens to enter and leave the territory easily, as immigration laws are like those of France. Non-EU citizens must put up with stricter procedures. The islands are financed by France and make their living through fishing. Tourism is virtually underdeveloped, but expats can easily find beautiful beaches and other places to relax in. The local prices are rather moderate, so the cost of living is not high.

## Countries with Low Tax Rates or Incentives for Expats

Expats looking for a low tax environment but do not want to live in the zero tax jurisdictions in the Caribbean, Middle East, or the Pacific Ocean which are mostly remote, will be surprised to learn that it is possible for almost anyone to live in Europe full-time and pay low taxes on their income without having to be a millionaire.

For many successful people, dragging a suitcase around the world just isn't their thing. They want a (nearly) full-time home in a bustling city with the benefits of minimal taxation.

The good news is that you don't have to move to the Bahamas or Dubai to enjoy low tax countries rates so long as you're able to invest some of your money in Europe.

Below is a list of some European countries with favorable tax policies for expats that could lessen your tax burden.

1. **Andorra**: This medieval village nestled into the mountainside not far from Barcelona is a countryside jurisdiction famous for its skiing and amazing mountain views. Pressure from the European Union caused Andorra to implement its first-ever income tax in 2015, but Andorra still remains a low tax haven conveniently nestled between high-tax Spain and France. Andorra is perfect for those with capital gains or generational wealth; it has no wealth tax, no gift tax, no inheritance tax, and the only capital gains tax is assessed on sales of local real estate. Income tax is exempt up to 24,000 Euros and the top rate is 10%. There are two ways to qualify for residence, make an investment or start a company. You need to live in Andorra for at least 90 days a year or own a property and maintain health insurance. To start a company, you must present your CV, and deposit 50,000 Euros in a local bond. If you want to choose an alternative and invest you need to invest 400,000 Euros which can also be in Real Estate.

2. **Bulgaria**: Bulgaria offers Eastern European city charm, plenty of beach resorts on the Black Sea, and a flat 10% tax rate with no minimum. Payroll taxes are capped at 19.6%. In order to become a tax resident, you need to live in Bulgaria for 183 days a year or persuade the local tax Authority that Bulgaria is your center of Life.

3. **Czech Republic**: Despite being a top tourist destination in Europe, Prague has one of the cheapest costs of living in central Europe. EU Citizens choosing to redomicile

themselves to the Czech Republic enjoy a flat tax rate of 15% and can claim a deduction for actual expenses. For most business owners, the lump sum can reduce the flat tax by 40% or 60%, leaving an effective tax rate of 6% to 9% on self-employed entrepreneurs. The Czech Tax authorities requires you or own an actual home, but this is surprisingly favorably priced.

4. **Georgia**: Georgia has a diverse tourism landscape. For instance, Mtskheta, Georgia is home to a UNESCO world heritage site. Georgia also happens to be the only European country with a largely territorial tax system, meaning properly structured foreign source income is not taxed in most circumstances.

Georgia's income tax is set at 1% for individuals with an annual income of up to $164,000 U.S. with 0% personal income tax on foreign-sourced income. You can even become a tax resident without living in Georgia if you can prove wealth or high income. While Georgia's capital of Tbilisi is not Paris, Georgia is one of the safest countries in the world.

5. **Malta**: Malta allows foreign citizens to pay an annual flat fee and exempt their foreign income from Malta tax. The island nation has developed some of the EU's most tax-friendly programs for both individual residents and corporations, with corporate tax rates as low as 5% possible for non-resident companies. Unlike Andorra and Monaco, Malta does not require any physical presence on its two Mediterranean islands, meaning you can establish residency but not live there at all. Maltese residents are not subject to tax in Malta on foreign-sourced income that is kept outside of the country. What's more, they are not subject to tax on foreign capital gains even if those gains are sent to a Malta bank account. Other income, including pensions, can be taxed once at

a flat 15% thanks to Malta's tax treaty network. The cost of maintaining the residence in Malta is a flat 15,000 euro "minimum tax" payable each year. With proper planning, this should also be the maximum tax. It is also possible to obtain a tax residence certificate.

6. **Monaco**: Monaco does not have any personal income tax. You can establish residence in Monaco just by proving wealth. Monaco's personal income tax still stands at a 0% tax rate, while its corporate income taxes are now set at 25% since the start of January of 2022. To become a tax resident, you are required to make a bank deposit of 500,000 Euros and purchase or rent a property there.

7. **Montenegro**: Montenegro has low corporate taxes and is one of the least expensive countries in Europe to start a company. Montenegro boasts about being one of the lowest personal income tax and corporate income tax rates in Europe, both pegged at a flat 9% for 2022. Montenegro allows foreigners who buy residential property to obtain a temporary residence card, renewable yearly. If you spend fewer than 183 days in Montenegro, you will generally not be taxed. If you live in Montenegro most of the time, you will become a tax resident and be liable to pay the flat 9% rate on your income. It also has a citizenship by investment program if you're looking into expanding your passport portfolio and your investment portfolio.

8. **Portugal**: Even though Portugal is a high tax country, foreigners can take advantage of a ten-year Non-Habitual Resident Tax exemption that exempts up to 100% of their income from Portuguese tax. Foreigners can take advantage of a ten-year Non-Habitual Resident Tax exemption that exempts up to 100% of their income from Portuguese tax. While this exemption doesn't allow you to live in

Portugal tax-free forever, it is long enough to allow you to claim Portugal citizenship if you meet the rather lenient physical stay requirements. The first step to living in Portugal is to obtain Portuguese residency; this can be done by purchasing real estate through the well-known Golden Visa program but can be done more easily by hiring people or by merely proving you have rental income overseas.

9. **Switzerland:** Switzerland was one of the first countries to allow wealthy taxpayers to negotiate a flat annual tax with its cantons at a maximum of 11.5%. Swiss residency offers an air of legitimacy that many other low-tax residencies can't match. Foreigners have two residency options to choose from:

   9.a  The first is to form a new company in Switzerland and hire local employees.

   9.b  The more common and lower tax method to living in Switzerland is the Lump Sum Taxation method, which requires a flat annual tax. Expect to pay at least $150,000 and up to $1 million in flat tax each year, depending on which canton you want to live in. If your income is in the millions, Switzerland could reduce your tax rate below 10%.

10. **The United Kingdom**: The UK is far from a tax haven, but there are certain exemptions from the rule when it comes to tax rates, which you can take advantage of if you're a wealthy entrepreneur. By exploiting the difference between domicile and residence, certain foreign citizens can live in London and pay an annual flat tax.

This "non-dom" system has been popularized thanks to Middle Eastern, Indian and Russian billionaires who take up residence in the United Kingdom yet claim they are not running their businesses from Kensington.(a wealthy part of London). Because their income is a foreign source, it is eligible to be taxed on a remittance basis; keep the income out of the UK and it is not taxed.

Obtaining residency in Britain requires a substantial investment, but for the right person, the tax benefits outweigh the initial costs. Claiming non-dom tax benefits may be free for up to six years, after which the remittance basis charge is anywhere from £30,000 to £90,000, depending on how long you've been a resident.

11. **Italy:** Recently, Italy introduced a massive expat tax relief known as "Decree of Growth", a bill seeking to help workers regardless of skill level willing to relocate to Italy. Under this law, during the first five years of employment in Italy, only 30% of your income is taxable, leaving 70% of your gross income as yours to keep. This bill increases the untaxed income bracket to 90% if you seek to relocate to southern Italy or the islands of Sicily or Sardinia, which are southern islands under the Italian domain. Furthermore, house ownership/mortgage or dependent children will extend this grant for an extra five years, with taxable income remaining at 50% for those extra five years. However, if three or more children are dependent on you, the five-year extra grant will stay at 90%. If you live in Italy as a non-resident, you're only taxed on income earned in Italy. However, if you're an Italian resident, spend more than 183 days a year in Italy, and your "center of economic interest" (i.e. your business and investments) is in Italy, your worldwide income is subject to Italian taxes.

Italian flat-rate tax for expat retirees

Italy offers a 7% flat tax incentive for retirees moving to Southern Italy. To qualify, you must officially transfer your tax residency to a municipality with a population less than 20,000 that's located in a region of Southern Italy (Sicily, Calabria, Sardinia, Campania, Basilicata, Abruzzo, Molise and Puglia). Under this regime, pensioners with a foreign-sourced income are taxed at a flat rate of 7% for the first 9 years of residency. You will also be exempt from tax on property and financial assets, if you haven't been a tax resident in the past 5 years and come from a country that has a Tax Information Exchange Agreement, Double Taxation agreement, or Foreign Account Tax Compliance Agreement with Italy. Fortunately, the UK, USA, Canada and most other countries are valid.

### Italian Non-Dom Tax Status

In 2017, Italy introduced a special tax regime for higher net-worth foreigners willing to relocate to Italy.

This regime allows Italian non-domiciled residents to pay a flat rate of €100,000 per year on all foreign income for a maximum of fifteen years.

You are entitled to this benefit if:

- You have transferred your tax residence in Italy. This favorable tax regime can be enjoyed for a maximum of fifteen years, and you may revoke it at any time.

- You have not been a tax resident for 9 of the previous 10 years prior to the introduction or application of the bill.

- Italian Tax Authorities formally approve your request.

## Case study US Expat.

If you're a US citizen or a green card holder and you live somewhere outside the USA you have US tax filing obligations if you have personal income such as wages, salary, commissions, tips, consultancy fees, pension fund, alimony, US and/or foreign social security, interest, dividends, capital gains, rental property, farm income, royalties, gambling winnings, inheritance or payment in kind in the US or abroad. You are required to report this and pay tax in the US even if you do not live there.

You may have US tax obligations even if you haven't ever lived in the USA or left several years ago and all your income is from "foreign" sources.

You may have US tax obligations even if some or all your income was already taxed at source or is going to be taxed by a foreign country.

You may have US tax obligations even if you aren't earning any money but are married to someone who does.

FATCA (Foreign Account Tax Compliant Act) is a US law that requires all financial institutions globally to identify every US citizen who has a bank, savings, or retirement account and to report the balance in the account, the savings, and all withdrawals made to the Income Tax authorities in the US (the IRS).

The implications of this is that if any US citizen living abroad has not reported accurately his financial holding to the US they will tax the tax payer, add on interest and severe penalties and in more significant cases may even start a process of criminal charges.

In addition to the Issue of the accurate reporting there is also an issue of what kind of assets a US citizen is allowed to invest in (PFIC) and what will happen to him if he invests in a non-authorized asset allocation or PFIC (Passive Foreign Investment Company).

**What is a PFIC?** (Something which is a non-authorized investment and incurs the highest tax rates for the investor).

All Foreign Mutual Funds, Provident Funds and even Pension Funds seem to be a very common and innocent investment but are also classified as PFIC. All investment accounts that hold non-US stocks or bonds are PFIC.

The aggressive tax regime of the US will not only require paying the highest tax bracket on these investments but also may require a theoretical annual sale of these assets to pay immediate taxes.

This is not the case in other jurisdictions where the tax paid is limited to people who are defined as tax citizens of the country, they are working in.

For example, if you are British or German and working in Dubai, you are required to pay tax in Dubai only. If you have income in the UK or in Germany, you may be required to pay tax in the UK or Germany first.

## Can a US citizen relinquish tax citizenship?

Yes, a US citizen can relinquish their tax citizenship through a process called expatriation. Expatriation is the act of voluntarily giving up one's US citizenship or long-term permanent residency for tax purposes. When a US citizen expatriates, they are no longer subject to US tax obligations on their worldwide income. However, it's important to note that expatriation for tax purposes is a complex process with various legal and financial considerations.

To formally relinquish tax citizenship, a US citizen must meet certain requirements and follow specific procedures, which are governed by the Internal Revenue Service (IRS). Here are some key points to keep in mind:

- **Expatriation Certification:** The individual must file Form 8854, Initial and Annual Expatriation Statement, with the IRS. This form is used to provide detailed information about their expatriation's actions, assets, and financial history.

- **Tax Compliance:** Before expatriating, the person must ensure they are up to date with their US tax obligations. This includes filing all required tax returns and paying any outstanding taxes or penalties.

- **Net Worth and Tax Liability:** The IRS imposes specific requirements for individuals with high net worth or high average annual net income. These requirements include paying an exit tax on the unrealized gains of certain assets and meeting certain financial thresholds.

- **Intent:** It's essential to demonstrate a clear intent to relinquish US citizenship or long-term permanent residency. This can be achieved by taking actions such as obtaining citizenship in another country, renouncing US citizenship at a US embassy or consulate, or other actions that demonstrate a voluntary and intentional relinquishment.

- **Consultation:** Given the complexities and potential implications of expatriation, it's advisable to consult with a qualified tax professional or attorney who specializes in international tax matters. They can provide guidance based on an individual's specific circumstances and ensure compliance with all relevant laws and regulations.

It's important to note that expatriation for tax purposes does not automatically absolve an individual from all past tax liabilities or obligations. Additionally, the decision to relinquish US tax citizenship should not be taken lightly, as it may have long-term consequences for an individual's ability to enter or work in the United States in the future. In addition, it is important to stress that being a US Citizen is not only liabilities.

## Advantages of Being a US Citizen

Being a US citizen comes with several advantages, including:

**Legal Rights and Protections:** US citizens enjoy a range of legal rights and protections under the US Constitution. These include the right to vote, freedom of speech, freedom of religion, due process, and protection against unreasonable searches and seizures. Citizens also have access to the US justice system and can serve on juries.

**Passport and Consular Protection:** US citizens are entitled to a US passport, which allows for easy travel and access to consular services while abroad. US embassies and consulates can aid and protect citizens in case of emergencies, such as lost passports, arrests, or medical issues.

**Voting and Political Participation:** US citizens have the right to participate in the democratic process by voting in federal, state, and local elections. They can elect officials and have a say in shaping public policies and laws that affect their lives.

**Employment Opportunities:** Some employment opportunities, particularly in government agencies and certain industries, may be restricted to US citizens. Additionally, certain government benefits and programs are available exclusively to citizens.

**Access to Social Services and Benefits:** US citizens are eligible for various social services and benefits, such as Medicare (healthcare for the elderly), Social Security benefits, and certain welfare programs. These benefits provide financial security and support during retirement or in times of need.

**Educational Opportunities:** US citizens have access to federal financial aid programs, scholarships, and grants that can help offset the cost of higher education. They can also attend public schools and universities at in-state tuition rates in their respective states.

**Ability to Sponsor Family Members:** US citizens can sponsor certain family members for immigration to the United States. This includes immediate relatives such as spouses, parents, and unmarried children.

**Dual Citizenship:** The United States generally allows dual citizenship, meaning individuals can maintain their US citizenship while also acquiring citizenship of another country. This can provide additional benefits and opportunities associated with the second citizenship.

It's important to note that the advantages of US citizenship may vary depending on individual circumstances and are subject to change based on laws and policies.

## Protecting our wealth against aggressive tax policies aiming at middle class, mass affluent and high net worth individuals

Most Governments are witnessing WW2 scale deficits and eventually the bill for this will end up at our front door. Estate tax, capital gains taxes, wealth tax and the cancellation of exemptions in addition to other choices are all on the table.

## How should families prepare themselves for this raid on their assets and the future of their children?

A strong and prosperous middle class is crucial for any successful economy and society. The middle class sustains consumption, it drives investment in education, health and housing and it plays a key role in supporting social protection systems through its tax contributions. Societies with a strong middle class have lower crime rates, enjoy higher levels of trust and life satisfaction, as well as greater political stability and good governance.

However, the top 10% in the income distribution in the western world holds almost half of the total wealth, while the bottom 40% accounts for only 3%. The brunt of the taxes falls on small businesses and the mass affluent who are not often the beneficiaries of government policies.

Since the financial crisis, the implicit tax rate on labour has increased gradually but steadily. During the same period, taxes on capital have risen steeply in Germany and France.

Over the past 30 years, mass affluent households have experienced dismal income growth or even stagnation. This has fuelled perceptions that the current socio-economic system is unfair and that the mass affluent class has not benefited from economic growth in proportion to its contribution. In addition to this they will bear the brunt of most of the cost of the "Covid Crisis".

Furthermore, the cost of living has become increasingly expensive for the middle class, as the cost of core services and goods such as housing have risen faster than income. Traditional mass affluent opportunities for social mobility have also withered as labour market prospects become increasingly uncertain: one in six workers are in jobs that are at high risk of automation.

Uncertain of their own prospects, the middle class are also concerned about those of their children; the current generation is one of the most educated, and yet has lower chances of achieving the same standard of living as its parents.

## How will the Governments pay for this?

**Borrowing:** The first level of defence for Governments worldwide is borrowing. Bonds issued by Governments for 20 – 100 years are transferring the bulk of the cost of COVID to future generations.

**Cutting Spending:** Governments all over the world are promising cuts in public spending.

Spending in some areas, such as schools and health systems, are being protected - and it would be difficult to reduce health spending after a pandemic.

Pensions, another big spending item, are also in general protected.

Public salaries are rising very fast as they bounce back after the pandemic, which could make this a very expensive pledge to honour.

Freezing salaries and cutting foreign aid may serve this goal but it will be marginal.

## Taxes

But governments cannot keep borrowing forever, so they must also cut spending or increase income from taxes or both.

Before the UK Government was elected in 2019, the government promised not to raise the rates of the three biggest taxes - income tax, National Insurance and value added tax VAT).

However, the chancellor announced measures which will increase most people's tax bills in 2022.

Nation states are likely to respond by increasing efforts to coordinate tax policy, and/or make tax grabs across borders (e.g., FATCA, *CRS*).

## What is CRS?

CRS stands for the Common Reporting Standard. It is an international standard for the automatic exchange of financial account information between tax authorities of different countries. CRS was developed by the Organisation for Economic Co-operation and Development (OECD) and endorsed by the G20.

The primary goal of CRS is to combat tax evasion and promote tax transparency on a global scale. It requires financial institutions, such as banks, to identify and report financial accounts held by non-resident individuals and entities to their respective tax authorities. The tax authorities then exchange this information with the tax authorities of the account holders' countries of residence.

Under CRS, financial institutions collect a wide range of information about account holders, including their personal details (name, address, date of birth), tax identification numbers, account balances, and investment income. This information is reported to the tax authorities annually, and it allows tax authorities to identify individuals who may be evading taxes by holding undisclosed offshore accounts.

The exchanged information helps tax authorities enforce tax laws and ensure that taxpayers accurately report their income and assets. It also helps countries identify potential tax residency conflicts, prevent tax base erosion, and ensure fair and equitable tax collection.

Over 100 jurisdictions have committed to implementing CRS, including major financial centres. Many countries have enacted legislation to enable the collection and exchange of financial account information as per the CRS requirements. The exchanged information is typically used for tax purposes and may be subject to strict confidentiality and data protection rules.

It's important to note that CRS focuses on financial accounts and the exchange of information between tax authorities, primarily for tax compliance purposes. It does not impose any taxes itself or establish tax rates. The implementation and enforcement of taxes remain the responsibility of individual countries.

## What is the easiest way to pay for COVID and the impacts of the Ukraine war?

The easiest way for Governments to cover the immediate surplus cost of COVID is to impose a wealth tax.

Introducing a one-off wealth tax of 5 per cent on net assets above 500,000 USD for example would raise more than 260bn GBP if 8 M taxpayers were eligible.

Tax experts from think-tanks, the OECD, industry practitioners, lawyers, and policymakers, have said. "A one-off wealth tax would work, raise significant revenue, and be fairer and more efficient than any other alternative,".

So once again the mass affluent middle class and small business owners will have to pay the price for us all.

## Will being an expat help me?

This will greatly accelerate the trend towards higher tax rates on labour, except for those who are highly mobile. As more workers become more mobile, it will become harder to tax the capital that is associated with them (e.g., pension and retail investment funds).

The challenge will be to understand the impact of national and international tax rules, in a way that helps serve an increasingly mobile client base. Advisers must either become global tax experts or build partnerships with experts.

### *So how should families prepare themselves for this raid on their assets and the future of their children?*

In any scenario preparing for the inevitable would be wise. Preparing strategies for gifting assets to future generations, preparing trusts, and offshore accounts are all strategies that in the best scenario could save families that worked all their lives accumulating assets for future generations from transferring these assets to governments and could mitigate the damage.

## Case Study: the UK as a desirable jurisdiction for Expats

The United Kingdom (UK) is often regarded as a desirable jurisdiction for expatriates due to several factors that make it an attractive destination for individuals seeking new opportunities. Here are some reasons why the UK is considered favourable for expats:

Economic Opportunities: The UK is one of the world's largest economies, with a diverse range of industries and sectors. It offers numerous employment prospects across various fields, including finance, technology, creative industries, healthcare, and more.

Expats can find opportunities to advance their careers and access a dynamic job market.

**Education and Research:** The UK is renowned for its prestigious universities and educational institutions. It offers a high standard of education and research opportunities, making it an attractive destination for students and academics. Expats looking to pursue higher education or engage in research find the UK's academic environment appealing.

**Cultural Richness:** The UK boasts a rich history and vibrant cultural scene. It is home to world-class museums, art galleries, theatres, music venues, and a diverse range of cultural events. Expats can immerse themselves in the country's rich heritage and enjoy a wide array of cultural experiences.

**Multicultural Environment:** The UK is known for its multi-culturalism and diversity. Expats can experience a melting pot of cultures, interact with people from various backgrounds, and enjoy a cosmopolitan lifestyle. This diversity contributes to a vibrant social atmosphere and fosters a sense of inclusivity.

**Healthcare System:** The UK has a comprehensive and publicly funded National Health Service (NHS), providing affordable healthcare to its residents. Expats can access quality medical services and enjoy the peace of mind that comes with compre-hensive healthcare coverage.

**Travel and Connectivity:** The UK's geographical location makes it an excellent base for exploring Europe and beyond. It has well-connected airports and an efficient transportation network, allowing easy travel to other European countries. Expats can take advantage of the UK's strategic position to explore different cultures and destinations.

**Legal and Political Stability:** The UK has a robust legal system, providing individuals with a sense of security and protection of their rights. It has a stable political environment, a strong rule of law, and an independent judiciary, which are appealing factors for expats seeking a secure and predictable living environment.

**Social Welfare System:** The UK offers a comprehensive social welfare system that provides support to individuals during periods of unemployment, disability, or retirement. Expats can benefit from social welfare programs that ensure a safety net and a decent standard of living.

**Quality of Life:** The UK offers a high standard of living with access to quality infrastructure, public services, and amenities. It has well-developed public transportation, efficient healthcare, and a range of recreational activities. Expats can enjoy a comfortable and convenient lifestyle in the UK.

**Language Advantage:** English is the predominant language in the UK, making it easier for expats from English-speaking countries to adapt and communicate effectively. This linguistic advantage simplifies daily life, work interactions, and integration into the local community.

While the UK presents numerous advantages for expatriates, it's important to consider individual circumstances, such as visa requirements, cost of living, and personal preferences. It's advisable for potential expats to thoroughly research and seek guidance to ensure a smooth transition and successful experience in the UK.

## Case Study: Gibraltar

Gibraltar is fast becoming a favoured jurisdiction for high-net-worth individuals and businesses that are looking for a legitimate way to lower their tax bill in a properly regulated financial environment. Having signed more than 80 Tax Information Exchange Agreements and been whitelisted by the OECD and the EU, Gibraltar has completed a transition from offshore tax haven to a mainstream leading European financial services centre. Gibraltar also has a Double-Taxation Treaty with the UK and a Tax Understanding with Spain. Gibraltar offers compelling tax planning advantages for businesses and high net worth individuals considering a new country of residence.

## Why would someone choose to live in Gibraltar?

Whether this is for personal tax restructuring, estate planning or simply for a change of lifestyle there are significant benefits to being tax resident in Gibraltar. Businesses pay a flat rate of corporation tax which is set at 12.5% whilst being able to enjoy direct and easy access to the UK (especially useful post-Brexit), with English as its official language and modelled on the English legal system. Moreover, Gibraltar has the added advantage of being outside of the VAT (value added tax) zone, with VAT at 0%.

## What are the benefits for Expats who are considering living in Gibraltar?

There are two distinct tax residency categories suitable for high-net-worth individuals and high executives. Both offer tremendous tax advantages:

1. CATEGORY 2 Residency, Individuals who are looking to protect either their trading or earned income from higher rates of taxation in their country of residence or where they declare their income. The key conditions which must be fulfilled to obtain Category 2 Gibraltar residency status are as follows:

1.a The Category 2 individual must be of substantial and sound financial standing and have a minimum net worth of £2 million (including assets/property). There is no requirement to bring the funds to Gibraltar.

1.b The Category 2 resident must own or rent approved residential accommodation in Gibraltar. The property must be approved by the Gibraltar Finance Centre and be used exclusively by the Category 2 individual and large enough to house direct family (if applicable).

1.c The Category 2 individual cannot have been resident in Gibraltar during the five years immediately preceding the year of assessment.

1.d The Category 2 individual is not allowed to engage in a trade, business, or employment in Gibraltar unless it is in a sector or activity which is not in direct competition with a local business.

2. Category 2 status is granted on an indefinite basis, but the Category 2 residency certificates need to be sent to the Gibraltar Finance Centre for renewal every three years.

3. The Category 2 individual must have private medical insurance to cover them and their family in the event of illness in Gibraltar.

**How much tax will I need to pay as a tax Resident in Gibraltar.?**

- There is no minimum physical residence requirement in Gibraltar for a Category 2 resident, meaning the individual is not required to live in Gibraltar even 1 day a year to be eligible as a tax resident.

- Only the first £118,000 of the taxable income of a Category 2 Individual is considered when calculating the tax payable. Only income remitted to Gibraltar is considered, although an individual may elect for his/her worldwide income to be considered. Maximum tax payable of £44,740 and a minimum tax charge of £37,000, per annum.

## What are the benefits for the new Resident?

She/he will receive a Gibraltar Residency status and ID Card, No inheritance tax and no wealth tax, no capital gains tax and no gift tax. There is no taxation on interest savings, or on dividend income arising from companies quoted on a recognized stock exchange. They can apply for British citizenship after five years (compared to 10 years in the UK)

## What other alternatives are there in Gibraltar?

- There is the HEPSS Category Under the "High Executive Possessing Specialist Skills" residency category (styled a "HEPSS individual") in Gibraltar, an individual will only be chargeable to Gibraltar Income Tax on the first £160,000 earned. Thus, at prevailing rates, for the HEPSS individual, taxation will effectively be limited to a figure of about £43,140 (27%) a year.

Any income above the initial £160,000 will be tax-free. Eligibility for HEPSS status The criteria for entitlement for this special tax status is as follows:

- The applicant must possess skills which are necessary to promote and sustain economic activity of value to Gibraltar, or the establishment, development or growth of which the Gibraltar Government is seeking to facilitate and encourage.

- The applicant will be occupying a senior management position and will earn more than £160,000 per year.

- The skills possessed by the applicant are important for the economic benefit of Gibraltar.

- The applicant has for his "exclusive use" for the period covered by the certificate, residential accommodation in Gibraltar approved as such by the Finance Centre.

- The applicant has not been gainfully occupied or resident in Gibraltar for any part of the period of 3 years immediately prior to the making of the HEPSS Application (there exists a power to waive this criterion).

# Chapter Seventeen

## "A World of Possibilities: Exploring Retirement Options for Expats"

---

## Should I retire Overseas?

Retirement planning raises many questions:

When can I retire? How much should I save? Will I continue to work and/or volunteer? What shall I do to stay active? One factor that influences how you answer all these questions is *where* you plan to retire—either at home or some place abroad.

While most people spend their retirement at home, a growing number are opting to retire overseas. Here are the pros and cons of this dilemma:

### Retire at Home

Most retirees either stay in their existing homes or make in-country moves. For many people, family is a big reason to stay home—especially if there are grandkids in the picture.

### Advantages of Retiring in my home country.

- You already may have established professional connections. These help you secure part-time or less stressful full-time work during retirement.

- You already may have established social networks. These enable you to remain physically and mentally active without the need to make new friends.

- Family. It's easier to spend time with children, grandkids, and other family members.

- Support. You're not among strangers if anything goes wrong.

- Trusted providers. You can stay with familiar doctors and hospitals, car mechanics, hairstylists, etc.

- Stability and convenience. You can depend on a certain level of predictability for everything from infrastructure to the brand of toothpaste available at your local grocery store.

- Comfort zone. You can maintain your "normal" routine.

## Disadvantages of Retiring at home.

1. Expensive. The cost of living in your home country may be much higher than in many parts of the world.

2. Rising healthcare costs. While the standard of care may be sufficient, private healthcare costs are enormous. Estimates show that a healthy 65-year-old couple retiring in the U.S. in 2021 will need about $300,000 saved (after tax) just to cover healthcare expenses during retirement.

3. High assisted living costs. You may never need it, but if you do, the median cost for community and assisted living facilities in developed nations are around $4,300 per month.

4. Routine. Although considered a plus by many, staying in a routine may limit your opportunities to learn and enjoy new experiences.

Pros

- Established connections and social networks

- Family and friends

- Stability and convenience

- Comfort zone

Cons

- High cost of living

- High healthcare costs

- High assisted living costs

- Could get stuck in a routine.

## Retire Abroad

Moving out of your home country could undoubtedly be an adventure, but it can be so, depending on your destination. From quiet beaches in Vietnam to hip cities in South America, you can choose a place that matches your comfort level in terms of modern conveniences, access, climate, activities, cuisine, healthcare, culture, and customs.

## More Advantages of Retiring Abroad

- New experiences. Experts link new experiences to healthy aging—they provide physical, cognitive, and social benefits.

- **Realize your dreams.** You can fulfil your dreams to travel, pick up a new sport, or enjoy a hobby.

- **Lower cost of living.** Sometimes it's possible to retire abroad comfortably for a fraction of the cost of staying at home. This helps if your budget is limited. Your benefits usually will follow you anywhere in the world.

- **Access to affordable healthcare.** You may find public healthcare systems that provide good healthcare at a reasonable cost. Private coverage is available in many countries for significantly less than comparable plans at home.

- **Retiree incentives**. Many countries offer incentives to retirees, such as Panama, or Italy and Portugal which is open to retirees who meet modest minimum income standards and offers discounts on everything from restaurant meals to movies.

- Weather you can pick your paradise whether it's a warm, sunny beach or a tropical rainforest.

## More Disadvantages of Retiring Abroad

- **You're a long way from home**. Depending on where you go, a long, expensive flight could be between you and your friends and family.

- **Long-stay visas.** Some countries welcome foreign retirees and offer an easy path to residency, but others offer no retirement visa schemes. Wealth opens doors to many countries through the availability of so-called "golden visa" programs.

- **Double taxation.** If you are a US Citizen the U.S. taxes your income no matter where you live but with a tax break on the first 100K $. Depending on where you retire, you could end up paying taxes on your income both in the U.S. and abroad. Most countries avoid double taxation on ex-pats, but you still may have to file returns.

- **Language and cultural differences.** Are you up for learning a new language and immersing yourself in a new culture?

- **Instability.** Not all countries enjoy the same level of political and economic stability your home country does.

- **Daily challenges.** The goods, services, and conveniences you are used to may not be readily available—or available at all.

- **The reality of vacation versus living.** Your piece of paradise could be a great place to visit, but not so great for full-time living.

- **Support.** You might be among strangers if something goes wrong.

## The Bottom Line: Stay or Go?

Many retirees would never consider moving abroad, and others know for sure it's what they want to do. If that's you, be sure to start planning early since it can take months, a year, or even longer to get your paperwork and logistics in order.

If you're a retiree or near-retiree who's on the fence, you face a tough decision that will require some soul searching and research—and maybe a trip abroad (or several) to test the waters before you make any decisions.

Most retirees either stay in their existing homes or make in-country moves. For many people, family is a big reason to stay home.

# Chapter Eighteen

## "Mapping Your Expat Retirement: A Blueprint for Financial Freedom"

Retirement Planning is planning for the day we stop accumulating assets and start living off the assets we have accumulated.

By identifying all sources of income and all expenses and recognizing the timing of each, you can identify in any year when the client will have a shortfall (more expenses than income). In those shortfall years, the monies invested can be used to cover these shortfalls. These controllable variables include:

- Controlling expenses as much as possible.

- Reducing taxes

- Improving the rate of return on the investment portfolio by changing investment strategy

- Reducing or eliminating one or more of your goals in the future if need be.

Planning for retirement is essential for everyone, including expatriates. As an expat, there are specific factors to consider when preparing for retirement in a foreign country. Here are some key considerations to keep in mind when planning retirement as an expat:

**Financial Planning**: Start by assessing your financial situation and determining how much you will need to save for retirement. Consider factors such as the cost of living in your host country, healthcare expenses, and your desired lifestyle during retirement. Consider any potential currency fluctuations and tax implications that may affect your income and savings.

**Retirement Accounts and Investments**: Research the retirement account options available to you as an expat. Explore whether you can continue contributing to retirement accounts from your home country or if you have access to local retirement plans in your host country. Consider diversifying your investments to mitigate risk and maximize potential returns.

**Social Security and Pension Benefits**: Understand how your home country's social security system and any pension benefits will be affected by living abroad. Research whether there are agreements or treaties in place between your home country and your host country that allow for the transfer or continuation of social security benefits. This can impact your retirement income significantly.

**Healthcare Coverage**: Evaluate the healthcare system and insurance options in your host country. Determine if you will be eligible for local healthcare benefits or if you need to secure private health insurance for your retirement years. Consider factors such as coverage, costs, and access to medical facilities.

**Tax Considerations**: Familiarize yourself with the tax regulations in both your home country and your host country. Understand how your retirement income, investments, and any other sources of income will be taxed. Consult with a tax advisor who specializes in international taxation to optimize your tax planning and minimize any potential tax liabilities.

**Long-Term Residence and Visa Requirements**: Research the visa requirements and regulations related to long-term residence in your host country. Understand how these requirements may impact your ability to remain in the country during your retirement years. Determine if you need to apply for a specific retirement visa or meet certain financial criteria to qualify for long-term residency.

**Estate Planning**: Consider your estate planning needs and how you want your assets to be distributed in the event of your passing. Understand the inheritance laws and regulations in your host country, as they may differ from those in your home country. Consult with an estate planning attorney to create or update your will and establish any necessary trusts or arrangements.

**Cultural and Social Integration**: Retirement abroad offers the opportunity to immerse yourself in a new culture and community. Consider how you will integrate socially and build a support network in your host country. Explore local activities, clubs, and organizations that align with your interests and can provide a fulfilling retirement lifestyle.

**Language and Communication**: If your host country has a different language, consider investing time in learning the local language. This will facilitate your daily interactions, enhance your integration, and provide a more enriching retirement experience.

**Seek Professional Advice**: Given the complexity of retirement planning as an expat, it's advisable to consult with professionals who specialize in international financial planning, tax planning, and legal matters. They can provide personalized guidance based on your specific situation and help you navigate the intricacies of retirement planning in a foreign country.

Remember that retirement planning is an ongoing process, and it's important to regularly review and adjust your strategies as circumstances evolve. By considering these factors and seeking professional advice, you can make informed decisions and ensure a secure and fulfilling retirement as an expat.

By working with this methodology, an expat can go from a shortfall to a surplus. When you have a surplus (identified as an "Estate") it means that you would achieve all your goals and objectives, with something left over at the end of your planning horizon.

## Saving for Retirement

Saving for retirement is difficult under any circumstances, and it can be even harder to set money aside after taxes. Luckily, many retirement savings options allow you to set money aside without paying taxes on that income. Once that money has been placed in a separate account, it can gain value based on interest or investments. You will not be charged taxes on that money until you remove it from the retirement account. By that time, it's likely you'll be in a lower tax bracket and need to pay significantly less.

While these accounts do not let you exempt yourself from taxes entirely, deferring payment allows you to maximize your savings and minimize the amount of taxes that eventually need to be paid.

Saving for retirement as an expat is crucial for ensuring financial security in your later years. Here are some key considerations when it comes to saving for retirement as an expat:

**Set Retirement Goals**: Determine your retirement goals and the lifestyle you envision for your golden years. Consider factors such as the age at which you want to retire, the type of activities you want to pursue, and the level of financial independence you desire. Having clear goals will help you develop a savings plan tailored to your specific needs.

**Understand Cost of Living**: Research and understand the cost of living in your host country. Consider expenses such as housing, healthcare, transportation, and daily living costs. This will give you a realistic idea of how much you need to save to maintain your desired standard of living during retirement.

**Create a Budget**: Establish a budget that allows you to save a portion of your income towards retirement. Identify areas where you can reduce expenses and allocate those savings towards retirement savings. Regularly review and adjust your budget as circumstances change.

**Explore Retirement Accounts**: Investigate retirement account options available to you as an expat. Determine if you can continue contributing to retirement accounts from your home country or if there are local retirement plans in your host country that you can utilize. Consult with a financial advisor who specializes in expat finances to understand the best options for your situation.

**Go for Tax-Advantaged Accounts**: Maximize the use of tax-advantaged retirement accounts such as Individual Retirement Accounts (IRAs) or their equivalent in your home country. These accounts offer tax benefits and can help grow your savings faster. Be aware of any tax implications when it comes to contributing to these accounts as an expat.

**Consider Employer Retirement Plans**: If you are employed, inquire about employer-sponsored retirement plans available to you. Many companies offer retirement benefits, such as 401(k) plans or their equivalent, which often include employer matching contributions. Take advantage of these plans to boost your retirement savings.

**Regularly Review and Adjust Contributions**: Monitor your retirement savings progress and adjust as necessary. Increase your contributions whenever possible, especially as your income grows or you receive salary raises. Regularly review your investment portfolio to ensure it aligns with your risk tolerance and long-term goals.

**Diversify Investments**: Diversify your investment portfolio to spread the risk and increase potential returns. Consider a mix of stocks, bonds, mutual funds, and other investment vehicles that align with your risk tolerance and time horizon. Seek professional advice from a financial advisor who understands international investments.

**Plan for Currency Fluctuations**: Be mindful of currency fluctuations and how they can impact your retirement savings. If you are saving in a currency different from your home currency, fluctuations can affect the purchasing power of your savings. Consider strategies to hedge against currency risks, such as maintaining a diversified portfolio or using currency exchange products.

**Start Early and Stay Consistent**: The earlier you start saving for retirement, the more time your savings must grow. Make consistent contributions to your retirement accounts and take advantage of compounding returns. Even small contributions can add up over time.

Remember that saving for retirement is a long-term commitment, and it requires discipline and planning. You could professional financial advice and regularly reassess your retirement savings strategy to ensure you are on track to meet your goals.

**Take a long-term approach:** Saving using tax efficient vehicles can offer short and long-term benefits, but you'll want to take a long view of your financial situation to maximize savings. If you anticipate an increase or decline in your income during the next few years, start catering your financial plan to the upcoming shifts ahead of time. Figure out if it's best to pay taxes on that increased income right now, or if you should try and put it all into tax-deferred accounts that may incur taxes later.

This can result in massive savings for couples, but far too many people fail to consider this factor when they plan. By speaking with professionals before taking any financial action, you can prevent yourself from accidentally missing out on significant tax exemptions.

## Planning for Retirement as an Expat - A Framework for a family conversation.

The world's population is ageing and so are we all. This brings with it new planning challenges.

You may want to organize and analyse your economic reality in order to answer the many questions that lie ahead. We want to make sure you have asked ourselves the right questions and every detail has been investigated.

So how do you create a framework for a family conversation ahead of the challenge of retirement and planning the passage of wealth from generation to generation?

There are those who think that planning the transfer of wealth from generation to generation is only for the ultra-wealthy, but this is not true. Everyone accumulates wealth throughout their lives and most leave wealth for future generations (apartments, savings, pensions) and without planning a large part of this wealth will not pass smoothly to them. Whether it's family asset planning or building a tax strategy, planning will save a lot and make sure our assets arrive where we want them to.

The needs and issues of Families are divided into four main categories:

1. Physical

2. Cognitive and Psychological

3. Family

4. Economic

Look at each of the categories with questions and advice that may bring value:

**Physical**: This means the physical effects that the ageing process has on our body. Chronic conditions can include limitations in movement, hearing, vision, heart problems, diabetes, and more. These problems lead to concerns about where to live and who will take care of us.

**Relevant questions:**

1. What effects do you think physical ageing will have on you?

2. How do you plan to deal with healthcare decision-making in the future?

3. Have you been concerned about having sufficient resources given the rising prices of healthcare?

4. What kind of decisions will you have to make about your living situation?

5. What types of transportation decisions will you need to make?

6. Do you understand the implications of the insurances you have?

**Cognitive and psychological**: Most of us are looking forward to retirement and see it as an opportunity to enjoy travel, well-being, community service, and perhaps even start a second (or third) career or start a small business. As time goes on, many senior citizens experience periods of sadness, worry and depression. Memory loss and unfortunately, dementia and maybe Alzheimer's develops.

Relevant questions:

1. What do you want to do or are you already doing to maximize your enjoyment of your retirement years?

2. Has your family made plans to plan in case of a decline in cognitive abilities?

Additional topics for discussion:

1. What do you do with your free time?

2. How should you prepare to avoid scams?

3. Have you thought about employment opportunities for senior citizens.

4. How to identify signs of dementia and cognitive decline.

5. How to prepare for the reality of declining cognitive ability.

## Family issues:

Over the past few decades, many changes have arisen in family structures and even the meaning of what a family is in general. Adult children may continue to live with us at home or on the other side of the world. The changes may affect relationships and family communication.

There may be a reality in which the children have multiple families, due to divorce. Multiple relatives from different legal jurisdictions will further complicate the problem.

## Relevant questions:

1. What is troubling you about your intra-family relationships?

2. Could geographic distancing be a problem in family communication in the future?

3. Have you decided on a family representative to be in charge of family communications?

## Additional topics for discussion:

1. Understanding intergenerational differences.

2. How to improve family communication.

3. How to arrange family meetings.

4. How to handle intergenerational wealth transfer from multiple jurisdictions.

5. How to choose a trustee for making decisions on matters of inheritance, health, and generality.

## Economic:

Although the elderly population have a lot of issues that concern them related to their finances, the main issue that worries most of us is whether our assets can be enough for us to live the life we are accustomed to. We all want to make the right decisions about pensions, withdrawing allowances, tax planning and allowances but we must see the big picture otherwise every little decision we make becomes extremely difficult and can affect our destiny.

Relevant questions:

- How do you want to manage your assets so that they last your lifetime?

- What help do you need to achieve this goal?

- What happens if the moment comes, when you are no longer able to make your financial decisions?

Topics for discussion

- Social Security (or the equivalent in your country of residence), pension withdrawals, creating income from our portfolio.

- Wills and Trusts

- Building a legacy.

## In a World of Uncertainty, Reliable Retirement Outcomes Matter

History buffs often say that history has a way of repeating itself. Lessons from the past can become blueprints for the future. While we can't predict the future or guarantee outcomes, we can build a strategy to create a sustainable retirement outcome that will enable families to live the life they dream of and provide for their next generation.

Every retirement journey is unique. Not all of us are alike—and not all paths to retirement are the same but the methodology for building a strategy is the same.

It will always begin with defining goals – from my experience the process of defining goals can be emotional, mostly in life we go from event to event, in our careers, bringing up our family caring for our loved ones, we do the best we can, hoping that withholding our values and just doing the best we can will lead us to a life of dignity and security.

But the reality is that this is just not enough, in short, passive income is important because it creates stability, security, and freedom in our financial life. Additionally, since passive income is not limited by our time and effort, it can have a positive, and significant, effect on your ability to build wealth and live the life you aspire to.

The first stage in the process of planning passive income is to ask ourselves the following questions.

What kind of life do we envision for ourselves after we stop working?

Defining the kind of life, you want to live is essential when preparing a plan. Accumulating wealth and passive income mean more sources of wealth to spend on the things that matter most to you.

Here are five additional questions to ask when thinking about your plan.

### Do you plan to stay in your current home?

Housing accounts for about 35 percent of annual expenditures for average families. Some families relocate to an area with a lower cost of living, or higher quality of life, but that has its own challenges—including necessitating travel to visit friends and family.

### Will you need extensive health care?

Even the healthiest person will have to contend with the rising costs of health care. Ensuring that you'll have enough to live comfortably means planning and choosing a strategy that you feel confident in.

### What kind of lifestyle do you envision?

From food to transportation to vacations to helping the kids, living expenses can add up. It's always a good idea to plan so that there's enough in your budget to treat yourself to the life you deserve.

### How will you spend your leisure time?

After spending your whole life working, this is the time to enjoy the fruits of your labour. A good plan includes fun, whether that's traveling the country in your camper or going on a family vacation studying or cruising the world.

### What will you leave behind?

Most families strive to plan to leave something behind for the next generation, many people hope to leave a legacy. Your plan might also include designating beneficiaries of your estate.

Time is one of our most precious resources, which is why we need to use it as wisely as possible. Unlike money, you can't earn back the time that's already been spent – once it's gone, it's gone.

When we start a business, our top priorities are likely profit and success, and part of that involves making the most of your time, using it in the right areas to grow our business in the most effective way, and creating freedom.

Creating passive income is something that most families aspire to achieve. It's a regular form of income that requires little maintenance or effort, and most importantly, it's not reliant on you inputting your time on a daily or hourly basis.

Creating a passive income for your family should be a priority, for it may be the difference between living the life you deserve and strive for and being dependent on your family and the state. Creating passive income will help you sleep better on your life journey.

## Converting my accumulation in a pension to guaranteed annuity in an Insurance Company.

Converting savings into income during retirement involves determining the conversion rate, which is the percentage or factor used to calculate the amount of income that can be generated from a given amount of savings. The conversion rate is a key factor in determining the sustainability and adequacy of retirement income. However, it is important to note that the conversion rate may vary depending on various factors and individual circumstances. Let's explore some considerations related to the conversion rate:

Ultimately, the conversion rate should be determined through careful consideration of personal factors, financial goals, and risk tolerance. It is essential to strike a balance between generating sufficient income for retirement needs and ensuring the sustainability of savings throughout the retirement period. Regular monitoring and adjustments to the conversion rate may be necessary to adapt to changing circumstances and maintain financial security during retirement.

## What has happened to the insurance companies' conversion (annuity) rates for pensions over time?

The conversion rates offered by insurance companies for pension plans have declined over the years due to various factors, including changes in market conditions, interest rates, and regulatory require-ments. Here are some key developments related to conversion rates for pension plans offered by insurance companies:

In the 1980s and 1990s, insurance companies used mortality tables from the 1950s to calculate the conversion. Since the average life expectancy in those years was lower than that of today, the policies marketed at the time had significantly better guaranteed conversion rates.

## Is this good for us?

There are pros and cons to this. On the one hand, it is an income stream that is guaranteed (by the insurance company or the pension fund) for life and this is reassuring, but on the other hand, investors who have accumulated money throughout their lives gave up their assets to receive the promised revenue. And this did not generally change with inflation.

The alternative of course is any investment that yields 6% (the equivalent of a conversion rate of 200) with the option to pay out the income created over the years, for example an investment in real estate that yields 6%. In this case the client will receive the same 6% throughout his life but in addition he will inherit the property in full.

So, if I own a property that is worth $500,000 and it is creating income of $2,500 a month, if I sold the property and bought an annuity (guaranteed lifetime income for an insurance company) I would get $2,272 income a month.

## What happens when I die?

In the scenario that I own the property it will pass on to my beneficiaries and in the scenario that I purchased an annuity my beneficiaries would be eligible to get nothing

**Decline in Guaranteed Conversion Rates:** In the past, many insurance companies offered guaranteed conversion rates for pension plans, which provided a specific income stream in retirement based on the accumulated savings. These conversion rates were often fixed and predetermined, providing retirees with a stable and predictable if not inflation proofed income. However, over time, insurance companies have shifted away from offering guaranteed conversion rates due to various reasons, including the challenges of managing long-term financial obligations and market volatility.

**Shift towards Variable Annuities:** Insurance companies have increasingly shifted towards offering variable annuities, which provide retirees with the opportunity to invest their savings in a range of investment options. With variable annuities, the income generated during retirement is based on the performance of the underlying investments, rather than a fixed conversion rate. This allows retirees to potentially benefit from higher investment returns, but it also exposes them to investment risk and market fluctuations.

**Impact of Interest Rates:** Insurance companies' conversion rates are influenced by prevailing interest rates. When interest rates are high, insurance companies can offer more attractive conversion rates because they can generate higher returns on the invested funds. However, in a low-interest-rate environment, insurance companies may lower the conversion rates to reflect the reduced income-generating potential of the invested assets. Fluctuations in interest rates can affect the competitiveness of conversion rates offered by insurance companies.

**Regulatory Changes**: Insurance companies are subject to regulatory oversight, and changes in regulations can impact on the conversion rates they offer. Regulatory requirements may be introduced to ensure the financial stability of insurance companies and the sustainability of the income they provide to retirees. These regulations may influence the methodology used to calculate conversion rates, the level of reserves required, or the risk management practices of insurance companies.

**Individual Factors**: Insurance companies consider various individual factors when determining the conversion rates for pension plans. These factors may include the individual's age, gender, health status, and life expectancy. Insurance companies use actuarial calculations and mortality tables to estimate the expected longevity of retirees and adjust the conversion rates accordingly.

**Competition and Market Dynamics**: The competitive landscape within the insurance industry can also influence conversion rates. Insurance companies may adjust their rates to remain competitive in the market or attract new customers. Changes in market dynamics, such as the entry of new players or shifts in customer preferences, can impact the conversion rates offered by insurance companies.

It is important to note that specific trends and developments regarding insurance companies' conversion rates can vary by region and country. Additionally, conversion rates may differ among insurance companies based on their individual business models, investment strategies, and risk management practices.

Individuals considering pension plans from insurance companies should carefully review the terms, conditions, and conversion rate provisions to understand the income they can expect during retirement. Seeking advice from financial professionals can provide valuable insights and help individuals make informed decisions based on their specific needs and circumstances.

## The Tax Consideration

Many pensioners think that once retirees arrive at pension age Social Security and income tax payments end. They are partly right. You may not pay tax on Social Security, but most tax authorities keep requiring tax on the pensions as if this was regular income.

In fact, in the eyes of tax authorities, pensions are active income and not passive income, so you may be required to pay a regular tax according to the tax levels of the jurisdiction you live in.

In a world where we are solely responsible for our own destiny and must take care of ourselves for income on the day, we stop generating income, passive income will play a major role in our lives. As the Saying goes: "By failing to prepare, you are preparing to fail".

## Pensions and Expats

Moving overseas may have impact on your retirement savings depending on how your pensions are structured and your status as an expat.

## Why do expats contribute to a pension?

A pension is simply a tax-efficient way of delaying the spending some of your income now to improve your lifestyle after retirement.

The money goes into an investment wrapper – the pension.

From a defined age (usually 55 or over), expats can then decide how to access the cash – which can also depend on the type of pension.

To urge people to save, the government offers tax breaks, such as topping up contributions and no tax on fund growth.

However, the money may be taxed on withdrawal from the pension.

Despite freedoms globally promising to make pensions easier, the choices are confusing for many expats who manage their money from another country.

Add to that the complications of local taxes, different inheritance laws where you live, and you can see why many expats are confused.

An important aspect of moving overseas for many expats is the benefit of paying little or no tax on income and savings.

Your original pension pot is not lost if you move overseas. The money sits safely in a vault until you decide what to do.

The world is aligning itself with new directives to allow pensions to be transferred freely between jurisdictions, this however is at a very primary stage and usually is very complicated and full of challenges.

A few examples of new laws that allow the free movement of pensions.

## European Union

European Union Retirement Benefits Scheme (EURBS) allows European citizens living overseas to transfer their accumulated pension savings into a more tax-efficient jurisdiction.

EURBS has their origin in pan-European pension law adopted in 1998 and subsequently added to, which enabled occupational pensions to be moved freely between member states whenever a pension holder retired to live in another EU jurisdiction.

However, the adoption of EURBS has been slow, mainly because they have been more difficult to arrange.

Even now, some would not normally be attempted, such as the transferring to another European country of a French pension, for reasons having to do with the French pension system.

Also, unlike the British System, EURBS are limited to Europe. This means that at this moment an EURBS could not be set up in New Zealand, say, for an emigrating Dutchman keen to bring his pension there with him.

According to recent studies, over 2.2 million emigrants have left Europe in the last two years alone, and they are looking to invest their employment and future aspirations in their new juris-diction or in a tax-free environment, and this figure is only going to increase over time. This trend may also be due to the ongoing global economic instability and the potential for people to create a better future abroad.

With the European economy becoming increasingly unstable, working abroad presents many significant advantages for EU citizens, and it may soon become the only option for some who want to invest in a specific area or provide themselves more constant and diverse growth.

## UK Legislation on Pension Transfers

The most popular private pensions for UK expats are self-invested personal pensions (SIPPs). These are often called 'direct contri-bution' pensions because the saver pays the provider directly.

The value of a direct contribution pension is based on the value of the underlying investment, which is generally mutual funds, stocks, and bonds. The fund value varies daily depending on stock market or fund performance. Personal pensions are not generally index linked.

Most personal pensions pay benefits in Sterling into a UK bank account with tax deducted at source. This can lead to currency juggling to find the best exchange rate, but specialist brokers offer discount fixed rates over 12 months to take away some of the stress.

## UK Citizens Retiring overseas transferring to a QROPS.

UK citizens who are retiring overseas have the option to transfer their UK pension benefits to a Qualifying Recognised Overseas Pension Scheme (QROPS). QROPS is an HM Revenue and Customs (HMRC) approved pension scheme located outside the UK that can receive transfers from UK-registered pension schemes. Here are some key points to know about transferring to a QROPS:

**Pension Portability:** Transferring to a QROPS allows UK citizens to have their pension benefits follow them when they move abroad. It provides greater flexibility and control over their retirement savings, enabling them to manage their pensions in the country where they plan to retire.

**Tax Advantages:** Transferring to a QROPS can offer potential tax advantages. It allows individuals to take advantage of the tax rules and regulations in the country where the QROPS is established. Depending on the jurisdiction, this may include benefits such as reduced taxation on pension income, inheritance tax planning, or more favourable tax treatment on withdrawals.

**Investment Flexibility:** QROPS often provide a wider range of investment options compared to UK-based pension schemes. This increased flexibility allows retirees to tailor their investments according to their risk appetite, retirement goals, and the specific investment opportunities available in the jurisdiction of QROPS.

**Currency Flexibility:** QROPS can be beneficial for individuals who plan to retire abroad as they provide the option to receive pension benefits in local currency, reducing exposure to currency exchange rate fluctuations and potential currency conversion costs.

**Regulatory Considerations:** It is important to consider the regulatory environment and legal protections when choosing a QROPS. Different jurisdictions have varying regulations and oversight of pension schemes. Retirees should ensure that the

**Reporting Requirements:** UK citizens transferring to a QROPS need to comply with reporting requirements set by HMRC. Both the individual and the QROPS provider are responsible for reporting relevant information to HMRC to maintain compliance with UK tax regulations.

Provided the QROPS they select is appropriately regulated, the system offers strong consumer protections, and can align with retirement objectives.

## Retiring overseas with a QNUPS as opposed to a QROPS.

QNUPS (Qualifying Non-UK Pension Schemes) and QROPS (Qualifying Recognised Overseas Pension Schemes) are both types of pension schemes that offer benefits for UK residents and citizens who are planning to retire or live abroad. While they share some similarities, there are also key differences between QNUPS and QROPS. Here's an overview:

### Purpose and Eligibility:

**QNUPS:** QNUPS are designed to provide individuals with a tax-efficient way to save for retirement or inheritance planning. They are available to both UK and non-UK residents, including those who have already used their lifetime allowance for pensions or individuals who are not eligible for QROPS.

**QROPS:** QROPS are primarily intended for individuals who are leaving or have left the UK and want to transfer their UK pension benefits to an overseas scheme. They are available to UK residents and citizens who are planning to retire or live abroad.

## Tax Treatment:

**QNUPS:** QNUPS offer potential tax advantages, including the ability to receive income and growth free from UK inheritance tax (IHT), as well as potential exemptions from income tax, capital gains tax, and lifetime allowance limits.

**QROPS:** QROPS can provide tax benefits depending on the jurisdiction. They allow individuals to potentially avoid or reduce UK income tax, capital gains tax, and lifetime allowance charges. However, tax treatment depends on the specific rules of the QROPS jurisdiction and any applicable double tax treaties between the UK and that jurisdiction.

## Contribution Limits:

**QNUPS:** There is no specific limit on the contributions that can be made to a QNUPS. However, contributions must be justifiable, and they should not be made with the intention of avoiding UK taxes.

## Reporting Requirements:

**QNUPS:** While there are reporting obligations for trustees of QNUPS, there are no specific reporting requirements for individuals who hold a QNUPS.

**QROPS:** Both the individual and the QROPS provider are responsible for reporting certain information to HM Revenue and Customs (HMRC) to comply with UK tax regulations.

## Investment Flexibility:

**QNUPS:** QNUPS generally offer a wider range of investment options compared to traditional pension schemes. This flexibility allows individuals to choose investments based on their risk appetite and investment objectives.

**QROPS:** Similar to QNUPS, QROPS can provide investment flexibility depending on the rules and regulations of the specific jurisdiction where the QROPS is established.

It is crucial for individuals considering QNUPS or QROPS to seek professional advice from qualified financial advisors or pension specialists. They can provide personalized guidance based on individual circumstances, retirement objectives, and the specific rules and regulations of each scheme.

## Transferring Pension savings from the US

If you lived and worked in the US you may have some funds accumulated in a US pension scheme that you want to transfer or to pay into your local account in your local jurisdiction.

This simple request, however, may be tricky.

What you probably have in the US is a "deferred annuity scheme". The way this work is that you save into them while you are working, and when you retire, the pension provider can offer you a guaranteed income for life or a drawdown (taking a controlled income from the pension pot aligned with US directives).

You may have not been drawing this income, so it has been rolling up in the pension. You have the option, however, to start taking it. The pension fund manager should pay it into a US or Foreign bank account for you.

That income will be taxed, so you will receive about $70 for every $100 of income you are paid. You might be able to get a refund on some of this aligned with the local treaty with the US, as pensioners globally would be expected to pay less than 30 per cent tax.

If you have health issues that you believe may shorten your life, or if you plan to use this money as part of any legacy you will structure to enable your beneficiaries to avoid inheritance tax you may look for an alternative strategy.

A "pension transfer" is a mechanism where you move your retirement pot from one provider to another. It is relatively easy to do globally, providing the pension company feels you have taken the necessary financial advice, but it could be a lot harder with a US pension.

The first and most simple issue is that you will get a US tax bill for transferring the money, which could be 30 per cent of the value of the funds in your US pension pot.

The second problem is that it is practically very difficult to convert a US pension into a local one. It is almost impossible to find financial professionals who can advise on US pension schemes because US regulations are complex, and most advisers are not trained in them or authorised to work with them.

To transfer the pension from the US to your jurisdiction, then, you would have to find an adviser who is based here but trained in both systems. This is a very specialist type of work which is done by large accounting firms with international reach. Their fees will be many hundreds of dollars an hour, so you must judge the potential profit you can make from transferring the value of the pension against what you will pay for accounting work.

A pension transfer is simple from a tax perspective, however, as you would just be taxed once in the US, at 30 per cent, for taking the pension pot across the world you may be eligible for a tax refund in your country of origin.

# Chapter Nineteen

## The Expatriate's Guide to Estate Planning: Safeguarding Your Legacy

Estate planning is the process of planning for the management and distribution of our assets and wealth after our death. It involves creating a comprehensive plan that ensures the smooth transfer of assets to beneficiaries, minimizes tax liabilities, and protects our wishes regarding our property and healthcare decisions. Estate planning typically includes several important components:

**Will**: A will be a legal document that outlines how a person's assets will be distributed upon their death. It allows individuals to specify their beneficiaries, designate an executor to manage the distribution process, and provide instructions for any other specific matters, such as guardianship of minor children.

**Trusts**: Trusts are legal arrangements that hold and manage assets on behalf of beneficiaries. They can be used to protect and distribute assets according to specific instructions, provide for the needs of family members, minimize estate taxes, and ensure long-term financial security for loved ones. Trusts can be revocable (modifiable during the individual's lifetime) or irrevocable (cannot be modified after creation).

**Power of Attorney**: A power of attorney grants someone the authority to make financial or legal decisions on behalf of another person if they become incapacitated or unable to manage their affairs. This ensures that a trusted individual can handle important matters such as bill payments, property management, and financial transactions.

**Advance Healthcare Directive**: Also known as a living will or healthcare power of attorney, this document outlines an individual's wishes regarding medical treatment and end-of-life care. It designates a healthcare proxy to make medical decisions on their behalf if they are unable to do so themselves.

**Beneficiary Designations**: Assets such as life insurance policies, retirement accounts, and bank accounts often allow individuals to designate beneficiaries who will receive those assets upon their death. Ensuring that beneficiary designations are up to date and aligned with overall estate planning goals is crucial.

**Tax Planning**: Estate planning also involves strategies to minimize potential tax liabilities, such as estate taxes, gift taxes, and generation-skipping transfer taxes. This may involve techniques like gifting assets during one's lifetime, establishing trusts, or utilizing tax-saving vehicles.

**Charitable Giving**: Estate planning can include provisions for charitable donations, allowing individuals to support causes or organizations they care about and potentially receive tax benefits for their philanthropic contributions.

Estate planning is not solely for the wealthy; individuals at various stages of life and with varying asset levels can benefit from creating an estate plan. It helps ensure that one's assets are distributed according to their wishes, protects loved ones, minimizes tax burdens, and can simplify the administrative process for the family after one's passing.

Like any planning, the process of creating an Estate Plan includes the following steps:

- Identify your estate planning objectives.

- Gather information about your current situation.

- Analyse your current situation.

- Document an appropriate strategy and the eventual outcome of that strategy.

- Identify Action Steps required to implement the strategy.

- Make decisions for action.

The implementation of an Estate Planning Strategy is achieved using a variety of devices. The fundamentals of estate planning are the execution of a Will and Powers of Attorney (for Property and Personal Care).

Before a strategy becomes effective, the appropriate legal documents must be executed. Lack of careful planning or faulty execution of legal documents can alter or even invalidate the intentions of a well thought out strategy.

## Estate Planning –Goals & Objectives

There are four Principles of Estate Planning that are fundamental. These are:

- Principle #1: Provide for your own needs for life – Ensure that your personal lifestyle needs are provided for so that you don't have to ever worry about running out of money.

- Principle #2: Safeguarding your estate to the maximum extent possible – By building an investment strategy that can sustain your lifestyle.

- Principle #3: Protect your estate from the erosion caused by taxes and other expenses.

- Principle #4: Distribute your estate in an orderly fashion – To identify and implemented a distribution strategy that ensures that your beneficiaries receive what you intended for them to receive and that the distribution strategy is tax effective.

- In addition to these principles, there may be some specific concerns that must be taken into consideration to ensure that an Estate Planning Strategy fulfils personal goals and objectives. These are as follows:

## Last Will and testament:

- The applicable law on inheritance is the law of the deceased's place of residence at the time of their death. The applicable law is the law of the deceased's place of residence at the time of making their will. A will is valid with respect to its form if it is made according to Local law.

- The laws of the place where it was signed; or

- The laws of the place of residence or citizenship of the testator when they signed the will or at the time of their death.

- As regards real estate, a will is valid with respect to its form if it is made according to the laws of the place where the real estate is located.

- Occasionally It could be worthwhile to divide assets as best as can be between beneficiaries so as to avoid unnecessary exposure to local taxes and conflicts of interest.

## Estate Planning Challenges for Expats

Estate planning for expats can present unique challenges due to the complexities of living abroad, varying legal systems, and potential tax implications. Here are some specific challenges that expats may face when it comes to estate planning:

**Multiple Jurisdictions**: Expats often have assets, properties, and financial accounts in multiple countries. Navigating the legal and tax systems of different jurisdictions can be complicated, as each country may have its own rules regarding inheritance, estate taxes, and property rights. It is essential to understand the laws of both the home country and the country of residence to ensure that the estate plan is effective and legally enforceable.

**Cross-Border Taxation**: Expats may be subject to both home country and host country tax laws. Double taxation treaties between countries can help mitigate tax liabilities, but it is crucial to understand the tax implications of owning assets and transferring wealth across borders. Consulting with tax advisors who specialize in international taxation can help optimize tax planning strategies and minimize potential tax burdens.

**Succession Laws**: Different countries have varying rules regarding inheritance and succession. In some jurisdictions, forced heirship laws may dictate how assets are distributed, often requiring a portion of the estate to be allocated to certain family members. Understanding the local succession laws is crucial to ensure that the estate plan aligns with one's intentions and that any potential conflicts are addressed.

**Language and Cultural Barriers**: Language barriers and cultural differences can add complexity to estate planning for expats. It is essential to work with professionals who are familiar with the local language, customs, and legal systems to ensure clear communication, accurate documentation, and proper implementation of the estate plan.

**Currency Considerations**: Expats often have assets and income in different currencies. Fluctuating exchange rates can impact the value of assets and affect estate planning decisions. It is important to consider currency risks and explore strategies for managing currency exposure, especially if beneficiaries reside in a different country or have financial obligations in a specific currency.

**Documentation and Record-Keeping**: Expats should ensure that their estate planning documents, such as wills, trusts, and powers of attorney, are up to date and reflect their current circumstances. It is crucial to maintain organized records of assets, investments, and liabilities in different countries to facilitate the administration of the estate and help executors or trustees carry out their duties.

**Coordination with Local Advisors**: Engaging professional advisors who are well-versed in both international and local estate planning laws is essential. These advisors may include attorneys, tax professionals, financial planners, and trust experts who can work together to develop a comprehensive estate plan that considers the unique challenges faced by expats.

Given the complexities involved, expats should prioritize estate planning and seek professional guidance from advisors with expertise in international estate planning. They can provide tailored solutions and ensure that the estate plan considers the specific circumstances, goals, and challenges faced by expatriates.

## The Importance of Preparing a Healthcare Power of Attorney and Living Will is crucial for expats.

Preparing a Healthcare Power of Attorney and Living Will is crucial for expats, as it ensures that their healthcare decisions and wishes are respected and legally protected, regardless of their location. Here are some key reasons why these documents are important for expats:

**Empowerment and Control**: A Healthcare Power of Attorney and Living Will give expats the power to make their own healthcare decisions and appoint a trusted individual to make medical choices on their behalf if they become incapacitated or unable to communicate their wishes. This allows expats to maintain control over their medical treatment, ensuring that their values and preferences are respected even if they are unable to express them.

**Healthcare Consistency**: As expats, you may find yourself living in different countries with varying healthcare systems, cultural norms, and legal frameworks. By having a Healthcare Power of Attorney and Living Will in place, you can ensure consistent healthcare decision-making, regardless of your location. Your appointed healthcare agent can act in accordance with your wishes, bridging any potential gaps or discrepancies between different healthcare systems.

**Customization to Individual Circumstances**: Each person's healthcare preferences and circumstances are unique. Expats may have specific concerns, cultural beliefs, or medical conditions that require special attention. By preparing a Healthcare Power of Attorney and Living Will, expats can clearly outline their preferences for medical treatments, end-of-life care, organ donation, and other important healthcare decisions. This customization allows for personalized care that aligns with individual beliefs and values.

**Legal Recognition and Protection**: Different countries have varying legal requirements and recognition of healthcare decision-making documents. By having a Healthcare Power of Attorney and Living Will prepared in accordance with local laws, expats can ensure that their documents are legally binding and enforceable in their country of residence. This legal protection provides peace of mind that their wishes will be respected and followed.

**Reduction of Family Disputes and Burden**: In the absence of clear healthcare directives, family members may disagree on medical decisions, leading to conflicts and emotional distress. By having a Healthcare Power of Attorney and Living Will in place, expats can relieve their loved ones from the burden of making difficult decisions during challenging times. It can also prevent potential disagreements among family members and help maintain harmonious relationships.

**Simplified Administration**: In the event of incapacity, having a Healthcare Power of Attorney and Living Will can streamline the administration of medical decisions. The appointed healthcare agent can work closely with healthcare providers, ensuring a smooth process and reducing delays or complications in receiving appropriate care.

Given the unique circumstances faced by expats, it is important to consult with an attorney who specializes in estate planning or healthcare law in the relevant jurisdiction. They can provide guidance on the specific legal requirements and help tailor the documents to your individual needs as an expat.

Preparing a Healthcare Power of Attorney and Living Will allows expats to proactively address their healthcare wishes and ensure that their values and preferences are respected, regardless of their location. It provides peace of mind and empowers individuals to maintain control over their medical treatment and decisions.

## Things to think about when preparing a will for an expat.

When preparing a will, it is important to consider several key factors to ensure that your wishes are accurately reflected and legally enforceable. Here are some important things to think about when preparing a will:

**Assets and Beneficiaries**: Take stock of your assets, including properties, investments, bank accounts, retirement accounts, and personal belongings. Consider who you want to inherit these assets and determine the beneficiaries of your will. Be specific in identifying individuals or organizations as beneficiaries and include contingent beneficiaries in case your primary beneficiaries predecease you.

**Executor**: Select a trustworthy and capable executor who will be responsible for managing your estate, distributing assets according to your wishes, and handling any administrative tasks. Discuss your choice with the person beforehand and ensure they are willing to take on the role.

**Guardianship**: If you have minor children, think about who you would want to be their legal guardian in the event of your death. Consider their suitability, values, and parenting style. It is crucial to discuss this responsibility with potential guardians and seek their consent before naming them in your will.

**Debts and Liabilities**: Consider any outstanding debts, mortgages, or loans you have. Consider how these should be handled and whether you wish for them to be repaid from your estate or if you want to specify how they should be managed after your passing.

**Digital Assets**: In the digital age, it is important to consider your digital assets, such as online accounts, cryptocurrencies, and social media profiles. Determine how you want these assets to be managed, transferred, or closed after your death. Provide instructions, including relevant account information and access details, to your executor or a trusted individual.

**Funeral and Burial Wishes**: Consider any specific wishes you may have regarding your funeral or burial arrangements. Although not legally binding, including your preferences in your will can serve as guidance for your loved ones.

**Charitable Bequests**: If you wish to leave a portion of your estate to charitable organizations or causes, identify the charities, and specify the amount or percentage you would like to donate. Ensure that the charities are properly identified and use their official names and contact details.

**Updating and Reviewing**: Regularly review and update your will to reflect changes in your circumstances, such as marriages, divorces, births, deaths, or significant changes in your assets. Keep your will in a safe place, inform your executor of its location, and consider having a digital or physical backup copy. **Legal Advice:** Consult with an experienced estate planning attorney to ensure that your will complies with local laws, addresses any specific legal requirements, and accurately reflects your intentions. They can provide guidance on the drafting and execution process and help you navigate any complexities or potential challenges.

Itemize Jewellery, and all assets of sentimental or fiscal value that you own including Cars, art etc.

Make a Memberships List. (For your beneficiaries to cancel). And don't forget passwords so someone can recover your online life!

Prepare a list of professionals that the beneficiaries can approach to get full information.

Make many copies of your lists. Perhaps give a copy to the lawyer who prepares the will.

## Additional Considerations

Do you want to leave your children all your assets in equal shares?

Do you want to leave anything for grandchildren or create a trust for education or marriages of children/ grandchildren/ great grandchildren?

Have you gifted any of your children or do you want to gift to any of your children anything while you are alive?

Do you want to take this into account in the will?

What are the chances that one of your children/ grandchildren will contest the will?

Do you want to include an Inheritance Act clause in your will?

## What is an Inheritance Act Clause?

An Inheritance Act clause, also known as a Family Provision clause or a Maintenance clause, is a provision included in a will that addresses potential challenges to the distribution of assets by certain individuals who may not be adequately provided for in the will.

In some jurisdictions, including the United Kingdom, Australia, and some Canadian provinces, there are laws that allow certain individuals, typically close family members or dependents, to make a claim against an estate if they believe they have not received reasonable financial provision. These laws are commonly referred to as Inheritance Acts or Family Provision Acts.

By including an Inheritance Act clause in a will, the testator (the person making the will) can express their intention that they are aware of these laws and wish to limit the ability of certain individuals to challenge the distribution of their assets. The clause may state that the testator has considered the potential claims under the applicable inheritance law and has made provisions in the will that they believe are reasonable and adequate for the intended beneficiaries.

While an Inheritance Act clause can indicate the testator's awareness of the potential claims and their intentions, it does not necessarily prevent a person from making a claim or override the legal requirements of the inheritance law. The court still has the authority to assess any claims made and determine whether further provision should be granted to the claimant based on their needs and the circumstances of the case.

Including an Inheritance Act clause in a will can serve as evidence of the testator's consideration of the relevant laws and their intentions, but it is important to consult with an estate planning attorney to understand the specific laws and requirements in your jurisdiction. They can provide guidance on drafting the clause and ensure that it aligns with the legal framework of your jurisdiction.

You may have liquid and illiquid assets in your estate. How do you want to divide the estate up between the children considering illiquidity and potential tax events.

Please note that transferring your home to a beneficiary who is a family member is almost completely tax free in some jurisdictions, however the beneficiary may inherit the tax exposure and will have to pay it when he/she sells the assets.

You may want to check the tax implications for children who are US citizens for US tax.

Explore conditioning the transfer of assets only to beneficiaries who have a financial agreement with their spouses/ life partners. This will ensure that if at any stage they part with their spouses/ life partners they will not have any claim to your gifts or inheritance.

Remember, the specific considerations for preparing a will may vary based on your jurisdiction and personal circumstances. It is always advisable to seek professional legal advice to ensure that your will is valid, enforceable, and aligned with your wishes.

## Case Study: UK Estate Planning for 'Non-Dom's

Estate planning is all about protecting your loved ones and part of this is transferring assets to your heirs in a way which is tax efficient.

Taking advice on estate planning can enable couples to reduce the tax burden on their estate, but the issues for international families connected to the UK are complex.

There are many challenges when preparing an estate plan, one of them is understanding the concept of "domicile", which under English law is not just determined by citizenship or residence.

### What does it mean to be a 'non-domiciliary'?

A non-UK domiciliary (sometimes called a "non-dom") is an individual who is domiciled outside the UK for the purposes of English common tax law.

"Domicile" is a concept in law which is different from the tax concept of residence. It is also unrelated to nationality. It is perfectly possible for an individual to be resident in one country, domiciled (for English law purposes) in a second country, and a national of a third.

Non-UK domiciled status can persist for a long time (up to seventeen years) after an individual has become a resident in the UK. Under English tax law, an individual may have been UK resident for decades, and may even have acquired British nationality, and yet have a domicile outside the UK. This will be the case if the individual had a "domicile of origin" outside the UK and he or she has never acquired a "domicile of choice" in any part of the UK.

### What is a domicile of origin?

Every individual is born with a "domicile of origin". If your parents were married at the time of your birth, their domicile of origin will have been the domicile of the father at that time. An individual can however acquire a "domicile of choice" in a different country, if they move to a different country and form an intention to reside there permanently or indefinitely.

So a domicile of origin means the home of an individual's parents and not where the child was born when the parents were working or on a visit or journey. It is not a place where a child happens to be born. Thus, domicile of origin is different from an accidental place of birth.

An individual with a non-UK domicile of origin will remain non-UK domiciled for as long as they can credibly say that they intend to cease residing in the UK at some point in the future. For example, it is common for individuals with foreign domiciles of origin to intend to leave the UK when their children cease to be in full-time education in the UK, on the termination of a particular job with a UK employer, on the sale of a particular UK company, or on their retirement. If the intention to leave the UK is realistic, the domicile of origin will be retained in these scenarios. However, if an individual moves to the UK late in life, an assertion of a foreign domicile may be more susceptible to challenge.

It is also possible for an individual with a domicile of origin in the UK to become a non-UK domiciliary, by residing in another country and forming the intention to reside there permanently or indefinitely. This will result in the acquisition of a domicile of choice in the other country. However, it's unusual for a person with a UK domicile to acquire a domicile of choice elsewhere as soon as they leave the UK. A domicile of origin has an adhesive quality, and it is difficult to cast off. There is a heavy evidential burden to show that a domicile of origin has been displaced with a new domicile of choice and keeping connections with the UK (like owning UK real estate) can undermine the claim to have acquire a domicile of choice elsewhere.

In principle, a domicile of choice in another country may be retained if the individual ceases to reside in that other country, and even if he begins to reside again in the UK. However, if an individual who has a UK domicile of origin and was born in the UK becomes a UK resident, they will be deemed domiciled and therefore ineligible for the tax benefits that normally attach to non-UK domiciled status.

Determining an individual's domicile is not necessarily straight-forward, but where an individual was born abroad, or his parents lived abroad, or he himself has lived abroad for a long period, it is likely to be worth investigating his domicile further to see whether he may be a "non-dom". It needs to be stated that UK non-dom status is politically contentious and may be abolished in the future.

## Why is domicile so important?

The significance of domicile goes beyond tax. A foreign domicile can affect succession to "movable" assets such as bank accounts and shares. The way such assets pass on the individual's death may be affected by the succession law of his country of domicile. That law may contain "forced heirship" provisions which prevent the individual from disposing of his assets on death in the way that he wishes.

However, it is probably fair to say that the most immediate impact of a foreign domicile is in relation to tax. Non-doms (who aren't deemed domiciled) have a reduced exposure to UK taxation, in recognition of the fact that they are less closely connected to the UK than individuals who are domiciled within the UK. The tax advantages of being a non-dom are essentially threefold:

1. The remittance basis of taxation; Under the remittance basis of taxation, you pay tax on local income and gains for the tax year in which they arise, but you only pay on foreign income and foreign gains when they are brought into your

tax residency. In practice, the remittance basis can help to prevent double taxation.

2. The restriction of inheritance tax to local assets.

3. The scope to create a non-resident trust from which the individual can benefit, without the creation of the trust giving rise to inheritance tax, and without various anti-avoidance rules applying to the trust's assets and income/gains generated within the trust.

## What is the advantage of being a non–dom where inheritance tax is concerned?

When a UK domiciliary dies, his or her estate is subject to inheritance tax on a worldwide basis. Inheritance tax applies at 40% to assets both within and outside the UK, except to the extent that they are protected by the exemption for assets passing to a surviving spouse or fall within the individual's "nil rate band". At £325,000, the latter is not exactly generous and has not changed for years.

By contrast, when a non-dom dies, then if he or she is not deemed domiciled in the UK for inheritance tax, the tax generally applies only to UK assets; generally, there is no inheritance tax on assets situated outside the UK.

The only notable exception to this relates to non-UK assets which derive their value from UK residential property or have been provided as collateral for a loan used to acquire or improve such property. This means that the value of a non-UK company which holds UK residential property will still be within the scope of inheritance tax, and that the value of the benefit of a loan can also be subject to inheritance tax, if the funds were used to buy UK residential property. Such assets are effectively deemed to be UK assets for inheritance tax purposes.

The same principles apply if a non-dom (who are not deemed domiciled) makes a lifetime gift of non-UK assets. Notwithstanding any connection with UK residential property, there is no inheritance tax on such a gift, even if the gift is one which would potentially give rise to an immediate inheritance tax charge for a UK domiciliary. Examples are gifts to trusts, gifts to trust-like entities such as private foundations and gifts to charitable entities outside the UK.

## What is the "deemed domicile" concept?

The concept of deemed domicile limits the length of time for which the tax benefits of non-UK domiciled status are available. A deemed domicile in the UK is typically acquired by a non-UK domiciled individual once he has been UK resident in 15 of the 20 preceding tax years. It follows that an individual with a foreign domicile typically becomes deemed domiciled for UK tax purposes at the beginning of his 18th tax year of residence in the UK.

It is important to count tax years of residence correctly for these purposes. Under the rules which applied before the UK introduced its current statutory residence test, it was not uncommon for an individual moving to the UK to become taxable as a resident in a given tax year even if he only started spending time in the UK towards the end of the tax year; and indeed, an unlucky or ill-advised individual might become tax resident a matter of days before the end of the tax year in which he "arrived" in the UK.

This can also happen under the statutory resident test, for example if the individual becomes UK resident on commencing full-time work in the UK. There is no doubt that, where an individual became UK resident partway through a tax year, that whole tax year must "go onto the clock" for the purposes of the deemed domicile test (even if he was taxable as a resident, in that tax year, for just a few days). Deemed domicile can therefore arrive sooner than expected, sometimes little more than 14 years after the individual's "arrival" in the UK.

The effect of being deemed domiciled in the UK is that the remittance basis of taxation ceases to be available, and the scope of inheritance tax extends from UK assets to all assets on a worldwide basis. This is relevant not only in the event of the individual's death, but also if the individual makes lifetime gifts, especially gifts to trusts or trust-like entities.

However, where an individual has not yet become deemed domiciled, these effects can be countered by putting non-UK assets into what is known as an excluded property settlement. This is a trust, usually in discretionary form, of which the non-dom himself can be a beneficiary. The trust must be created and funded before the non-dom becomes deemed domiciled. If so, it can function as an indefinite shelter from inheritance tax, not just in the non-dom's lifetime but potentially for many generations after his or her death. It can also provide significant tax deferral benefits with respect to income and gains generated by the trust assets.

## How can a person get out of the "deemed domicile" rules?

Where an individual has already become deemed domiciled for inheritance tax purposes, his deemed domicile can in principle be "broken" by a period of non-UK residence. In a typical case, six entire tax years of non-UK residence are required if the individual plans to resume residence in the UK after the non-resident period.

## Are there any treaties that are relevant for inheritance tax?

Generally, an individual who has become deemed domiciled in the UK for inheritance tax purposes has the same status, where inheritance tax is concerned, as someone who is domiciled in part of the UK. However, in certain scenarios the position is modified by a double taxation treaty.

There are a few treaties that the UK has entered into with other countries, which can affect the scope of inheritance tax in relation to individuals who are domiciled outside the UK but are deemed domiciled for inheritance tax purposes. The effect of one of these treaties applying is that, on the individual's death, inheritance tax may not apply to non-UK assets, notwithstanding the individual's deemed domicile. Generally, these treaties only have effect in relation to transfers on death, and they do not (for example) affect the inheritance tax position if the individual makes a lifetime gift of non-UK assets to a trust.

## What are the domicile mismatch traps?

Non-dom status is generally beneficial, but there is one situation in which it can have unwelcome inheritance tax consequences – where there is a "domicile mismatch". This occurs when:

A UK domiciled spouse dies leaving his or her estate to a non-dom spouse who is not yet deemed domiciled; or

A non-dom spouse who is deemed domiciled for inheritance tax purposes dies leaving his or her estate to a non-dom spouse who is not yet deemed domiciled.

Normally, assets passing from one spouse to another are free of inheritance tax, by virtue of the spouse exemption. However, in the scenarios mentioned above, the spouse exemption is limited to £325,000 – unless the surviving spouse makes an election to be treated for inheritance tax purposes as domiciled in the UK. If so, the spouse exemption is unlimited, but the worldwide assets of the surviving spouse will be within the scope of inheritance tax on his or her own death (unless the surviving spouse then spends sufficient time outside the UK to shed his or her deemed domiciled status).

Mixed domicile couples, and non-dom couples who became UK resident at different times, should consider putting special Wills in place to cater for the possibility of a domicile mismatch on the first death. Consideration should also be given to transferring non-UK assets of the non-UK domiciled and non-deemed domiciled spouse into an excluded property settlement, to forestall the acquisition of deemed domiciled status if an election is required to avoid inheritance tax on the first death.

How establishing an excluded property settlement can work for a family?

As mentioned above, non-doms generally lose their favoured inheritance tax status once they become deemed domiciled, when their non-UK assets fall within the scope of inheritance tax.

However, if a non-dom gives non-UK assets to an excluded property settlement before he becomes deemed domiciled, these assets will remain ring-fenced from inheritance tax even after the individual becomes deemed domiciled and beyond his death, so that the assets are protected from inheritance tax for future generations. The individual can, and normally should, be a beneficiary of trust. It is also possible for trust to be revocable, so that the individual can bring it to an end at any time. These features of the trust do not affect its efficacy as a shelter from inheritance tax.

If the trust has non-UK resident trustees, it offers an additional advantage, because (provided that certain conditions are met) neither the non-UK domiciled settlor nor any other UK resident beneficiary will be liable to capital gains tax realized by the trustees, or liable to income tax in respect of non-UK income received by the trustees, until a benefit is received from the trust. This means that income and gains can, in principle, roll up inside the trust without tax being paid on them.

Although an excluded property settlement will save inheritance tax at 40% of the value of the assets on the settlor's death, there will be ongoing trustee fees. Prospective settlors should compare these costs against the cost of life assurance.

Where a non-dom might be interested in establishing such a trust, to ring-fence assets from inheritance tax, it is strongly recommended that advice is taken at the earliest opportunity. Ideally, an adviser should be consulted more than a year before the anticipated date of acquisition of a deemed domicile in the UK.

There are two reasons for this. One reason is that it can take some time to choose a trustee and establish and fund a trust, and it is not sensible to leave it to the last minute.

In addition, it is very common for individuals to have poor records and recollection of when they first became UK resident. Very often, it transpires that the individual became UK resident earlier than he or she had remembered, and/or that the totting up of years of UK residence has been done incorrectly. In either case, a surprisingly common outcome is that the professional adviser is consulted about establishing an excluded property settlement after the individual has already become deemed domiciled! This is deeply disappointing for the individual and adviser alike.

## What other issues should non-doms consider in their estate planning?

Other important issues for non-doms to consider include:

The possibility of (in effect) converting foreign income or gains into clean capital through gifts to family members.

The possible use of "wrappers" or structures and how foreign structures might be treated for UK tax purposes.

Estate planning for foreign assets – whether local Wills are necessary, and the impact of local succession laws (for example, forced heirship rules may apply).

Whether steps are needed to prevent any companies that the non-dom manages from becoming UK resident for tax purposes.

Specific issues which may arise due to an individual's domicile or nationality, or where his assets are situated (in particular, we work with a lot of US citizens, who are subject to US taxes on a worldwide basis and need specific advice to achieve the best result from the interplay of the International and US tax regimes); and

What would happen in the event of incapacity, as opposed to death. The UK has 'lasting powers of attorney' whereby you can nominate who should make decisions for you if you became unable to do so for yourself. Similar provisions may be needed for each jurisdiction in which there are substantial assets.

## What does the future hold for non-doms in the UK?

The tax rules for non-doms are very complex and specialist advice is almost always needed when moving to or from the UK, and to keep abreast of developments. It is quite possible that the rules on domicile will be subject to further changes in the future and so any planning should be as 'future-proof' as it can be.

# Chapter Twenty

## Embracing the Expat Journey: Navigating the Future with Confidence

What does the future look like for us?

Most expats are enjoying their lives and embracing their new communities. Most of us say we will continue to live abroad and reap the benefits.

In a recent report, expats experienced optimism for their future, and this is underpinned by the sense of stability within the new adopted country. Nearly all expats living in Australia (92%), Switzerland (92%), and Jersey in the Channel Islands (90%) feel optimistic that each respective location will be a stable place to live in the future.

Expats enjoy experiencing the local area, travelling more, and becoming more familiar with the local culture (47%).

Australia still tops the list for wellness, followed closely by Spain. And 9 in 10 expats in Switzerland, Australia, New Zealand, Cyprus, and Spain recommend moving there for its quality of life.

While living abroad as expats can enrich our lives, it also benefits our home country and creates openness and academic and business cooperations. It is my belief that working together cross borders, cross culture, creates new opportunities.

## And what does the future hold for all of us?

Economics is a social science that focuses on the production, distribution, and consumption of goods and services, and analyses the choices that individuals, businesses, governments, and nations make to allocate resources and as such, is totally unpredictable.

Just decades ago, it seems Japan would become the leader of Asia and now it is the turn of the Chinese.

For five hundred years the general global opinion was that capitalism would cease to exist and yet here we are today, mostly in a more socialist form.

The Italian economist Pareto said that 80% of the world's wealth is controlled by 20% of the people and of that 20%, 80% is again controlled by 20% of the people and of that 20% is again controlled by 20% of the people so according to that theory 0.6% of the world's population will control 38.4% of the world wealth. According to 2019 OECD figures the world's top 0.6% of the population controls 39.4% of the world's wealth.

## Will this change? Probably but also probably not in our lifetime.

In inscriptions deciphered in ancient Egypt we learn that they too thought that the world was "going to the dogs" (terminology that they invented) and in the recent past even our generation thought that with population growth it was inevitable that there would not be enough food to feed all of us. Then fertilizers arrived and we learnt to produce more food.

When I was a child in the sixties, the western world was threatened by nuclear war many people did not believe they would survive to sixty. Today we are threatened by global warming. Our evolution is so unpredictable it is virtually impossible to forecast anything.

Most of humanity's significant developments were accidents such as Fleming's discovery of penicillin and Archimedes discovering the buoyancy principle ("Eureka").

In the words of Charles Dickens from David Copperfield "Something will turn up".

In the meantime, we expats are mostly blessed, we have on our side opportunity, and discovery so just enjoy.

## Finally, a word of warning

Expatria is complex. Always seek advice. Even if it is expensive.

Made in the USA
Middletown, DE
06 November 2023

41819823R00195